Contemporary Issues in Criminal Justice

A RESEARCH-BASED INTRODUCTION

AN ANTHOLOGY BY

Carolyn D'Argenio
David Owens
Jeffrey Chin

Looseleaf
Law Publications, Inc.

43-08 162nd Street, Flushing, NY 11358
www.LooseleafLaw.com • 800-647-5547

Library of Congress Cataloging-In-Publication Data

Contemporary issues in criminal justice : a research-based introduction : an anthology / [edited] by Carolyn D'argenio, David Owens Jeffrey Chin.
    p. cm.
 Includes bibliographical references and index.
 ISBN 978-1-60885-034-1
 1. Criminal justice, Administration of--Research. 2. Criminal justice, Administration of. 3. Criminology. 4. Law enforcement. I. D'argenio, Carolyn. II. Owens, David. III. Chin, Jeffrey C. (Jeffrey Chuan-che)
 HV7419.5.C664 2012
 364--dc23

                                2012014487

Cover design by *Sans Serif, Inc.* Saline, Michigan

TABLE OF CONTENTS

ABOUT THE EDITORS

Carolyn D'Argenio is an Associate Professor of Criminal Justice at Mohawk Valley Community College in Utica, NY. For the 2011 – 2012 academic year, she is serving as a leave replacement faculty member in the Criminal Justice department at Onondaga Community College in Syracuse, NY. D'Argenio is the past president of the Criminal Justice Educators' Association of New York State (CJEANYS) and their current secretary. She is the New York State representative on the executive board of the Northeastern Association of Criminal Justice Sciences (NEACJS). She has also served on the Assessment Committee of the Academy of Criminal Justice Sciences (ACJS).

David F. Owens is a Professor of Criminal Justice at Onondaga Community College in Syracuse, NY. He has served as president of the Criminal Justice Educators' Association of New York State (CJEANYS) and the Northeastern Association of Criminal Justice Sciences (NEACJS). Owens has served as the Region One Trustee of the Academy of Criminal Justice Sciences (ACJS) and is currently the ACJS Treasurer.

Jeffrey Chin is a Professor of Sociology at Le Moyne College in Syracuse, NY and is the former chair of the Department of Anthropology, Criminology, and Sociology. He is a Carnegie National Scholar (a program of the Carnegie Foundation for the Advancement of Teaching and Learning) and a former editor of *Teaching Sociology*, an official journal of the American Sociological Association (ASA). Professor Chin is a member of Criminal Justice Educators' Association of New York State (CJEANYS) and the Academy of Criminal Justice Sciences (ACJS), where he serves as a certification reviewer. He can be reached at chin@lemoyne.edu.

i

PREFACE

Contemporary Issues in Criminal Justice: A Research-Based Introduction is more than just the title of our book; it is a vehicle for instructors to use in demonstrating the importance of discipline-based research to lower division criminal justice and criminology students. We know that critical thinking skills, paired with the ability to write well-organized reports, briefs, and position papers are essential attributes of the successful criminal justician. This book is aimed at assisting students in further developing those skills and is the perfect companion to introductory textbooks in criminal justice and criminology.

Within these pages you will find a diverse collection of articles authored by prominent criminal justice scholars, including many who have brought their practitioner's insight into focus as they demonstrate to students the value of qualitative and quantitative analysis of several major issues of our discipline. Many articles are the product of preliminary research as presented at professional conferences that include annual meetings of the Academy of Criminal Justice Sciences. Each contributor shares our goal of instilling in students the importance of information literacy and the application of criminal justice and criminological research.

The editors of *Contemporary Issues in Criminal Justice: A Research-Based Introduction* are united in the belief that criminal justice and criminology students need to understand early in their academic careers the importance of being able to think critically about crime theory and related policy development. This book will not only help them achieve success in those areas but also better prepare them for entry into related career fields. Therefore, unlike other companion books, we decided not to draw articles from news-based periodicals. It is important to note that scholars who are also classroom instructors have written each article. We are particularly proud of the fact that some articles have been co-authored by students and that this volume has contributed to a publication line on the CV of emerging criminal justicians and criminologists.

We were excited when James Finckenauer agreed to write the book's introduction about Criminal Justice Higher Education. As a distinguished criminologist, educator, and acknowledged leader in the discipline, Dr. Finckenauer is well positioned to provide students with a basic understanding of how criminal justice higher education has evolved and why their degree will have great value.

But for the book's unique introduction, we believe that the layout of this reader will facilitate the use of your primary textbook. You will find that articles have been separated into the following five parts:

- Criminal Justice Higher Education
- Crime Theory
- Law Enforcement
- Courts
- Corrections

This intentional feature follows the natural sequence of instruction common among most introductory criminal justice courses. At the same time, instructors will have no problem assigning articles in a random order if it better fits their own teaching style.

This book contains pedagogical tools that support the student's ability to think critically and to problem-solve. These devices reinforce the content of the corresponding articles, as well as develop an increased level of information literacy for each student. These aids include:

- Key Terms
- Section Introductions
- Article Abstracts
- End of Chapter Discussion Questions
- Instructor Test Bank
- Index

Contemporary Issues in Criminal Justice: A Research-Based Introduction will allow students grow as independent thinkers, form objective opinions, and arrive at logical conclusions. We have great expectations for this book and look forward receiving feedback from adopters and students alike.

This reader was truly the result of collaboration and cooperation from many. We sincerely thank Michael and Mary Loughrey, for their support of this project and flexibility throughout the process. Thanks to Rachel Polmanteer (Le Moyne College class of 2005), and to Jennie Crate, who assisted with some of the research needed for this project. Thanks also to Samantha Manno (Le Moyne class of 2012), who performed many clerical support duties. Thanks also to the authors who contributed their research. Finally, thanks to our families, friends, and colleagues, whose support came in many forms and was always greatly appreciated, even if not expressly stated at the time.

KEY TERMS

Aggregate—(a) To combine or cluster individual units. (b) A unit made of individual entities. Research presented in aggregate is based on a culmination of data from individual units. Descriptions of such data represent common characteristics representative of the whole, but do not indicate that each individual unit in the group has such characteristics. Presenting data in aggregate form protects the identity of research subjects.

Anonymity—The assurance that individual participants in research cannot by identified. The strictest kind of anonymity means that the identities of subjects are concealed even from researchers, as is possible when respondents return their completed questionnaires by mail with no identifying information. Many kinds of research, such as face-to-face interviews, make strict anonymity impossible. Then, confidentiality of information about individual participants, including their identities, becomes the standard. While anonymity means that the researcher does not know subjects' identities, confidentiality means that the researcher knows but promises not to tell.[1]

Bivariate—Denotes two variables. *Bivariate analysis* refers to the statistical analysis of two variables.

Census—(a) Complete count of an entire population. (b) Collection of data from all members of the population—in contrast to the survey of a sample (subset) of the population.[1]

Chi-Square Test—A test statistic for categorical data. Chi-Square as a test statistic is used as a test of independence, but the chi-square test also is used as a goodness-of-fit test. The chi-square test statistic can be converted into one of several measures of association, including the phi coefficient, the contingency coefficient, and Cramer's V. The chi-square test is known by many names: Pearson chi-square, X^2, chi^2, and c^2.

The simplest use of the chi-square test, illustrated in the following example, occurs when a researcher wants to see if statistically significant differences exist between the observed (or actual) frequencies and the expected (or hypothesized, given the null hypothesis) frequencies of variables presented in a cross-tabulation

---

[1] NOTE: From *Dictionary of Statistics & Methodology: A Nontechnical Guide for the Social Sciences,* 4th ed. (pp. 12 and 48) by W. P. Vogt and R. B. Johnson, 2011, Los Angeles: Copyright 2011 by Sage Publications. Reprinted with permission.

or contingency table. The larger the observed frequency is in comparison with the expected frequency, the larger the chi-square statistic. The larger the chi-square statistic, the less likely the observed differences do just a chance, and the more statistically significant the finding is.[1]

Coding—(a) "Translating" data from one language or format to another—often to make it possible for a computer to operate on the data thus coded. (b) Reducing textual and visual data (e.g., many pages of text or videos of observations) to summary codes and categories to aid in analyzing and understanding the large amount of data. (c) Writing a set of instructions telling a computer how to handle data.[1]

Comparison Group—Also known as the control group. In studies designed to evaluate the impact of a given "treatment" or "condition" on a group, two groups are formed: the experimental group and the comparison (control) group. The groups would be characteristically similar; however, only the experimental group would receive the treatment. The comparison group receives no treatment. Researchers base their conclusions on the significance of any observed changes in the groups after the treatment is given.

Composite Score—A "new" score calculated by adding or averaging other scores.

Conceptualization—Specifically clarifying the meaning on concepts/variables used. Helps others understand the exact nature of the research.

Confidentiality—A condition whereby the source of information is not revealed to the public but is known to the researcher. Generally, results of such studies are presented in aggregate form.

Content Analysis—A technique used to systematically analyze communications.

Control Group—See *Comparison Group*.

---

[1] NOTE: From *Dictionary of Statistics & Methodology: A Nontechnical Guide for the Social Sciences,* 4th ed. (pp. 51 and 57) by W. P. Vogt and R. B. Johnson, 2011, Los Angeles: Copyright 2011 by Sage Publications. Reprinted with permission.

Control Variables—Extra variables that researchers do not want to interfere with their studies. To "control" the impact of these variables, researchers take care in assigning subjects to control or experimental groups or applying specific statistical techniques, like regression analysis, when analyzing data.

Correlation—Refers to the way things are related to each other. Correlation is not the same as causation. Things with a causal relationship are also correlated, but establishing causality requires temporal sequencing (A is not just related to B, but A *always* comes before B) and exclusion of other possible reasons for the observed relationship.

Cost/Benefit Analysis—The process of evaluating effort against return.

Covariate—(a) Another term for a continuous independent variable. (b) A variable other than the independent (or predictor) variable that correlates with the dependent (or outcome) variable. Typically the researcher seeks to control for (statistically subtract the effects of) the covariate by using such techniques as multiple regression analysis (MRA) or analysis of covariance (ANCOVA).[1]

Cross-Sectional—Pertains to when data for a particular study were collected. In a *cross-sectional* study, analysis is based on data collected at a single point in time. This contrasts a *longitudinal* study, in which data are collected at two or more times before being analyzed.

Cross-Tabulations—A way of presenting data about two variables in a table so that their relations are more obvious. Also called a contingency table or a crosstabs table. A cross tabulation can be used for categorical variables only and shows the joint frequency distributions of the two variables.[1]

Database—An organized collection of data, typically stored electronically.

Demography—The study of variables in the human populations (such as death, fertility, and migration) and the social and economic

---

[1] NOTE: From *Dictionary of Statistics & Methodology: A Nontechnical Guide for the Social Sciences,* 4th ed. (pp. 83 and 88) by W. P. Vogt and R. B. Johnson, 2011, Los Angeles: Copyright 2011 by Sage Publications. Reprinted with permission.

variables that cause them to change. Demographic variables are often used by researchers and other disciplines as background variables.[1]

Dependent Variable—The variable whose quality is presumed to change in response to the introduction of or a change in another variable.

Dichotomized/Dichotomous Variables—A continuous variable that has been divided into two categories. For example, one might use income data to create two categories, poor and not poor. Compare dichotomous variable, in which two categories occur naturally; that is, they are not created by the researcher. [Example: male/female].[1]

Empirical—Observation- or experience-based data; data that can be verified.

Ethnographic Research—A major method of qualitative or mixed methods research focusing on the description of social or cultural life of particular groups of people based on direct, systematic observation, such as becoming a participant in a particular social system. Ethnographic research is most closely associated with anthropological research but is widely used in other fields as well.[1]

Exit Survey—An evaluation conducted at the end of a process, such as upon graduation from college.

Focus Group—A qualitative research tool pioneered in the 1940's and 1950's by Robert K. Merton, who called it the "focused group interview." The basic technique involves having about a dozen persons engage in an intensive discussion focused on a particular topic. It has been used extensively in market research among potential customers ("What would you think of this product?") and in planning political campaigns ("What do you see as this candidates main weakness?"). It is increasingly used by survey researchers to help them design questionnaires. Members of focus groups tend to be similar to one another, sharing a trait of interest to the

---

[1] NOTE: From *Dictionary of Statistics & Methodology: A Nontechnical Guide for the Social Sciences,* 4th ed. (pp. 102, 106 and 128) by W. P. Vogt and R. B. Johnson, 2011, Los Angeles: Copyright 2011 by Sage Publications. Reprinted with permission.

researchers, such as potential customers for a product or likely voters for a candidate.[1]

Frequency—The number of times something occurs. A count.

Generalizability—The ability to use information from a subset (like a sample) to draw conclusions about the characteristics of the larger context from which the subset was drawn (like a population).

Hypothesis—A tentative answer to a research question; a statement of (or conjecture about) the relationships among the variables that a researcher intends to study. Hypotheses are sometimes testable statements of relations. In such cases, they are usually thought of as predictions that, if confirmed, will support a theory.
For example, suppose a social psychologist theorized that racial prejudice is due to ignorance. Hypotheses for testing this theory might be as follows: (1) if education reduces ignorance, then (2) the more highly educated people are, the less likely they are to be prejudiced. If an attitude survey showed that there was indeed an inverse relationship between education and prejudice levels, this would support or confirm a theory that prejudice is a function of ignorance.[1]

Impact Assessment—A process whereby the effects of a program or policy are judged.

Independent Variable—The presumed cause in a study. Also, a variable that can be used to predict or explain the values of another variable. A variable manipulated by an experimenter who predicts that the manipulation will have an effect on another variable (the dependent variable).[1]

Index—(a) A number, often a ratio, meant to express simply a relationship between two variables or between two measures of the same variable. (b) A composite measure (a group of individual measures) that, when combined, is meant to indicate some more general characteristic. This type of index is similar to certain types of scales, and the terms are sometimes used interchangeably.
For example, (a), indexes measuring access to medical school for various groups could be calculated by dividing a group's percentage of students in medical school by its share of the population of

---

[1] NOTE: From *Dictionary of Statistics & Methodology: A Nontechnical Guide for the Social Sciences*, 4th ed. (p. 145, 173 and 178) by W. P. Vogt and R. B. Johnson, 2011, Los Angeles: Copyright 2011 by Sage Publications. Reprinted with permission.

medical school age. If, say, women made up 50% of the 21 to 25-year-olds and were 40% of the medical students, their access index would be 0.8 (40/50 = 0.8. Or, if white males were 40% of the 21 to 25-year-old population and were 56% of the medical students, their index would be 1.4 (56/40 = 1.4).

For example (b), in survey research, political tolerance might be measured by an index composed of six questions about whether the respondent favored such things as free speech for religious outsiders, the right to demonstrate for political radicals, and so on. Scores of the index could range from zero (for those answering none of the questions in the tolerant way) to six (for those answering all the questions in the tolerant way). This kind of indexes used to measure an ordinal variable. [1]

Institutional Review Board (IRB)—A screening panel for research projects that must, by law, be in place at any U.S. institution receiving federal funding. Its focus is protecting human subjects from potential harm caused by research. Research conducted by faculty must have IRB approval prior to being conducted.[1]

Interaction Effect—The combined effect of two or more independent variables on a dependent variable that is not accounted for by the simple sum of their separate effects. In other terms, interaction effects occur when the relation between two variables differs depending on the value of another variable. An interaction is present between two independent variables when the relationship between one independent variable and the dependent variable changes at the different levels of the other independent variable – the relationship, in a sense, "depends on" the level of second independent variable. The presence of a statistically significant interaction effect makes it difficult to interpret main effects.[1]

Interview—A person-to-person questioning session.

Levels of Measurement—A term used to describe measurement scales in terms of how much information they convey about the differences among values—the higher the level, the more information. There are four levels of measurement. Arranged in order of strength, from the highest to the lowest, they are: ratio, interval, ordinal, and nominal. It is possible to describe data

---

[1]   NOTE: From *Dictionary of Statistics & Methodology: A Nontechnical Guide for the Social Sciences,* 4th ed. (pp. 178-179, 181 and 182) by W. P. Vogt and R. B. Johnson, 2011, Los Angeles: Copyright 2011 by Sage Publications. Reprinted with permission.

gathered at a higher level with a lower level of measurement; but the reverse is not true. For example, one can express income in dollars and cents (interval level) or with ordinal descriptions like upper, middle, and lower class.

It is important to be aware of the level of measurement that you are using because statistical techniques appropriate for one level might produce ridiculous results at another. For example, in a study of religious affiliation, you might want to number your variables as follows: 1 = Catholic, 2 = Jewish, 3 = Protestant, 4 = Other, 5 = None. The religion variable is measured at the nominal level. The numbers are just convenient labels or names; one cannot treat them as if they mean something at the interval level; one should not add together a Jewish person (2) and a Protestant person (3) to get an atheist (5).[1]

Lexis/Nexis—A database used to look up topics that range from legal system to news articles.

Likert Scale—A widely used questionnaire format developed by R. Likert. (a) in its larger sense, it refers to a summated scaling technique pioneered by Likert in the late 1920s. Respondents are giving a series of statements and asked to respond to each by saying whether they 1 "strongly agree," 2 "agree," 3 "disagree," or 4 "strongly disagree." (b) in its smaller sense, a Likert scale refers to the use of an ordinal (some would say interval) for a five point rating scale with each point anchored or labeled. This usage probably arose because in addition to pioneering the use of the summative scaling procedure, Likert used a five-point approval rating scale.

Today the term "Likert scale" has become somewhat confused because it might refer to either (a) or (b), and the reader is sometimes left wondering. Wording on rating scales today varies considerably. The width of rating scales tend to vary from 4 to 11 points. By constructing the appropriate anchors, rating scales can be used to address many kinds of attitudinal variation, such as intensity about agreement, amount, effectiveness, important, satisfaction, and so forth.

Summated scales and rating scales are the most widely used attitude scale types in the social sciences. Summated scales are comparatively easy to construct and tend to have high reliabilities.[1]

Literature Review—A comprehensive review and interpretation of theories and research on a particular topic.

---

[1] NOTE: From *Dictionary of Statistics & Methodology: A Nontechnical Guide for the Social Sciences*, 4th ed. (pp. 205 and 208) by W. P. Vogt and R. B. Johnson, 2011, Los Angeles: Copyright 2011 by Sage Publications. Reprinted with permission.

Logistic Regression Analysis—Also known as logit regression and even sometimes logistical regression. A kind of regression analysis often use when the dependent variable is dichotomous and scored zero, one. The kind of regression analysis used with dependent variable is dichotomous and scored zero or one. It also can be used when the dependent variable is more than two categories, in which case it is called "multinomial") it is usually used for predicting whether something will happen or not, such as graduation, business failure, heart attack—anything that can be expressed as an event/non-event.[1]

Longitudinal Study—A study that looks at a variable or a group of subjects over a period of time. For example, researchers wanted to test the impact of drug court on recidivism. They surveyed a sample of drug court graduates upon graduation and every three years for a total of fifteen years. This is in contrast to a cross-sectional study in which subjects/variables are measured once.

Matching—Also known as "matched pairs." A research design in which subjects are matched on characteristics that might affect their reaction to a treatment. After the pairs are determined, one member of each pair is assigned at random to the group receiving treatment (experimental group); the other group (control group) does not receive treatment. Without random assignment, matching is considered a much weaker research practice because the groups are matched or equated on only a single variable. Also called "subject matching" for example, if professors wanted to test the effectiveness of two different textbooks for an undergraduate statistics course, they might match the students and quantitative aptitude scores before assigning them to classes using one or another of the tax. An alternative, if the professors had no control over class assignment, would be to treat the quantitative aptitude scores as a covariate and control it for it using an ANCOVA design.[1]

Mean—An average. The mean is calculated by adding the value of each case and dividing it by the total number of cases. This is expressed often as $\bar{x}$.

---

[1] NOTE: From *Dictionary of Statistics & Methodology: A Nontechnical Guide for the Social Sciences,* 4th ed. (pp. 241 and 223) by W. P. Vogt and R. B. Johnson, 2011, Los Angeles: Copyright 2011 by Sage Publications. Reprinted with permission.

Median—Midpoint. Calculated by taking the lowest to the highest and finding the middle score. If there is an even number of scores, then the two in the middle are averaged.

Meta-Analysis—Quantitative procedures for summarizing or integrating the findings obtained from a literature review on a topic. Meta-analysis is, strictly speaking, more a kind of synthesis than analysis, and it is also called "research synthesis." The meta-analyst uses the results of individual research projects on the same topic (perhaps studies testing the same hypothesis) as data for a statistical study of the topic. The main controversies about meta-analysis have to do with identifying the appropriate studies to synthesize, that is, with specifying which studies are truly studying the same hypothesis, treatments, and populations.[1]

Methodology—Research design; i.e., the "methods" used to collect data in support of hypotheses.

Mode—The most frequently occurring score in a set. For example, consider the following set of scores: 1, 3, 5, 5, 6, 6, 6, 6, 7, 8. The mode is 6.

Multicollineariary—In multiple regression analysis, multicollinearity exists when two or more independent variables are highly correlated; this makes it difficult, if not impossible, to determine their separate effects on the dependent variable.[1]

Multiple Regression Analysis (MRA)—Any of several related statistical methods for evaluating the effects of more than one independent (or predictor) variable on a dependent (or outcome) variable... MRA answers two main questions: (1) What is the effect (as measured by a regression coefficient) on a dependent variable (DV) or a one-unit change in an independent variable (IV), while controlling for the effects of all the other IVs? (2) What is the total effect (as measured by the R^2) on the DV of all the IVs taken together?[1]

Multivariate—Denotes three or more variables. *Multivariate analysis* (or *multiple variate analysis*) refers to the statistical analysis of three or more variables.

---

[1]   NOTE: From *Dictionary of Statistics & Methodology: A Nontechnical Guide for the Social Sciences,* 4th ed. (p. 229, 238 and 243) by W. P. Vogt and R. B. Johnson, 2011, Los Angeles: Copyright 2011 by Sage Publications. Reprinted with permission.

Needs Assessment—An evaluation of a situation in order to determine gaps in delivery of products, services, or processes. May be called a "gap analysis."

Negative Relationship—An inverse relation between two variables. In other words, when one variable increases, the other variable decreases.

Non-Random—Deliberately chosen.

Null hypothesis—The hypothesis that is directly tested in hypothesis or significance testing. A hypothesis that a researcher hopes to reject (nullify), thereby supporting its opposite. The null hypothesis is something like the presumption of innocence in a trial; to find someone guilty: the jury has to reject the presumption of innocence.[1]

Ordinary Least Squares (OLS) Regression Analysis—A statistical estimation method of determining a regression equation, that is, an equation that best represents the relationship between the dependent variable and the independent variables.[1]

Pilot Study—A "test run" of a study administered on a much smaller scale than the intended "main" study. Pilot studies provide researchers with the opportunity to discover and correct potential methodological problems before more resources are spent on the intended study.

Population—A group of persons (or institutions, events, or other subjects of study) that one wants to describe or about which one wants to generalize. In order to generalize about a population, one often studies a sample that is meant to be representative of the population.[1]

Positive Relationship—A direct relation between two variables. In other words, when one variable increases, the other variable increases, or, when one variable decreases, the other variable decreases.

Posttest—Data collected after a "treatment" and designed to assess the impact of the treatment on the group receiving it.

---

[1] NOTE: From *Dictionary of Statistics & Methodology: A Nontechnical Guide for the Social Sciences,* 4th ed. (pp. 262, 272 and 293) by W. P. Vogt and R. B. Johnson, 2011, Los Angeles: Copyright 2011 by Sage Publications. Reprinted with permission.

Predictive Research—Said of an investigation whose goal is to forecast (predict, but not explain) the values of one variable by using the values of one or more other variables. Usually contrasted with explanatory research, in which the goal is to understand the causes behind relations, to test theory-based hypotheses to develop a theory, or sometimes to compare the effectiveness of two theories to explain variance in a dependent variable. In other terms, the goal in predictive research is to estimate a future value of a deep ended variable; in explanatory research, it is to estimate the partial regression coefficients that are interpreted as showing the degree of effect or causal relation for each variable, controlling for other variables.[1]

Pre-Test—Data collected before a "treatment" and designed to assess the impact of the treatment on the group receiving it when compared to data collected after the "treatment" (posttest).

Process Evaluation—Analysis of the sequencing of events designed to produce an end.

Purposive Sampling—A sampling method in which the researcher purposely chooses the subjects of the sample. Usually, this is done to assure that the sample is made up of subjects with certain characteristics particularly relevant to the study.

Qualitative Research—Descriptive research based on subjects that cannot be quantified.

Quantitative Research—Numerical-based research.

Quasi-Experimental—A type of research design for conducting studies in field or real-life situations where the researcher may be able to manipulate some independent variables but cannot randomly assign subjects to control and experimental groups.
For example, you cannot cut off some individuals unemployment benefits to see how well they could get along without them or to see whether an alternative job-training program would be more effective. But you could try to find volunteers for your new job-training program. You could compare the results for the volunteer group (experimental group) with those of people in the regular program (control group). The study is quasi- experimental because

---

[1] NOTE: From *Dictionary of Statistics & Methodology: A Nontechnical Guide for the Social Sciences,* 4th ed. (p. 300) by W. P. Vogt and R. B. Johnson, 2011, Los Angeles: Copyright 2011 by Sage Publications. Reprinted with permission.

you were unable to assign subjects randomly to treatment and control groups.[1]

Random—Unpredictable. Occurrence based on chance. Random assignment of research subjects helps increase validity of the results.

Rate—A calculation of the number of events per a designated base.

Records Analysis—Study of data files, etc.

Regression Analysis—(a) Methods of explaining or predicting the variability of a dependent variable using information about one or more independent variables. Regression analysis can be used to answer three basic questions: (1) what is the predicted change in a dependent variable for each one unit increase in an independent variable? (2) what is the predicted change in the dependent variable associated with the one unit change in the particular independent variable – after controlling for other independent variables? (3) how much better can one explain or predict a dependent variable taking all the independent variables together?[1]

Reliability—Consistency of results. If measuring the same thing multiple times produces the same (or similar) results, the measurement instrument is reliable.

Respondents—People who responded to survey or interview questions.

Response Rate—The percentage or proportion of members of a sample who respond to a questionnaire. Low response rates are one of the more frequent sources of bias in social science research.[1]

Retrospective Study—Reflective research. Subjects of *retrospective studies* base responses to questions on memories.

Sample—A group of subjects or cases selected from a larger group in the hope that studying this smaller group (the sample) will reveal important things about the larger group (the population).[1]

Scale—(a) A set of numbers or other symbols used to designate characteristics of a variable used in measurement. For example, the

---

[1] NOTE: From *Dictionary of Statistics & Methodology: A Nontechnical Guide for the Social Sciences,* 4th ed. (pp. 316, 330, 341 and 347) by W. P. Vogt and R. B. Johnson, 2011, Los Angeles: Copyright 2011 by Sage Publications. Reprinted with permission.

numbers on a thermometer and the words 'low, medium, and high' on an air conditioner are scales. (b) A group of related measures of a variable. The items in a scale are arranged in some order of intensity or importance. A scale differs from an index in that the items in an index need not be in a particular order, and each item usually has the same weight or importance.[1]

Secondary Analysis—Analysis of data collected by others. Social scientists often use data collected in large studies—like the General Social Survey—to evaluate their research questions.

Selection Bias—Also called "selection threat (to validity)" and "self-selection defect." A problem that arises when the researcher cannot randomly assign subjects to control and experimental groups. For example, comparing the effects on academic achievement of attending two-year colleges versus attending four-year colleges would be difficult because (among other reasons) students who choose to attend two-year colleges might be indifferent in important ways (e.g., goals, income, motivation, aptitude) from those who selected four-year colleges.[1]

Self-Administered—As in a "self-administered questionnaire," it is an instrument that is completed by the respondent directly.

Significance—The degree to which a research finding is meaningful or important. Without qualification, the term usually means *statistical* significance, but lack of specificity leads to confusion (or allows obfuscation).[1]

Skewed—Abnormal or non-symmetrical unusual nontypical measurements.

Spurious Relation (for Correlation)—A situation in which measures of two or more variables statistically related (covariation) but are not in fact causally linked—often because the statistical relation is caused by a third variable. When the effects of the third variable are removed, they are said to have been partialled out.
For example, if the students in a psychology class who had long hair got higher scores on the midterm then those who had short hair, there would be a correlation between hair length and test scores.

---

[1] NOTE: From *Dictionary of Statistics & Methodology: A Nontechnical Guide for the Social Sciences,* 4th ed. (pp. 351, 357 and 360) by W. P. Vogt and R. B. Johnson, 2011, Los Angeles: Copyright 2011 by Sage Publications. Reprinted with permission.

However, not many people would believe that there was a causal link and that for example students who wish to improve their grades should let their hair grow. The real cause might be gender: women (who had longer hair) did better on the test. Or that might be a spurious relationship too. The real cause might be class rank: seniors did better on the test and sophomores and juniors, and in this class the women (who also had longer hair) were mostly seniors, whereas the men (with shorter hair) were mostly sophomores and juniors.[1]

Subjects—Who or what is studied. Most think of *subjects* in terms of people, but subjects can be animals, buildings, songs, etc. It is the unit of analysis being examined.

Survey Questionnaire—A set of questions given to subjects and from which data are collected and analyzed.

Theory—A statement or group of statements about how some part of the world works—frequently explaining relations among phenomena. W theories explain "how" and "why" (and they can be big, small, or medium-sized, and they can be about big objects all the way down to very small objects).[1]

Typology—A model whereby the items listed within each category has unique characteristics.

Validity—The quality, accuracy, intersubjective agreement/approval, or truth value of or about some "object" of discussion (e.g., a measurement instrument, a research design, and inference, a claim, a conclusion). Validity is viewed and defined differently in different knowledge domains. Validity requires reliability, but the reverse is not true. In research design, validity refers to the strength of the research design. In the evaluation of published research, validity refers to the degree to which the researchers gathered data appropriate for answering their questions and how much one should believe their inferences and conclusions. In qualitative research, validity has many additional definitions, but generally refers to the trustworthiness of the statements and findings provided by the research study.[1]

---

[1] NOTE: From *Dictionary of Statistics & Methodology: A Nontechnical Guide for the Social Sciences,* 4th ed. (pp. 374, 398 and 415) by W. P. Vogt and R. B. Johnson, 2011, Los Angeles: Copyright 2011 by Sage Publications. Reprinted with permission.

SECTION 1

THE IMPORTANCE OF CRIMINAL JUSTICE RESEARCH

SECTION 1
The Importance of Criminal Justice Research

INTRODUCTION

The first chapter in this introductory section is by James Finckenauer, an internationally recognized criminologist who, as President of the Academy of Criminal Justice Sciences (ACJS), held a leadership role in the establishment of the ACJS Certification Standards for Academic Programs. Finckenauer's article sets the tone for this volume perfectly. In it he discusses the value of a college education based in liberal arts, as opposed to a highly technical training program and shows why this is especially important for students whose interests are in criminal justice. This is due in part to the history of criminal justice as an academic field and in part due to the relationship between theory and practice. While it is almost always the case that a discipline must find the balance between theory and practice, it is especially important in the field of criminal justice because of the many misconceptions of what criminal justice is.

This section's remaining chapters provide students with a basic understanding of what scholarly research articles present, how they are used, and how they differ from the types of reading most people are familiar with. Jeffrey Chin's article is designed to provide students with an example of how educators are sometimes asked to serve as research consultants for criminal justice organizations and the unique ways in which researchers view the process of gathering information and finding solutions. This further establishes the value of research and its application to real-world problems.

Educating for Justice: Its Past, Present, and Future

In essence, there was no academic discipline of criminal justice in the United States until 1968 when the federal Omnibus Crime Control and Safe Streets Act created the Law Enforcement Education Program (LEEP). LEEP funding provided under that law stimulated a student consumer demand that in turn led to the creation of a variety of criminal justice higher education programs. Although there has been a nearly constant struggle for academic legitimacy over the four plus decades since then, criminal justice education continues because it has become institutionalized. It became institutionalized because it filled a critically important niche and need in society. Thousands of such programs exist today, awarding associates, bachelors, masters, and doctoral degrees. Criminal justice higher education has helped professionalize criminal justice. It has helped create whole new professions. And it has educated thousands of students about the profound issues of crime, law, and justice. Now in its fifth decade, new challenges for criminal justice include transnational crime, terrorism and counter-terrorism, security management, and the expanding role of forensic science. Criminal justice education has and must continue to evolve and grow to meet these challenges.

The Case for Sound Social Science Research

This provides a real-life example of why social science research is useful and even essential to all criminal justice practitioners. Regardless of what field in criminal justice one chooses, the need to have accurate and reliable data is essential for making decisions that relate to policy. Dr. Chin illustrates this by drawing from a research project conducted while under contract by a municipality concerned about having a better understanding of how its police officers treated minority populations. It provides a clear example of the importance of planning and implementing an evaluation project effectively, as well as how such planning and implementation can impact a project's outcomes and value of its results.

A Beginner's Guide to Reading Research Articles

The articles presented in scholarly journals are much different than what most students have previously been exposed to in popular magazines, newspapers, and the web. These articles follow standards in terms of what they are designed to do, as well as what it takes to even get published in professional journals (peer-review). The sequencing of sections commonly found among such articles form the foundation needed for understanding the research project presented. This brief guide introduces students to the key elements of research articles and will aid in their ability to comprehend the chapters that follow.

Chapter 1
EDUCATING FOR JUSTICE: ITS PAST, PRESENT, AND FUTURE

James Finckenauer, Ph.D. Rutgers University School of Criminal Justice

Introduction

For students studying criminal justice and perhaps considering careers in the field, it should be enlightening and useful to understand the history and development of criminal justice as an academic discipline in the United States. Where, how, and why did criminal justice education begin? Where do things stand today? Where is criminal justice likely to be going in the future? What roles will education play in that direction? Let's begin by looking back to a little over four decades ago.

The Past

Throughout most of U.S. history, men and women working in criminal justice fields have had to meet limited education and training requirements. The exceptions have been the judges and lawyers with their law degrees and a variety of others, such as parole and probation officers and counselors, who mostly had four-year college degrees, which often could be in any discipline. For instance, I recall many years ago when I was contemplating a job as a probation officer; a degree in animal husbandry would have been sufficient!

For years, most line police and corrections officers only had to have a high school diploma or its equivalent. Police officers received their technical and operational training in police academies. Training for corrections officers was very spotty, if there even was any.

Despite its rarity and although it was not called specifically "criminal justice," teaching various matters of criminal justice actually has quite a long history in the United States. Some law faculties in American universities studied criminology as well as criminal law at least as early as the early 1900s. With very few exceptions, e.g., the University of California at Berkeley, the University of Chicago, and Michigan State University, most colleges offered no courses in law enforcement or criminal justice. Consequently, until the middle of the twentieth century, there was no such academic discipline as "criminal justice." Beyond specialty areas like counseling and social work and the few schools that offered the study of police science or law enforcement, students generally had only sociology and criminology to learn about the myriad issues of crime, law, and justice. Indeed, as both an undergraduate and graduate student, I studied sociology, with as many courses in criminology, juvenile delinquency, and the like as I could find or could fashion into independent studies—and this was not at all unusual.

It was this situation that the President's Commission on Law Enforcement and Administration of Justice was responding to in its 1967 report called The Challenge of Crime in a Free Society. The Commission recommended that all police personnel with general enforcement powers (in essence, all sworn police officers) have baccalaureate degrees. The Commission recommended that university curricula include attention to corrections and that universities provide fellowships and stipends to students interested in corrections and to correctional employees wanting university training. The Commission also called for support for internships and field placement programs developed with correctional agencies.

A year after the release of the Commission report, President Lyndon Johnson signed into law the *1968 Omnibus Crime Control and Safe Streets Act*. Among its many provisions was the creation of the Law Enforcement Education Program, known popularly as LEEP. LEEP funded college education for police and corrections officers, paying for their tuition, fees, and books. Suddenly, there were hundreds and then thousands of law enforcement personnel nationwide with the financial ability to go to college, and they took advantage of the opportunity.

Because of the limited offerings specifically related to their interests, the new LEEP students initially studied in whatever subjects the colleges and universities offered. Soon, however, these students clamored for areas of study that were more "relevant," which meant mostly courses on policing. Consequently, being entrepreneurial and recognizing this new pool of applicants, colleges began to create such courses.

Two-year and four-year programs in police science and law enforcement sprouted across the country in the late 1960s and early 1970s. Many later evolved into criminal justice programs, as their curricula grew beyond policing to include courses in law, the courts, corrections, criminology, etc. Students in these courses were generally of three kinds: in-service students, those already working in the field and taking advantage of the LEEP funding; pre-service students, those majoring in criminal justice because they were thinking about a job in law enforcement; and students from other subject majors, who took elective criminal justice courses out of interest.

The dramatic growth of criminal justice programs during the 1970s proved to be a period of struggle for legitimacy within criminal justice higher education. Many programs began in haste in order to respond quickly to student demand and to capture the applicant pool fueled by LEEP. Practically the only model for teaching criminal justice practitioners at that time—notwithstanding the few exceptions already mentioned—was the police academy. As I indicated earlier, teachers, social workers, and psychologists working with criminal offenders had their own educational disciplines. Professions such as probation and parole accepted college degrees in virtually any subject. The FBI wanted accountants and lawyers, and, in general, law school was the required preparation for judges, prosecutors, and defense counsel. Thus, police academies became the source of instructors for undergraduate college and university criminal justice programs. These instructors naturally taught what they knew: what they had themselves been taught. Consequently, as a variety of criminal justice programs blossomed, there was often little to distinguish what was being taught on many college campuses from what had been offered in the police academy. The principal difference was that this "training" was now called "education" and was awarded college credit.

Unfortunately, many colleges and universities did not move beyond these humble beginnings and commit the necessary planning and resources to ensure higher quality programs. On the one hand, traditional academic disciplines such as sociology, political science, and so on did not view criminal justice studies as a real discipline, accusing the latter of being simply "cop shops" that were teaching "Handcuffs 101." On the other hand, program administrators contributed to this lack of credibility and low regard by hiring unqualified or underqualified faculty (often police academy instructors), by offering courses with few requirements that were little more than what the typical police academy curriculum included, and by treating the programs as "cash cows" that could bring in a lot of students and money for few resources. Criminal justice education therefore became tainted and stigmatized in a way that unfortunately continues today. At the core of the troubled state of criminal justice education is the juxtaposition of low quality programs with high quantities of students.

Despite its shortcomings and failings, however, there have been and continue to be reasons for pride and optimism. For example, many weaker criminal justice programs dropped by the wayside, and stronger ones evolved and expanded. Even when funding for LEEP stopped in 1978, criminal justice higher education continued. This was because the students and student interest did not go away. In fact, despite often being under-resourced, criminal justice programs became established parts of the institutional structures at colleges and universities. The courses were very popular with students, and they filled a critically important niche and need in society. One of the most important achievements of criminal justice education was that the subjects of crime and justice became recognized as appropriate, even necessary, areas of study for college students. This is a bedrock foundation, in my judgment, for criminal justice education. As witness to the popularity of these programs, when I was hired at New Jersey's Trenton State College to develop its criminal justice program back in 1971, there were nine students interested in studying in the program. Just three years later, there were approximately 900 students taking courses!

Typical undergraduate criminal justice courses and programs of study in typical undergraduate criminal justice programs have been very much focused on U.S. policing, courts, and corrections. Criminal justice students typically have learned, for example, about the FBI Uniform Crime Reports; about police administration and management; about patrol and police-community interactions. They learn about prosecution, the courts, criminal law, sentencing, etc.; about community corrections, prisons, and the death penalty; about juvenile delinquency and juvenile justice; and sometimes about such more arcane subjects as criminological theory, victimization surveys, self-report studies, violence, the role of race and gender in crime, etc.

The in-service students then, as now, saw the degree in criminal justice as the route to advancement and promotion in their agencies, or as the ticket to a second career as a college instructor following retirement. The pre-service students likewise saw the degree as opening the door to a career in law enforcement—often in the usually more prestigious and better paying agencies of the federal government—or as a precursor to law school. In either instance, criminal justice education was the fulfillment of the President's Crime Commission recommendations. Many more police and correctional personnel attained college degrees, and in the process, they studied subjects that were directly pertinent to their jobs. For example, police officers better understood the causes of crime and violence, how the community viewed them, and what their roles as police officers in a constitutional democracy were.

Besides the many 2-year and 4-year undergraduate programs, some universities developed graduate and doctoral programs—also beginning in the early 1970s. The latter development was especially significant because it meant that for the first time there could be teaching faculty steeped in research and the study of criminal justice at the highest levels. This too was a major step in the institutionalization of criminal justice as an academic discipline.

The Present

So where are we now? Hundreds of colleges and universities in the United States offer undergraduate and in some cases graduate programs in criminal justice. Many places have more than one program (for example, at my institution—Rutgers University—we have six spread over three campuses). There are now more than 35 doctoral programs offering PhD degrees in criminal justice or criminology. For the first time, in 2005, doctoral programs in criminal justice/criminology were included in the national magazine *US News & World Report* ratings of higher education in the United States. In their assessment of the quality of these doctoral programs, the magazine observed that criminology has emerged as a field of its own and provides an impetus for the scientific study of crime and criminal justice systems (*US News & World Report*, 2005). The criminal justice/criminology programs were also included in its second set of rankings, published in 2009. This must say something about criminal justice education coming of age!

As with many other disciplines in higher education, criminal justice has moved dramatically in the direction of distance learning and online education. This means that criminal justice practitioners in particular, who may work in far-flung areas inaccessible to campus sites, can study criminal justice via the Internet. Although this obviously expands opportunity, there is a need to be wary of trying to do more with less— trying to teach too many students in too many places with too few resources. Granted, this problem is not unique to criminal justice education, but given our history, it is one to which we must be particularly sensitive.

Before we turn to the future, a quick assessment of where we are now will help to understand where we are going and where we need to be in the future. First, higher education in criminal justice has had and is continuing to have great impact in professionalizing criminal justice practice and policy. Although not completely realized, the goal of the President's Crime Commission that every police officer would have a baccalaureate degree has seen substantial progress toward its accomplishment. Without question, policing is much more a profession than it was 40 years ago. The capabilities of college-educated officers helped build police specialties such as Compstat, crime mapping, hostage negotiations, crime scene analysts, and more.

Second, as important as the impact upon practitioners and the criminal justice system specifically has been, a largely unanticipated benefit has come in the form of the thousands and thousands of students made aware of the profound issues of crime, law, and justice that exist in our society. This has produced a better-informed and educated citizenry—irrespective of whether these student/citizens actually work in the field of criminal justice. For any who firmly believe in the critical importance of these issues, this is a great achievement. Understanding is an important element in establishing the foundations for a society governed by the rule of law—a society with an independent judiciary and with its police and prisons operating in accordance with democratic principles and with due concern for human rights.

Third, the opportunity to study criminal justice has helped create new professions. These include criminal-justice planners, crime analysts, evaluation specialists, forensic scientists, and security specialists, as well as criminal justice professors. As I indicated, the latter means there is now a specially educated faculty cadre of criminal justice experts—academics, scholars, and researchers—who stand on the same level with scholars from all the other academic disciplines.

Finally, criminal justice has moved far along the road of being an accepted academic discipline. Its enormous popularity is evidenced by the fact that many high schools are now offering criminal justice electives. The scholars and researchers referred to above have not only held their own in academe, but have studied some of the most profound issues facing our society. Such issues include racial profiling, domestic violence, terrorism, human trafficking, treating sex offenders, hate crimes, corporate crime, juvenile gangs, public corruption, and many others. It is the existence of criminal justice programs, particularly doctoral programs, which have facilitated these studies and gained the necessary financial support to carry them out.

The Future

It seems clear that we now need new and expanded subject-matter coverage in criminal justice. Criminal justice educators must recognize (as many practitioners and policy makers already have) that the face of crime has changed—it has become increasingly transnational and international in nature. Consider cybercrime, drug trafficking, human trafficking, other forms of trafficking and smuggling, and money laundering. Although global in nature, these sorts of crimes have significant state and local impact. Twenty-first-century criminal justice professors and students need to recognize and understand those impacts.

Increasingly, crime and criminals do not respect national borders. As a result, national borders cannot bind policing and prosecution. The United States has criminal justice operatives situated in the world's trouble spots. Because the U.S. Department of Justice has primary responsibility for representing the United States in global crime and justice matters, a significant proportion of its work involves transnational and international crime. Policy-makers and practitioners in U.S. law enforcement increasingly need to work with their counterparts in other countries. This means they must have a basic understanding of such legal mechanisms as extradition and mutual legal assistance treaties (MLATs) and of such international entities as the United Nations, civilian policing initiatives (CivPol), the International Criminal Court, and so on.

CivPol and the International Criminal Court are two excellent examples of hot topics for the kind of critical thinking and acknowledgment of cultural and societal diversity that need to be incorporated into criminal justice courses. Both are highly controversial: CivPol because of such concerns as jurisdiction, authority, cultural conflict, etc., and the ICC because of the U.S. refusal, so far, not to be bound by its jurisdiction. These sorts of controversies demand in-depth discussion and debate.

One of the major concerns I have heard expressed by Federal law enforcement operatives is what they perceive to be an inadequate understanding (ignorance) of the different roles and responsibilities of Federal versus State and local law enforcement in dealing with international crime and justice issues. Should, for example, the New York City Police Department have officers assigned overseas, as is currently the case? What are the pros and cons of that? What about the U.S. government's highly controversial "extraordinary rendition" of terrorism suspects to foreign countries for detention and interrogation? Do the ends justify the means? I believe that criminal justice curricula must address these sorts of issues.

A second priority for criminal justice education is the need to recognize the increasingly pervasive and sophisticated role of science in law enforcement and the administration of justice. This role includes developments in DNA testing and forensic evidence, the use of less-than-lethal weapons, increasingly sophisticated means of identification, and crimes such as identity theft and frauds. The use of scientific evidence and expert witnesses is also a significant issue in the prosecution and adjudication of offenders. Although not all students need extensive and intensive study in the science of forensics, all students should have a grounding in the fundamentals that goes beyond what they gain from watching *CSI* television programs and movies about criminal profilers.

A third development and priority is unfortunately quite familiar to all of us—namely the necessary emphasis on public security and terrorism engendered by the events of September 11, 2001, and their aftermath around the globe. This emphasis continues to shape criminal justice (and consequently criminal justice education) in a variety of ways. Given the nature of terrorism and terrorists, the earlier stressed priority given to international issues is pertinent here as well. It clearly behooves practitioners, policy-makers, educators, and students to get ahead of the curve on issues related to terrorism. This includes the legal and constitutional questions surrounding the handling of terrorism suspects, racial and ethnic profiling, infrastructure security, the roots of terrorism, domestic and international terrorism, and the unique challenges presented to criminal justice and criminology by this phenomenon.

The fourth priority on my list is to recognize that the current move toward evidence-based criminal-justice policy requires applying rational-empirical methods to improve crime control and prevention efforts and, therefore, effectively reduce the impact of crime on individuals, families, and communities. We spend billions of dollars on crime control and prevention, but is it money well spent? We need to do a much better job of finding out what works. Knowledge of planning and problem solving are thus critical, as is the understanding that all this must be accomplished within the strict parameters set by our constitutional standards of justice and by the rule of law. Many steps may be effective and may "work," but are they steps we really want to take? Are they the "right" thing to do?

What then are the implications of all this for criminal justice education? In my view, and I emphasize it is only one person's opinion, the implications are many. Tomorrow's (if not today's) criminal justice students must have knowledge of comparative criminal justice. Such a requirement will present a rather dramatic shift from the current curricula at most colleges and universities. Several years ago, I reviewed an Educational Testing Service (ETS) survey of criminal justice programs and learned that very few programs included "international criminal justice" as part of their core content or recognized it as an important competency for criminal justice majors. This flies in the face of current global developments with respect to crime and justice concerns. Students must have some knowledge of cultures other than their own in order to understand the roles of formal and informal social control systems in controlling crime and deviance. If they aspire to careers in law enforcement and the administration of justice, they need to know legal traditions other than ours.

Another must for graduates of criminal justice programs is knowledge of languages other than English. Language skills are increasingly important not only because of the transnationalization of crime and terrorism, but also because of the changing makeup of our own domestic population that increasingly requires criminal justice professionals to interact with non-native English speakers. Further, to be most effective, language training must provide students with oral language skills, and must move beyond traditional language education available to students. What will be the lingua franca of this and succeeding generations? Arabic, Chinese, Russian, and Spanish certainly top the list.

As previously indicated, today's criminal justice students must be acquainted with the subjects of terrorism and counter-terrorism. This includes some knowledge of the nature and origins of terrorism and of the variety of preventive and responsive efforts employed to combat it. The subject matter of public security must be expanded to encompass these topics. Similarly, criminal justice students must have an appreciation and understanding of evolving scientific applications in criminal justice. This includes the collection, preservation, and presentation of physical evidence, including new identification techniques. It includes information technology, and it includes understanding some of the juxtaposition of science and the law. At a minimum, that would seem to mean a survey course in forensic science for all criminal-justice majors.

The evidence-based policy developments demand attention to policy, planning, and evaluation. Although the most intensive efforts in this area will probably occur at the graduate level, undergraduates should also be exposed to these developments. Criminal justice practitioners at all levels need to know something about the effectiveness of various policies and practices.

As we look to the future of criminal justice education in the United States and to its expansion and evolution elsewhere in the world, we must be mindful of a few more things—beginning with accountability. All walks of life are demanding greater accountability. With higher education, part of this accountability comes in the form of consumer and constituent demand—from students, parents, alumni, legislators, criminal justice officials, etc. This I call the "so what" question—so what does having a degree in criminal justice mean? We clearly need a better answer to this question than we have now.

As defined by the certification standards of the Academy of Criminal Justice Sciences (ACJS is an international organization of teachers and students of criminal justice), the purpose of undergraduate programs in criminal justice should be to educate students to be critical thinkers who can communicate their thoughts effectively in oral and written form, as well as to instill a comprehensive knowledge of the causes, consequences, and responses to crime and its interrelatedness to other areas of inquiry (see ACJS Certification Standards for Academic Programs). Programs are supposed to strive not only to familiarize students with facts and concepts but also, more importantly, to teach students to apply this knowledge to related problems and changing situations. As delineated in the certification standards, the primary objectives of all criminal justice programs should include the development of critical thinking, communication, technology and computing skills; quantitative reasoning; ethical decisionmaking; and an understanding of diversity. Achieving these objectives is obviously no small task. Let us take just three of them to illustrate the challenges they present.

Critical Thinking

Nearly all college faculty and administrators would agree that critical thinking is a primary goal of a college education in general. Exposing criminal justice students to critical thinking and encouraging them to think critically demands approaches and formats that are extremely difficult to achieve in most current programs. To really encourage and engage students in critical thinking, colleges need the luxury of small group exercises in which, for example, students are able to dissect the reasoning with respect to such weighty issues as capital punishment, punishing juvenile offenders as adults, indefinite preventive detention, electronic surveillance, and more. Criminal justice is ripe with thorny issues where there is widespread dissent in the society; where there are emotional, ideological, and moral overtones; and where there is a strong case to be made either way as to whether or not the ends justify the means.

In these small group interactions, students need to be pushed to acknowledge, but then put aside any preconceived notions, stereotypes, or biases, and to be open to the arguments and evidence of the other side. The point is not necessarily to change attitudes and opinions, but to encourage students to think carefully through the issue, to examine and weigh its various elements, and to consider the rationales behind them. A related format for stimulating critical thinking is the use of debates, in which students have to develop arguments and evidence in support of a position that they might have initially opposed. Or, perhaps there could be a critical issues seminar in which students take U.S. Supreme Court cases on major issues and critically examine the arguments and reasoning used by the assenting and dissenting justices.

The difficulty with each of these approaches is that they require students to work in small groups in which intensive and interactive discussion and debate can occur. Critical thinking is not and cannot be stimulated in large lecture sessions where there is little if any discussion. It cannot happen in courses that depend upon pre-packaged textbooks or where students absorb and regurgitate just enough facts to pass the test. It cannot happen in settings where instructors lack the knowledge and skill to manage the kind of emotionally charged interaction that can and should occur around these sorts of issues. Moreover, it cannot be accomplished through typical online/distance learning methods.

Ethical Decision making

According to the ACJS standards mentioned above, criminal justice programs are expected to teach students "to employ ethical perspectives and judgments in applying [their] knowledge to related problems and changing fact situations." As with critical thinking, teaching ethical decision making requires intensive and interactive approaches. For example, in an approach designed to engender what they called "legal socialization," Tapp (1987) and others proposed four socializing strategies: (1) providing knowledge about rules, rights, and remedies; (2) presenting ethical dilemmas which generate conflicting perspectives and call conflicting values into play; (3) providing role-taking opportunities where participation emphasizes reciprocity; and (4) stimulating comparisons of the various rule and law-based systems in which everyone lives. Again, trying something like this requires the commitment of adequate resources.

Understanding of Diversity

Criminal justice programs are supposed to include "a systematic examination of the issues of diversity in criminal justice through either specific required courses and/or the integration of these issues within the program's curriculum," according to the ACJS standards. Given the long history of the roles of race and gender in crime and justice and current concerns about immigration and crime, having criminal justice students confront these issues in an in-depth way is also obviously vital. As with critical thinking and ethics, however, there is a need for resources and special approaches in order to be able to do it.

These ideas are not meant to exhaust the list of possibilities. I am sure that creative minds can come up with other approaches. What all should agree on, however, is the recognition that the criminal justice field does not look as it did in the 1960s and 1970s, the time when many criminal justice programs began. It does not even look as it did as recently as the 1990s. Criminal justice curricula and programs, faculty, and students must continue to evolve to meet new challenges and demands. If the past is prologue, I am confident that they will be able to do so.

References

Academy of Criminal Justice Sciences (25 October, 2008). ACJS certification standards for academic programs. Retrieved from http://www.acjs.org/pubs/167_664_2906.cfm.

Butler, C. K. (2005). A good time to study crime. *US News & World Report,* America's Best Graduate Schools, pp. 78–80.

President's Commission on Law Enforcement and Administration of Justice. (1967). *The Challenge of Crime in a Free Society.* Washington, DC: Government Printing Office.

Tapp, J. L. (1987). The jury as a socialization experience: a socio-cognitive view. *Advances in Forensic Psychology and Psychiatry,* Vol. 2, pp. 1 – 32.

Discussion Questions

1. Every educational program, as well as each course within the program, should have clearly articulated student learning outcomes (SLOs), i.e., skills that a student will have acquired after successfully completing the course/program. Often, these are listed in course outlines, syllabi, or college catalogs. (For example, 1. Students will be able to identify the key parts of a research proposal, 2. Students will be able to construct a survey questionnaire, etc).

    Compile a list of three student learning outcomes that students majoring in criminal justice should possess having completed that program. Discuss these SLOs in the context of Finckenauer's comments.

2. Consider your response to question #1. How would you measure success? Identify the criteria you would use to measure whether students achieved the goals expressed in each of the student learning outcomes you created. (For example, 1. Students will take a comprehensive final exam. The criteria for success is a score of 70% or higher on this exam. 2. Students will create and administer a 10-question survey. The instructor will grade the survey according to a rubric.)

3. As a member of a criminal justice advisory board for a local college, you are to suggest areas where the program should focus future efforts. Based on this chapter, what might you suggest?

4. Why should criminal justice courses incorporate cultural and societal diversity?

5. Describe the factors that contributed to criminal justice higher education being stigmatized as "cop shops" teaching "handcuffs 101." Do such labels accurately portray the discipline today?

6. What is the value of an organization such as the Academy of Criminal Justice Sciences (ACJS)?

Chapter 2
THE CASE FOR SOUND SOCIAL SCIENCE RESEARCH

Jeffrey Chin, Ph.D. Le Moyne College

Introduction

Although many people don't find the topic of "research" particularly "sexy," the ability to understand research is a desired attribute of today's graduates and emerging professionals. It is part of becoming "information literate." Information literacy is a key student learning outcome of many college and university programs, including criminal justice. In today's "information age," students must not only know when it is important to find information on something, but they must also be able to understand where to find it, how to evaluate it, and what to do with the knowledge gained.

When you're given a research paper assignment, what is the first thing you do? Years ago, many would probably say, "head to the library and search the academic indexes." Today's students would likely respond quite differently. Information is literally at their fingertips, and it can be accessed 24 hours a day, seven days a week, through computers, tablets, e-readers, and cell phones. While most college libraries have magnificent online database services, the first inclination of many students is to go right to an Internet search engine. Type a few key words into the Google search bar, and voila! Pages and pages of stuff! As wonderful as that may be, buyer beware. Not all "stuff" is created equal. Anyone can put up a website. That means it is up to the consumer to research the origin of a website's content. What person or organization is responsible for this website? Where did the information come from? Does the responsible party present any credentials? Is there reason to believe the content is biased? When was the information posted or last reviewed? Knowing the answers to these questions will not guarantee that the information on the website is current or accurate, but it will increase your ability to sift through that virtual pile with a critical eye.

Although a complete discussion of research methods is beyond the scope of this chapter, it is worth noting that many social science baccalaureate curricula (criminal justice included) devote at least one full semester to the study of research methods. Some require two semesters. Most graduate programs require more than that. At undergraduate and graduate levels, students are often required to write research proposals or theses. This should indicate how important it is.

Research helps us understand the world around us. Research has very real, practical implications. Our world is surrounded by research ... from the material in the shoes we put on, to the chemicals in our pain reliever, to the car we drive, to the location of the light fixtures in the college parking lot, to the lesson plans taught in school, to the presence of the school resource officers, to the Friday night city-sponsored basketball league for teenagers. The list could go on and on. Research helps us answer questions about some of life's most serious questions, and those answers help us make tough decisions on things like policy development, program elimination, project funding, and legislative developments.

The Role of the Police Research Consultant

In this chapter, I will draw on my experience doing contract research for a medium-sized city's police department. In 2003, a Common Counselor (a member of a governing body for our city government) asked me to serve as a consultant for a project on racial profiling. In the decades preceding, and especially after the terrorist attacks of September 11, 2001, public criticism on the use of racial profiling—targeting individuals for police intervention based solely on race or ethnicity—placed increased pressure on police administrators nationwide to address the issue within their own departments and communities. The police department that I was asked to consult had begun collecting data for this purpose in 2001.

The department created a form for officers to complete each time they had contact with a citizen. The form contained fields for the officer to record demographic information on the citizen (e.g., apparent sex, race, age, etc.) and the purpose and details of the stop. This information was loaded into a database at the end of each officer's shift. By the time I was approached, the department had acumulated more than 200,000 records. It was my job to analyze these data. I assembled a research team to do this.

Whether you have had formal training in research methods or not, you should be thinking that this was no easy task. Perhaps you're already thinking about some obstacles I faced. My first concern was with the data collection process that had been established. Each officer had been responsible for collecting data and submitting the forms. These officers were likely not educated as researchers. They were trained to be police officers. Both researchers and police officers require special sets of skills and tactics, and while there may be similarities in terms of the "scientific method" used to formulate, test, and analyze hypotheses in research and theories about the way crimes occurred, the nature of the police officer's job is far different from that of researcher.

Here are some problems with having officers, untrained in research methods, collect data:

1. The work of an officer varies from being extremely busy—including life-and-death circumstances—to extremely slow and sometimes monotonous. Could we be certain that every officer filled out the form, even when things were extremely busy? If some forms didn't get completed during times of chaos, how might that impact results? Is it possible that those were times when officers were more likely to have been in contact with citizens from more diverse populations?

2. Any officer will tell you that the bane of her/his existence is paperwork, even if it can now be done on a laptop. Having to fill out this police-citizen encounter form means more paperwork. If you can avoid doing it, why not? How clear were instructions given to officers about exactly what police-citizen interactions would require this extra paperwork? For example, if citizens approach officers for directions, must they complete the form? Did they? How about if a citizen approaches the officers to tell them that she can't unlock her car and there's a sleeping baby inside? The problem being described here is that each officer, someone whose primary job description does not include collecting data for a research project, was deciding whether to collect data needed for this study.

3. Officers were asked to make judgments on demographics that might not have been always obvious. What do you call a multi-racial individual? What about a transsexual? This is not to suggest that officers can't make these determinations; some can, but others can't, or don't, see this as important. Yet, this determination was vital to the purpose of the study.

Given the issues just mentioned, the dataset was at best an imperfect measure of racial profiling. There needed to be a more reliable set of data to review. Therefore, my report recommended that the department install cameras on every car and analyze a representative sample from each of the three shifts, randomly selecting officers so there is no self-selection bias, etc. Then, you would have trained researchers go through the video records and code each incident. This would produce a much more accurate dataset from which conclusions could be drawn.

In addition to my concerns about officers collecting data, another major problem arises from police procedures. Police-citizen encounters are the product of two processes: directives to respond to situations or decisions to stop citizens (called "on-view") based on what the officers see. Some refer to this distinction as reactive (reacting to a request by others) versus proactive (acting on their own directives) policing. Is it possible that these different processes impact the ability for racial profiling to be exhibited? If so, in what ways?

Compared to reactive police actions, on-view encounters are of far greater value in terms of analyzing the police-citizen contact records for evidence of racial profiling. It is far less likely that there would be racial bias in a dispatched call. The officer does not know the race of the citizen she/he is about to have contact with, and there is no discretion in responding. The officer has to respond. This does not mean that racial profiling cannot exist in these cases, as officers exercise discretion in how they deal with the situations they are dispatched to. There may be some officers for whom race is factored into their decisions on how to handle those cases they are sent to. Unfortunately, in the dataset I inherited, there was no way to disaggregate these two types of calls. My recommendation was to add a code to the form that would allow disaggregation between dispatched and on-view calls. This would provide a more meaningful comparison between the two forms of police procedure.

Discussion

Another recommendation that I might have made was to create the research design *before* collecting data. Since I was brought on board a few years after the data collection had begun, I did the best I could with what was given to me and in my report suggested ways they could move forward. The police department made the recommended changes, which would improve the value of the data from that point on. I recommended that the person who succeeded me in the data analysis consider the first few years of this overall study a "pilot" project. A pilot project is explicitly intended as a trial ... to try things out, fix what didn't work well, and keep what did. Data collected during a pilot is not included in the final analysis. Ultimately, changing the methodology proved worthwhile, as my successor was able to reach a conclusion based on the improved dataset.

These are just some of the problems that a researcher needs to think about when doing work in the field. You may notice some others as you critically read through the chapters in this volume. Often, researchers will acknowledge and accept limitations to their study and suggest future research. For example, you will find that a number of chapters present survey research. Some are surveys of students (e.g., Dodson and Cabage) while others are surveys of entities outside the home institution (e.g., Smith and Moore). There are other chapters that provide information gleaned from interviews (e.g., Brewster). There are chapters based on analysis of existing data (e.g., Noga-Styron and Rubble). Researchers choose from a variety of possible methods to study problems, and each comes with its own set of costs and benefits. Ultimately, researchers choose the best, most feasible method given access to population, costs, and time constraints. All of this is to say there is never one perfect way to gather data to answer a question. In the best of all worlds, you might approach a research question using multiple methods. These kinds of studies are rare because most researchers do not have training in multiple methodologies, and very few have the time and resources to conduct what amounts to multiple parallel research projects, one using one method, one using another, etc. (Again, it is a matter of feasibility.)

One final note: every research project, whether conducted by a student or a faculty member, should have the approval of their school's Institutional Review Board (IRB). This is a group of people whose job it is to make sure that the research does not harm the subjects of that research. You will notice that some authors specifically mention this in their chapters.

This chapter was designed to get you thinking further about how a better understanding of research methods can make you a more informed criminal justice student and in turn, a more informed citizen. Hopefully, you have a research methods course in your curriculum. If you do, pay close attention to the material—it will make all the difference in helping you recognize and later construct good research design that will produce results you can rely on ... *the first time around.*

Discussion Questions

1. What problems could have been avoided if the police department had sought consultation prior to starting data collection?

2. When critically assessing website information, what features help determine the site's value?

3. How might installing cameras in police cars impact officer behavior?

4. What is the purpose of a pilot study?

5. What is an Institutional Review Board?

6. What is the value of sound social science research?

Chapter 3
A BEGINNER'S GUIDE TO READING RESEARCH
ARTICLES

Carolyn D'Argenio, M.S. Onondaga Community College

Introduction

Today's criminal justice students are preparing to enter a workforce plagued by uncertainty. Social scientists, educators, political leaders, and others continue to search for what works in criminal justice. It is a time of budget restriction and economic insecurity. It is a time of greater demand for social services, for get-tough crime policies, for more protection, and *for solutions*. This time of "more," however, must do it with "less."

In terms of capital management (both human and monetary), who decides where the resources will go? How do community-based non-profits secure funding? How do we know what prisons to close, what offices to merge, what services to expand, what schools need resource officers, or what security measures to take to reduce property crimes? How do we know when to intervene with a family whose child is using alcohol or drugs? How do we know how best to handle domestic violence incidents?

"Criminal justice" doesn't just happen. Promoting safety, security, individual rights, and respect for law requires efforts of many public and private agencies. The leadership of those agencies are responsible for making tough choices, especially with allocating resources. Often, agency operation is dependent on available government funding or grants. Grants are competitive awards that provide funds for certain projects or for operating programs for a certain period of time. Grants come with expiration dates, meaning the funding will end at a set time. Agencies must reapply or find alternate means of funding services provided.

What does this all mean? It means that for today's students, it is vital that they be information literate. Competition for limited funds and greater demands to provide evidenced-based assessment of program and policy initiatives require that agency leaders be able to locate, comprehend, and critically evaluate research. In what some dub the "information age," the readiness of information cannot be taken for granted. Nor can all information be treated alike. An information literate person can distinguish among the various types of documents available on any given subject. There are books, magazines, newspapers, trade journals, government reports, discussion boards, scholarly journal articles, and more. The research, writing, and publication process differs among them. Most entries in this book are examples of research articles similar to those found in academic journals. This chapter provides an overview of the purpose and layout of scholarly journal articles.

Professional, Scholarly Journals

Scholarly research articles are typically published in what's known as professional academic journals. As a criminal justice student, you may be familiar with some of them already, such as *Criminology, Journal of Criminal Justice, Social Problems, Journal of Research in Crime and Delinquency,* and *Justice Quarterly*. Professional journals are designed to present information to particular audiences; they are published on a regular basis. Typically, articles published in them are written by scholars or experts in the field and present new research or analyze existing research to provide an evidence base to support a position.

Most professional journals are very strict about what goes inside them. Articles found in them typically went through a rigorous evaluative process called "peer review" or "refereeing." This means that before publication, all articles are reviewed by a panel of field experts. They judge the study's overall value, paying particular attention to quality, timeliness, and relevance. It is not unusual for a reviewed article to be returned to the author for revision before being reevaluated and published. This may seem overwhelming, but it is this peer review process that ensures quality and integrity.

These are serious readings. One article alone could easily span 30-40 pages and culminate with a reference list of more than twenty sources. Because these articles are published in journals devoted to particular disciplines, they often are written using discipline-specific vocabulary and abbreviations and assume that readers will understand the language as well as the mathematics used to establish the significance of observed correlations among variables.

Scholarly journals contribute to ongoing discussions and controversies within disciplines. They provide a place for researchers to apply theory—some old and some new—and research design—again, some old and some new—to social problems. They also allow the authors to present a synthesis of research already done on certain topics. Scholarly journals provide a platform for researchers to put forth their ideas and share what was learned from their study. That's the beauty of scholarly sources …everything's out there. You know why the authors are writing, what work has contributed to their ideas, what researchers/theorists they agree and disagree with, how they have conceptualized and operationalized their variables, how they did the study, what they learned from their results, and what they acknowledged as their own limitations.

The transparency of the research presented in scholarly journals is key to advancing the discipline toward a more solid knowledge base. This knowledge, in turn, contributes to the changes in polices and program development. This knowledge contributes to the momentum for social, legal, and political changes. This knowledge helps criminal justicians, non-profit workers, community organizers, and others secure funding for projects or direct their limited resources in significant ways.

The Structure of Scholarly Research Articles

Research articles in scholarly journals tend to be structured similarly. Typically, they contain an abstract, an introduction to the problem, a literature review, a presentation of hypotheses, a description of the methodology, conclusion, discussion, and a reference list. See Table 3-1 for a description of each of these parts.

Table 3-1. Parts of Scholarly Journal Articles

Parts of Scholarly Journal Articles
Abstract
Briefly presents the basics of the research presented: the goal, the primary methodology, key results, and implications of the research. It's usually just a few sentences.
Introduction
Provides a broad overview of the problem, setting the context, theoretical basis, and significance of the research to follow. This validates the problem and establishes the need for the current study.
Literature Review
Presents an organized synthesis of prior research on the topic, carefully addressing any shortcomings of the studies described. Prior research provides the conceptual or theoretical basis for the current study. Some authors combine the literature review with the Introduction.
Research Questions/Hypotheses
Briefly describes the expected relationships between variables. From this point on, these are the questions that the researcher will focus on. Some authors don't list this part separately; rather, they work this into the Methodology section.
Methodology (Methods)
Explains what the key variables in the hypotheses/research questions mean and describes how they will be measured (conceptualization & operationalization). This part defines the population and describes how the sample was chosen. It specifies the methods used to collect data.

Results
Describes sample characteristics and results found. Presents statistical evidence used to establish the results. Often includes tables presenting such statistics.
Discussion
Explains the results, linking them to the original research questions/hypotheses.
Conclusion/Summary/Implications
Evaluates the value of the current research in the understanding of the problem described earlier. Authors sometimes acknowledge limitations of their study here. Presents possible uses for the information learned, in terms of programs, policies, future research endeavors, etc.
References
Lists the sources used by the authors as reference sources for their writing. These are full listings, written in discipline-preferred formats (like APA, ASA, or MLA) that correspond to the shorter, parenthetical citations included in text of the article. Some authors will use footnotes or endnotes with reference listings and/or additional information.

Reading Research Articles

Because of the length of most research articles and the obvious inclusion of statistics, reading them can be a daunting task. Novice readers often find that their first few times reading take them a long time. It may be helpful to have a pencil and paper in your hand to take notes and a dictionary to look up words that you don't know. Knowing the key elements in the anatomy of a research article will direct your attention certain parts in certain order. With practice, you'll learn how to process the information much more quickly. It also helps to remind yourself why you are reading the article in the first place.

The obvious place to start is at the top: with the title of the article. Titles of scholarly journal articles differ from the titles of magazine or newspaper articles; they're much more specific and technical. Then, look for the author's name and credentials. Authors of scholarly articles include their credentials that not only establish the author's authority as an expert but also provide a potential point of contact for those who read the article and may want to contact the writer at some point.

Next, read the abstract. That will shed light on what the intent of the researcher was in writing the article. The author may be presenting data to support a new theory or to refute an existing one. The researcher may be replicating a previous study. The researcher may be synthesizing studies to evaluate the body of research on a particular topic as a whole, serving also as a gap analysis to guide future researchers. Abstracts are short, usually fewer than 250 words, and usually will provide you with enough of a snapshot to determine if the article does indeed suit your needs.

If the article fits, skim it. Get a layout of the land. You'll be able to notice the writing style and vocabulary level upon quick glance. Then, read the introduction. You'll want to identify the purpose of the article, which is typically a statement embedded in the introduction. You may think of this in terms of the "thesis statement." Look ahead to the hypotheses.

Many suggest reading the discussion next. Don't worry about "spoiling" the story. In between the purpose and the conclusion is the evidence. The evidence of the need for the study emerges upon reading the literature review and theoretical basis. The evidence supporting the conclusion arises from the methods used and statistical analysis of the data. Finally, notice the reference list. You might find this part especially useful in "snowballing" your research by identifying other sources on the topic or exposing you to different keywords to type into search engines.

Perhaps the most important part of the research article is the methodology section. How variables were defined, how questions were asked, how samples were chosen, how data were collected, and how results were analyzed directly impact a study's value and hence, the quality of the research. From the methods section, future researchers find guidance for replication or with formulating their own studies on the topic. Finally, the strength of the research can be used to determine potential policy/program implications, something that criminal justice students must be able to do.

Discussion Questions

1. What is peer review? What is the value of having a peer review process?

2. What types of articles would you likely find in scholarly journals?

3. How would you go about searching for scholarly articles using your library's resources?

4. Where would you look in a scholarly article if you wanted to determine the purpose of the research?

5. How might you be able to use the reference list/bibliography to your benefit if you were researching a similar topic?

SECTION 2

RESEARCHING CRIMINOLOGICAL THEORY

Section 2
Researching Criminological Theory

INTRODUCTION

Theory is a set of assumptions about the world. Why do people commit crime? This question has plagued criminologists, criminal justicians, and many others for eons. People have drawn from their experience in various disciplines to formulate hypotheses and establish theories to explain crime. Do people commit crime because they have sociopathic personalities? There are a number of psychologically based theories that try to explain crime using personality theory. Do people commit crime because they were abused as children? There are a number of sociologically based theories that try to explain crime using socialization theory. Do people commit crime because of economic necessity? Again, there are a number of theories, some sociological, some based in economics, that try to explain crime using concepts like relative deprivation. You will likely be exposed to theory in several of your courses. Ultimately, we are left to conclude that no theory explains all activities in all situations.

Each of the three chapters in this section focus on behaviors that are quite familiar to college students and asks you to think about them in terms of some well-established social theories. Dodson and Cabage discuss the topic of risky sex and use control theory as an over-arching theoretical framework. Their conclusions are based on a survey of undergraduates. Ricketts, Vegh, Marcum, and Higgins present the use of Facebook in the framework of nonsocial reinforcement theory. Their research is also based on survey responses from college students. Finally, Noga-Syron and Ruble discuss crime in a much broader perspective of economy. Their work is based on a very ambitious secondary analysis of existing data.

We hope that when students are finished reading these chapters, they will have a better understanding not only of the specific theories these authors present, but also an appreciation of the use of theory in general.

Explaining Risky Sexual Behavior Among College Students: A Test of Hirschi's Revised Self-Control Theory

Risky sexual behavior can carry serious consequences. For example, there is an increased risk of contracting sexually transmitted infections and unplanned pregnancies. Understanding the cause of risky sexual behavior might help us to reduce it. The purpose of this study was to empirically test Hirschi's revised measure of self-control as an explanation of risky sexual behavior among college students. Risky sex was defined as respondents' participation in unprotected sex, casual sex, and number of lifetime sexual partners. A survey was administered to two nonrandom samples of undergraduate students in a northeastern university in the United States. The findings indicate that the revised self-control measure is related to reports of risky sexual behavior in our college samples. In other words, individuals with low self-control are more likely to report involvement in unprotected sex, casual sex, and have more lifetime sexual partners.

The Role of Nonsocial Reinforcement on College Student Fear Using Facebook

College student use of the Internet for online social networking purposes is increasing in popularity. Facebook is one social networking website that college students use with current estimates of over 7.5 million users spanning over 2,000 colleges and universities. Facebook usage offers both rewards and risks. While college students can provide vast amounts of information on personal profiles in which they may receive positive feedback from others, they are also concerned with general privacy issues on Facebook. The purpose of this study is to examine the role nonsocial reinforcement plays on college students' fear using Facebook. Using self-report data from college students, we examine several factors to determine if nonsocial reinforcement outweighs the perceived risk of victimization in college students' fear of victimization on Facebook. OLS regression analysis demonstrates that the intrinsic rewards of Facebook trump privacy concerns. This finding and the use of security features and selection of Facebook friends are discussed.

Crime and the Great Recession: An Analysis of Economic and Crime Variables from 2002 to 2010

The public consensus is that criminal behavior increases during difficult economic times. This opinion is substantiated by a six-month survey of randomly selected subjects across the country. The media, as well as scholarly articles, seem to concur and help to perpetuate this impression, particularly as it relates to high unemployment rates. Yet, our study shows that there is little, if any, correlation between crime and the economy. In other words, crime rates do not necessarily rise as unemployment rates go up, and current criminal behavior is not necessarily motivated by negative economic circumstances.

Chapter 4
EXPLAINING RISKY SEXUAL BEHAVIOR AMONG COLLEGE STUDENTS: A TEST OF HIRSCHI'S REVISED SELF-CONTROL THEORY

Kimberly D. Dodson, Ph.D. Western Illinois University
LeAnn N. Cabage, M.A. Western Illinois University

Introduction

Gottfredson and Hirschi's (1990) general theory has become one of the most widely cited (Cohn & Farrington, 1999) and tested theories of crime (Pratt & Cullen, 2000; Vazsonyi, Pickering, Junger, & Hessing, 2001). A growing body of empirical research has demonstrated at least moderate support for the theory's central proposition (Hirschi, 2004) that low self-control predicts a variety of criminal and noncriminal deviant behaviors (see e.g., Arneklev, Grasmick, Tittle, & Bursik, 1993; DeLisi, Hochstetler, & Murphy, 2003; Gibbs, Giever, & Martin, 1998; Grasmick, Tittle, Bursik, & Arneklev, 1993; Keane, Maxim, & Teevan, 1993; LaGrange & Silverman; 1999; Tittle, Ward, & Grasmick, 2003; Wood, Pfefferbaum, & Arneklev, 1993). A meta-analytical review of the empirical status of Gottfredson and Hirschi's (1990) theory revealed that self-control is "one of the strongest known correlates of crime" (Pratt & Cullen, 2000, p. 952).

Gottfredson and Hirschi (1990) define self-control as "the differential tendency of people to avoid criminal acts whatever the circumstances in which they find themselves" (p. 87). The decision to commit a crime or equivalent act when presented with an opportunity is related to the individual's calculation of costs and benefits. This reflects the individual characteristic or trait of self-control. Crime and equivalent acts appeal to those lacking self-control because they lack the capacity to consider the long-term consequences of their behavior for themselves and others.

As far as Gottfredson and Hirschi (1990) are concerned, self-control is the primary characteristic that accounts for consistent individual rate differences in the commission of criminal acts and crime equivalents. Specifically, people who lack self-control tend to act impulsively, to take risks, and to seek short-term, immediate pleasures; they tend to prefer simple tasks over complex ones and physical activities over mental or cognitive pursuits. People lacking self-control tend also to be short-tempered, self-centered, insensitive to the wants and needs of others, and likely to resort to aggressive coping strategies when faced with frustrating situations.

Recently, Hirschi (2004) indicated that a "shift" in the conceptuali-zation of self-control was necessary because, as he sees it, he and Gottfredson presented a conceptualization of self-control that misled researchers, who in turn misinterpreted the meaning of the self-control construct (see also Marcus, 2003; 2004; Taylor, 2001). As a result, Hirschi (2004) argues that the current measures of self-control are inconsistent with what he and Gottfredson intended.

The primary purpose of this research is to test a revised measure of self-control based on Hirschi's (2004) most recent conceptualization of the self-control concept as an explanation of risky sexual behavior. In general, those testing self-control theory have not examined risky sexual behavior, although Gottfredson and Hirschi (1990) indicate that those lacking self-control will engage in a variety of illicit sex acts. In addition, Hirschi (2004) indicated that his reconceptualization of self-control can explain a wide variety of criminal and deviant behaviors that would undoubtedly include risky sex. To our knowledge, this study is the first to test a measure of self-control based on Hirschi's (2004) revised conceptualization as an explanation of risky sexual behavior.

Redefining Self-Control

In a recent essay, Hirschi (2004, p. 543) revised his definition of self-control, describing it as "the tendency to consider the full range of potential costs of a particular act" (p. 543, italics in original). This new definition is much broader than Gottfredson and Hirschi's (1990) original definition of self-control because it acknowledges a much wider range of factors that affect how and why individuals make decisions, especially decisions to offend. This revised definition of self-control is more con-sistent with the original intent of the theory, which stated "the dimen-sions of self-control …are factors affecting the calculation of the conse-quences of one's acts" (Gottfredson & Hirschi, 1990, p. 95). From this perspective, self-control refers to an internal "set of inhibitions" that influence the choices people make (Hirschi, 2004, p. 543). These inhi-bitions are best described in the social bond because, according to Hirschi (2004, p. 543), "social control (bond) and self-control are the same thing."

The social bond is comprised of four elements: attachment, com-mitment, involvement, and belief (Hirschi, 1969; 2004). These elements act as inhibiting factors, all of which reduce one's likelihood of choosing to engage in criminal or deviant behavior. Put another way, the elements of the bond represent an internalized value system that guides behav-ioral choices.

Risky Sexual Behavior

For the purpose of our study, risky sexual behavior is defined as one's participation in high risk behaviors such as casual sex (e.g., one-night stands, weekend flings, or having sex with unfamiliar or unknown partners), sexual activity with multiple partners, and unprotected sex (e.g., failure to use contraceptives including birth control pills or condoms). It is important to understand why people engage in risky sexual behavior, given the potential for serious and potentially negative consequences. For example, those who participate in risky sex increase the likelihood of contracting sexually transmitted infections (STI) or having an unintended pregnancy (Hoyle, Fejfar, & Miller, 2000). Even though most individuals realize that pregnancy and STIs can be prevented by condom use, research suggests that most individuals do not use condoms during sex (Hays, Kegeles, & Coates, 1990; Hingson, Strunin, Berlin, & Heeren, 1990; Thurman & Franklin, 1990). Reducing the number of sexual partners greatly reduces the risk of contracting STIs, but studies indicate that many people have had multiple sexual partners. For instance, Arnett (1998) found that 25% of a sample of unmarried, sexually active people in their twenties had sex with two or more partners in the previous year.

In a recent study, Jones and Quisenberry (2004) examined the relationship between self-control and several measures of risky sexual behavior. They gathered information from a nonrandom sample (n = 254) of college students attending a large Midwestern state university and enrolled in sociology courses. They measured self-control using the most popular measure of self-control within criminology, namely the Grasmick et al. (1993) scale. This scale uses responses from four questions to measure risky sex: (1) "How many times have you had sexual intercourse without a condom?"; (2) "How many times have you had sexual intercourse without using any form of contraception?"; (3) "How many times have you had sexual intercourse with someone you did not really know very well?"; and (4) "How many sexual partners have you had in your lifetime?" (Jones & Quisenberry, 2004, pp. 408-409).

Jones and Quisenberry (2004) used multiple regression as the statistical method to analyze their data. The goal of multiple regression is to estimate the effect of several independent variables on one dependent variable. Jones and Quisenberry (2004) wanted to know whether their measure of self-control was related to risky sexual behavior. They found that individuals with high self-control had fewer sexual partners and were less likely to engage in sex with an unfamiliar or unknown partner or without a condom or contraceptives. The findings support Gottfredson and Hirschi's (1990) argument that those who lack self-control are more likely to be involved in risky sexual behavior.

In a related study, Love (2006) examined the relationship between
self-control and sexual deviance, using data collected from a nonrandom
sample (n = 705) of undergraduates enrolled in entry-level sociology
classes at one of three Southwestern universities: one rural, one com-
muter, and one Carnegie I research institution. Like Jones and Quisenberry (2004), Love (2006) measured self-control using the Grasmick et
al. (1993) scale.

Love (2006) created two scales to measure deviant sexual behavior.
The first sexual deviance scale measured illicit sexual behavior that can
be engaged in without the support or aid of another individual (e.g.,
masturbation, use of sexually explicit materials, and a preoccupation
with sexual thoughts). The second sexual deviance scale measured acts
that require the presence of others (e.g., affairs outside of a primary
relationship, cross-dressing, and sexual exposure). Love (2006, p. 521)
used one additional measure of illicit sexual behavior: "Before college
how many sexual partners would you say you have been with?"

Love (2006) used logistic regression as the statistical technique to
analyze her data. Logistic regression is a correlational technique that is
used for dependent variables that are dichotomized (i.e., have two
categories). The results of the logistic regression showed that those who
had low self-control were more likely to report engaging in masturbation,
using sexually explicit materials, and being preoccupied with sexual
thoughts. Logistic regression also revealed that those who lacked
self-control were more likely to report engaging in affairs outside of a
primary relationship, cross-dressing, and exposing themselves. Unex-
pectedly, self-control was not significantly related to respondents
reported number of sexual partners. However, based on the overall
results, Love (2006) concluded that low self-control has a significant
correlation with participation in deviant sexual behaviors, which is
consistent with Gottfredson and Hirschi's (1990) general theory.

Hope and Chapple (2005) examined a random sample (n = 709) of
adolescents age 15-17 from the National Longitudinal Survey of Youth
79 (NLSY79). The survey asked respondents to report if they had ever
engaged in sexual activity. Of the 709 respondents, 223 reported that
they had engaged in sexual activity. Hope and Chapple (2005) further
analyzed these 223 respondents to determine their involvement in risky
sexual behavior.

Hope and Chapple (2005) did not use the Grasmick et al. (1993) scale
to measure self-control. They used parental reports of self-control that
included bullying behaviors, lack of remorse after misbehaving,
disobedience at home and school, restlessness and overactivity,
irritability, temperament, and inability to follow teacher instruction. The
measure of risky sexual behavior included three items: ever had sexual
intercourse, number of sexual partners in the past year, and relationship
to last sexual partner.

Hope and Chapple (2005) conducted a regression analysis on risky sexual behavior and self-control. They found that individuals higher in self-control were less likely to report that they had engaged in sexual intercourse. In addition, those with higher self-control had fewer sexual partners and greater reported familiarity with their sexual partner. Again, these findings are consistent with Gottfredson and Hirschi's (1990) general theory.

Although these described studies support self-control theory, they each used the Grasmick et al. (1993) measure or similar measures of self-control. Our study uses the revised measure of self-control based on Hirschi's (2004) most recent conceptualization of self-control. As previously stated, this is the first known study to use the revised self-control measures as an explanation of risky sexual behavior.

Methods

Sample
We administered a survey to a nonrandom sample (n = 404) of undergraduate students enrolled in introductory criminology survey courses in a mid-sized, northeastern university. Compared to the university population, the sample was similar on age, race, and class status but not gender (females were underrepresented).

Measures
Dependent Variable—We used responses from three questions to measure risky sex: "How many sexual partners have you had in your life?" and "How many times have you had unprotected sex?" and "How many times have you had casual sex or what some people would call a 'one-night stand' or 'weekend fling'?" The response categories ranged from "0 = None" to "3 = Many." We used the risky sex measures individually and summated the three items to form a risky sex scale.

Independent Variable—The proposed self-control scale intended to measure the current level of self-control of college students. The self-control scale consisted of 48 items that designed to capture the concepts of self-control that include attachment, commitment, and belief. We summated these items to create a composite measure of self-control.

According to Hirschi (2004), attachment is the emotional bond or the degree of love and respect between an individual and conventional people such as parents, teachers, and peers. In fact, he indicated, "the principal source of control is concern for the opinion of others" (Hirschi, 2004, p. 545 [emphasis in the original]). Our attachment measures included items designed to capture the degree to which respondents care about the opinions of significant others (e.g., parents, professors, and peers) as indicated by Hirschi (2004). For example, we asked respondents to indicate how strongly they agreed with items such as "I care a lot about what my parents think of me," "Generally, I have a lot of respect for my professors," and "It is very important to me to be respected by friends whose values I respect" (Dodson, 2009, p. 99).

Commitment "refers to the individual's aspirations and expectations, to investments in a line of activity" (Hirschi, 2004, p. 539). Hirschi (2004) argued that commitment captures the "...idea that we are controlled by what we are, and by what we wish to be" (p. 539). The commitment concept includes both individual and group identity components. College students who see themselves as "good students" are more likely to be committed to educational and occupational goals. In addition, college students who associate with prosocial peers are more likely to identify themselves as prosocial. Our commitment measures included items designed to assess respondents' commitment to college and prosocial peers. Examples of the items used for the survey include "Grades are important to me," "Graduating from college is a very high priority for me," and "Doing well in school is important to most of my friends" (Dodson, 2009, p. 101).

According to Hirschi (2004), those who hold beliefs that are similar to those of the conventional society are less likely to engage in criminal or deviant behavior. Hirschi (2004) also claimed that the "acceptance of the moral validity of rules ...vary at the individual level. Some people believe more than others. Some believe fully; others, not at all" (p. 539). Therefore, "beliefs matter" because some beliefs restrain individuals from engaging in criminal and deviant acts while others free individuals to commit criminal and deviant acts (Hirschi, 2004, p. 539). Our belief measures included items designed to tap respondents' beliefs about various violations of university policies and minor law violations. Examples of statements used to assess level of belief included: "Rules restricting alcohol use on campus should not be strictly enforced," "Law enforcement officers should look the other way when people exceed a posted speed limit of 55 mph by 10 mph," and "Marijuana possession and use is against the law, but authorities should let it go when a few friends get together to smoke" (Dodson, 2009, p. 103).

Noticeably missing from our measure of self-control is the involvement component. This self-control measure performed poorly in the analysis of our pretest. Hirschi (1969) admitted that involvement items tend to perform poorly. In addition, researchers have found that, although involvement in conventional activities should be related to a decrease in deviant behavior, it is actually related to an increase in deviant behavior (Hirschi, 1969; Wright, Cullen & Williams, 1997). Because of the pretest finding and the theoretical arguments made in other studies, we dropped the involvement items from the self-control measure.

Control variables—We included age, gender, and race as control variables. We measured age at the interval level by asking respondents to indicate their age at their last birthday. We dichotomized gender, with males = 1 and females = 0, and race, with White = 1 and nonwhite = 0.

Results

We begin our analysis of the relationship between the self-control scale and the risky sex items using a simple bivariate correlation. A bivariate correlation tells us the strength (weak, moderate, or strong) and direction (negative or positive) of the relationship between two variables. Table 4-1 presents the bivariate correlation of self-control and risky sexual behavior for the sample is presented. Each of the risky sexual behaviors is negatively and significantly related to self-control. To be more precise, respondents with greater levels of self-control reported having fewer lifetime sexual partners and lower involvement in casual and unprotected sex. We also performed a bivariate correlation for self-control and a composite measure of risky sex. Self-control is negatively and significantly related to risky sexual behavior. These findings support Gottfredson and Hirschi (1990) claim that low self-control is related to a variety of risky sexual behaviors.

Table 4-1. Bivariate Correlations Among Study Variables

	1	2	3	4	5	6	7
1. Bond-Based Self-Control							
2. Lifetime Sexual Partners	-.31**						
3. Unprotected Sex	-.25**	.50**					
4. Casual Sex	-.30**	.70**	.33**				
5. Gender	-.19**	.13*	.04	.18**			
6. Age	-.06	.20*	.19**	.17**	.08		
7. Race	-.01	-.01	.06	.10*	.26**	.13**	

** Significant at the .01 level
* Significant at the .05 level

To test the effects of self-control on risky sexual behavior, while controlling for age, gender, and race, we employed multiple regression. Table 4-2 presents the regression models for the sample. Self-control is significantly related to the four risky sex dependent variables.

Table 4-2. Regression Models Examining the Effect of Self-Control on Risky Sexual Behaviors

	Self-Control		Age		Gender		Race	
	Coeff.	S.E.	Coeff.	S.E.	Coeff.	S.E.	Coeff.	S.E.
Lifetime Sexual Partners	-.28***	.00	.19***	.02	.09	.09	-.09	.04
Unprotected Sex	-.24***	.00	.18***	.03	.01	.12	-.09	.05
Casual Sex	-.26***	.00	.15**	.02	.12*	.09	.05	.04
Risky Sex Composite	-.31***	.01	.21***	.05	.08	.23	-.06	.10

***Significant at the .001 level
**Significant at the .01 level
*Significant at the .05 level

In the first model, self-control is negatively and significantly related to the number of lifetime partners reported by respondents. Our measure of self-control is also negatively and significantly related to reports of unprotected sex and casual sex. In the final model, we summated the three risky sex measures into a risky sex scale. The findings indicate that self-control also is negatively and significantly related to our composite measure of risky sexual behavior. The results support Gottfredson and Hirschi's (1990) assertions that those high in self-control are less likely to participate in risky sex.

Conclusion

The primary purpose of this chapter was to investigate whether Hirschi's (2004) revised measure of self-control was related to risky sexual behavior. To our knowledge, we are the first to test a revised measure of self-control based on Hirschi's (2004) most recent conceptualization of self-control as an explanation of risky sexual behavior. The results of the bivariate correlations and regression models show that self-control is significantly related to risky sexual behavior as predicted by Gottfredson and Hirschi (1990).

Our findings are consistent with the work of Jones and Quisenberry (2004) who also found self-control to be negatively related to risky sex, although they used the Grasmick et al. (1993) scale for the measurement of self-control. The results of our study are also consistent with those of Love (2006) who found that self-control, also measured using the Grasmick et al. (1993) scale, was negatively related to a variety of deviant sexual behaviors (e.g., masturbation, viewing pornography, cross-dressing, number of sexual partners, affairs outside of primary relationship, and sexual exposure). Our findings are similar to those of Hope and

Chapple (2005), whose research indicates that self-control, measured using parental reports, is related to participation in sex, number of sexual partners, and relationship to one's sexual partner. Of course, our work extends prior research on the relationship between self-control and risky sexual behavior because we employed a revised measure of self-control based on Hirschi's (2004) most recent conceptualization.

Our measure of self-control provides an initial step toward understanding the applied measurement of Hirschi's revised concept of self-control (for a similar conclusion, see Piquero & Bouffard, 2007). Researchers should continue to develop and test measures based on Hirschi's revised conceptualization. In addition, researchers should continue to expand the measure of risky sexual behavior to include other behaviors not investigated here (e.g., unplanned pregnancy). Finally, researchers should continue to explore the relationship between self-control and risky sexual behavior.

References

Arneklev, B. J., Grasmick, H. G. Tittle, C. R., & Bursik, R. J. (1993). Self-control theory and imprudent behavior. *Journal of Quantitative Criminology*, 9 (3), 225-247.

Arnett, J. J. (1998). Risk behavior and family role transitions during the twenties. *Journal of Youth & Adolescence*, 27, 301-320.

Cohn, E. G., & Farrington, D. P. (1999). Changes in the most-cited scholars in twenty criminology and criminal justice journals between 1990 and 1995. *Journal of Criminal Justice*, 27 (4), 345-359.

DeLisi, M., Hochstetler, A., & Murphy, D. S. (2003). Self-control behind bars: A validation of the Grasmick et al. scale. *Justice Quarterly*, 20 (2), 241-263.

Dodson, K. D. (2009). *The metamorphosis of Gottfredson and Hirschi's general theory of crime*. Saarbrucken, Deutschland: VDM Verlag.

Gibbs, J. J., Giever, D., & Martin, J. S. (1998). Parental-management and self-control: An empirical test of Gottfredson and Hirschi's general theory. *Journal of Research in Crime and Delinquency*, 35 (1), 42-72.

Gottfredson, M. R., & Hirschi, T. (1990). *A general theory of crime*. Stanford, CA: Stanford University Press.

Grasmick, H. G., Tittle, C. R., Bursik, R., & Arneklev, B. (1993). Testing the core empirical implications of Gottfredson and Hirschi's general theory of crime. *Journal of Research in Crime and Delinquency*, 30 (1), 5-29.

Hays, R. B., Kegeles, S. M., & Coates, T. J. (1990). High HIV risk-taking among gay men. *AIDS*, 4, 901-907.

Hingson, R. W., Strunin, L., Berlin, B. M., & Heeren, T. (1990). Beliefs about AIDS, use of alcohol and drugs, and unprotected sex among Massachusetts adolescents. *American Journal of Public Health*, 80, 295-299.

Hirschi, T. (1969). *Causes of delinquency*. Berkeley: University of California Press.

Hirschi, T. (2004). Self-control and crime. In R. F. Baumeister & K. D. Vohs (Eds.), *Handbook of self-regulation: Research, theory and applications*. New York: Guilford Press.

Hope, T. L., & Chapple, C. L. (2005). Maternal characteristics, parenting, and adolescent sexual behavior: The role of self-control. *Deviant Behavior: An Interdisciplinary Journal*, 26 (5), 25-45.

Hoyle, R. H., Fejfar, M. C., & Miller, J. D. (2000). Personality and sexual risk taking: A quantitative Review. *Journal of Personality*, 68 (6), 1203-1231.

Jones, S., & Quisenberry, N. (2004). The general theory of crime: How general is it? *Deviant Behavior*, 25, 401-426.

Keane, C., Maxim, P., & Teevan, J. (1993). Drinking and driving, self-control, and gender: Testing a general theory of crime. *Journal of Research in Crime and Delinquency*, 30 (1), 3-46.

LaGrange, T. C., & Silverman, R. A. (1999). Low self-control and opportunity: Testing the general theory of crime as an explanation for gender differences in delinquency. *Criminology*, 37 (1), 41-72.

Love, S. R. (2006). Illicit sexual behavior: A test of self-control theory. *Deviant Behavior*, 27, 505-536.

Marcus, B. (2003). An empirical examination of the construct validity of two alternative self-control measures. *Educational and Psychological Measurement*, 63 (4), 674-706.

Marcus, B. (2004). Self-control in the general theory of crime: Theoretical implications of a measurement problem. *Theoretical Criminology: An International Journal*, 8 (1), 33-55.

Piquero, A. R., & Bouffard, J. A. (2007). Something old, something new: A preliminary investigation of Hirschi's redefined self-control. *Justice Quarterly*, 24 (1), 1-27.

Pratt, T. C., & Cullen, F. T. (2000). The empirical status of Gottfredson and Hirschi's general theory of crime: A meta-analysis. *Criminology*, 38 (3), 931-964.

Taylor, C. (2001). The relationship between social and self-control: Tracing Hirschi's criminological career. *Theoretical Criminology*, 5 (3), 369-388.

Thurman, Q. C., & Franklin, K. M. (1990). AIDS and college health: Knowledge, threat, and prevention at a northeastern university. *College Health*, 38, 179-184.

Tittle, C. R., Ward, D. A., & Grasmick, H. G. (2003). Gender, age, and crime/deviance: A challenge to self-control theory. *Journal of Research in Crime and Delinquency*, 40 (4), 426-453.

Vazsonyi, A. T., Pickering, L. E., Junger, M., & Hessing, D. (2001). An empirical test of a general theory of crime: A four-nation comparative study of self-control and the prediction of deviance. *Journal of Research in Crime and Delinquency,* 38 (2), 91-131.
Wood, P., Pfefferbaum, B., & Arneklev, B. (1993). Risk-taking and self-control: Social psychological correlates of delinquency. *Journal of Crime and Justice,* 16 (1), 111-130.
Wright, J. P., Cullen, F.T., & Williams, N. (1997). Working while in school and delinquent involvement: Implications for social policy. *Crime and Delinquency,* 43 (2), 203 222.

Discussion Questions

1. Compare Hirschi's revised concept of self-control to the original one.

2. What other factors might explain risky behavior other than the ones included in this analysis?

3. What is an independent/dependent/control variable? In an ideal world, how are they related to each other? What did Dodson and Cabage use as their independent/dependent/control variables?

4. Design a project that eliminates the kinds of problems that a human subjects review board might object to but that will give you a more definitive conclusion that what it typical in social science research. Hint: Discuss your subjects as if they were rats and you could control every aspect of their lives.

5. Would you expect different results from students from other majors? Explain.

Chapter 5
THE ROLE OF NONSOCIAL REINFORCEMENT ON COLLEGE STUDENT FEAR USING FACEBOOK

Melissa L. Ricketts, Ph.D. Shippensburg University
Deborah T. Vegh, Ph.D. Central Connecticut State University
Catherine Marcum, Ph.D. Georgia Southern University
George E. Higgins, Ph.D. University of Louisville

Introduction

Facebook is a social networking site (SNS) that is increasing in popularity among college students. Recent reports indicate that Facebook has more than 500 million active users (e.g., users who have returned to the site in the last 30 days), with more than 50% accessing their account each day (Facebook, 2010). Since its inception in 2004, Facebook continues to broaden its user-base, especially among younger users. Nearly half the 103 million Facebook users in the United States are between the ages of 18 and 25, which include students from more than 2,000 colleges and universities. The typical Facebook user has over 130 friends and spends fifty-five minutes on Facebook each day. Female users of Facebook continue to outnumber male users in every age bracket. Facebook has become so popular that it is the second most popular site on the web, behind Google.

Facebook's simplified navigation gives its users easy access to core site functions and applications. For instance, users can create a richly detailed profile, accumulate friends, and subscribe to a variety of Facebook applications—photos, notes, groups, events, and posted items—that other registered users may view. Facebook provides an outlet for its members to send and receive messages from other members and allows "friends" to post comments on each other's pages. The site is tightly integrated into the daily media practices of its users. The typical user writes 25 comments on Facebook each month, is invited to 3 events per month, and is a member of 12 networks (Facebook, 2010). In addition, more than 200 million active users currently access Facebook through mobile devices.

Although college students have responded positively to Facebook, this popular social networking site does not come without some controversy (Madrid, 2005). Much of the academic research on Facebook has focused on identity presentation and privacy concerns (Gross & Acquisti, 2005; Stutzman, 2006; Young & Quan-Haase, 2009). Given the amount of personal information Facebook participants post, the relatively open nature of the information, and the under-utilization of privacy controls, users may be putting themselves at risk for victimization both offline and online (stalking, harassment, identify theft, etc.) (Fox et al., 2000; Gross & Acquisti, 2005, 2006; Young & Quan-Haase, 2009).

Our study examines the role that nonsocial reinforcement plays in the amount of information placed on Facebook users' profiles. We begin by providing an overview of privacy concerns among Facebook users. Next, we provide a summary of the criminological theories and relate corresponding literature to the use and consequences of Facebook. Finally, using self-reports from a cross-section of undergraduates at a southeastern university, we present the results of our examination of links among nonsocial reinforcement, the amount of personal information placed online, and the perceived risk for victimization among Facebook users.

Privacy Concerns Among Facebook Users

Facebook users can actively construct their identity on the site through the disclosure of personal information including name, address, birth date, e-mail address, class information, interests, political views, and relationship status. Facebook's privacy feature gives its users tools to control the information they share and with whom they choose to share it. In doing so, users can share and restrict information based on particular "friends" or "friend lists."

The literature on privacy online suggests that Internet users are generally concerned about unwanted audiences obtaining personal information. Fox et al. (2000) reported that 86% of Internet users are concerned that unwanted audiences will obtain information about them or their families, 70% are concerned that hackers will access their credit card information, and 60% are concerned that someone will discover personal information from their online activities. Acquisti and Gross (2006) found similar results, showing that students expressed high levels of concern for general privacy issues on Facebook, such as strangers learning their address, the location and schedule of their classes, their sexual orientation, the name of their current partner, and their political affiliations.

However, and most importantly, despite these concerns, research has shown that users continue to disclose personal information and often disclose accurate personal information online (Acquisti & Gross, 2006; Fox et al., 2000; Govani & Pashley, 2005; Gross & Acquisti, 2005; Tufekci, 2008; Viseu, Clement, & Aspinall, 2004). For instance, in their examination of information sharing and privacy on Facebook, Acquisti and Gross (2006) revealed that 89% of students used their full name on their profiles, 87.7% disclosed their birth date, and 50.8% listed their address. Therefore, despite users' noted concern for their privacy, their behaviors suggest otherwise, putting them at risk for potential victimization.

Researchers are paying closer attention to online victimizations, particularly cyberstalking (Alexy, Burgess, Baker, & Smoyak, 2005; D'Ovidio & Doyle, 2003; Finkelhor, Mitchell, & Wolak, 2000; Fisher, Cullen, & Turner, 2000, 2002; Lee, 1998; Pathé & Mullen, 1997; Spitzberg & Hoobler, 2002). Recent studies suggest that the prevalence of cyberstalking is expanding at a rapid pace, especially among college students and young adults. They attribute this to the desire to create new friends, which often leads many to put too much personal information online, allowing the potential stalker to learn a great deal about a person (Alexy et al., 2005).

A second form of victimization prevalent among college-aged students is identity theft. According to the Federal Trade Commission (2003), young people ages 18-29 experienced the highest levels of victimization, comprising 31% of the total thefts. With technological advances such as Facebook, young adults spend more time online, putting themselves at an ever-increasing risk for identity theft victimization. In addition, Facebook's public linkages between individual profiles and the real identities of their owner and Facebook's perceived connection to a physical and presumably bounded community of college students make its users a particularly interesting population for our research.

Although Facebook has generated a substantial amount of interest among college students and although media coverage of it has risen, there has been little academic research exploring the phenomenon. Most of the current thinking is based on anecdotal evidence as opposed to empirical data (Acquisti & Gross, 2006; Ellison, et al., 2006; Stutzman, 2006; Gross & Acquisti, 2005; Marshall & Tong, 2005; Martucci, 2005; Paquin, 2005; Sealy, 2005; Woo, 2005; Zelkowitz, 2005). Because of its large number of users, its important target audience (e.g., college students), its high visibility, widespread public concern, and lack of empirical research, there is a need to investigate college students' use of Facebook and to consider the possible consequences of posting behaviors.

Theoretical Explanations

Nonsocial Reinforcement

Nonsocial reinforcements are part of social learning theory (Akers et al., 1979). According to Akers (1998), nonsocial reinforcements are narrowly confined to unconditioned physiological and physical stimuli. They are the intrinsic rewards that an individual experiences after performing a behavior without any direct contact with others.

People may experience nonsocial reinforcements such as thrill, excitement, self-esteem, and a sense of accomplishment. They interpret these sensations as positive occurrences and desire that they re-occur, thus motivating them to continue their behavior. Wood et al. (1997) suggest that habitual behavior is to some degree maintained through the physiological sensations the behavior produces. In other words, individuals who are high on nonsocial reinforcement see those acts as being intrinsically pleasurable; internal gratifications (as positive or negative reinforcement) implies the further production of those behaviors. Nonsocial reinforcements give people internal rewards, rather than a social reward from their peers. Thus, those high on nonsocial reinforcement may see some behaviors as more intrinsically rewarding than other behaviors. Akers (1998) views reinforcement as a social phenomenon and, as such, as more important than nonsocial reinforcement, but Wood et al. (1997) makes the case that nonsocial reinforcement may be just as important. In either event, support for nonsocial reinforcement supports social learning theory.

The literature on nonsocial reinforcement seems to support the nonsocial premise and shows that it is an understudied part of social learning theory. For example, Wood et al. (1997) showed that thrill seeking and immediate gratification had strong links with illegal drug and alcohol use among adolescents. Arnett (1995) showed an interaction effect—between nonsocial reinforcement and social environment—that explained reckless behavior. May (2003) showed nonsocial reinforcement as having a stronger connection with violence than differential association and social bonds. Although these findings indicate that nonsocial reinforcement is valid, researchers have not used nonsocial reinforcement to explain other behaviors, such as college students' willingness to use and to post information on Facebook. The focus of our study was to provide a clear understanding of the link between nonsocial reinforcement and college students' use of the SNS Facebook.

Peer Association

Peer association is another fundamental element of social learning theory (Akers, 1998). Essentially, if your friends engage in certain behavior, then you are more likely to do so. Friends play an important role in understanding various behaviors, especially crime (Akers, 1998; Warr, 2002) and victimization (Schreck, Wright, & Miller, 2002), as well as Internet behaviors (Higgins & Makin, 2004; Skinner & Fream, 1997). Given the use and support for social learning theory for many Internet behaviors, including software piracy (Higgins, Fell, & Wilson, 2006), peer association is an important factor in understanding undergraduate students' use of Facebook, especially with regard to the amount of information placed on the site. Thus, positive findings would lend support to social learning theory.

General Model of Fear

Ferraro's (1995) general model of fear assumes that people are rational and weigh the costs and benefits of actions prior to engaging in them. Thus, it would hold that people become fearful when they perceive that they are at risk. Fear is an emotional reaction of alarm or trepidation (Ferraro, 1995). In order to produce a fear reaction, an individual must acknowledge a situation has some potential dangerousness to his or her welfare (Ferraro, 1995; Ferraro & LaGrange, 1987, 1992; Ricketts, 2007). In other words, the individual recognizes perceived risk of victimization (Ferraro, 1995; Ferraro & LaGrange, 1987, 1992). Ferraro (1995) places perceived risk of victimization as the most important measure that generates fear.

The examination of perceived risk and fear among college students is important for several reasons. First, college students are victims of various crimes both on and off campus (Baum & Klaus, 2005; Fisher & Sloan, 2003) and as such, are likely to fear for their safety. Second, undergraduates engage in risky behavior without much, if any, forethought regarding the consequences of their actions (Mustaine & Tewksbury, 1999). Third, college students are rather inattentive in monitoring and disclosing personal information both online and off (Higgins et al., 2006). Therefore, college students are likely to be at risk and to have some level of fear, making them suitable for potential online victimization.

Routine Activities Theory

Routine activities theory posits that lifestyles or behavior patterns increase vulnerability to victimization by increasing contact with potential offenders (Jackson, Gilliland, & Veneziano, 2006). The profile page of Facebook does not require any mandatory information. Users decide the amount and type of information seen by others and which privacy options to use. Facebook profile pages can include an array of information, from the rather mundane (favorite books, movies, music, etc.) to the highly sensitive and invasive (profile status, relationship status, provocative pictures, phone numbers, addresses, etc.) (Stutzman, 2006). The prevalence of the latter may indicate the relative low expectation of any perceived risk and the belief that there is some sort of an online omnipresent suitable guardian protecting users from harm (Felson, 1998). Given the vast amount of time spent on Facebook daily (Facebook, 2010), the amount of information shared, and the interaction with various levels of "friends"—from those they know well to virtual strangers—college students may be decreasing their guardianship in pursuit of more intrinsic rewards. We expect that nonsocial reinforcements (e.g., thrill, excitement, and positive feedback) will be essential and will positively influence students who post more information (e.g., address, photos, cell phone numbers, class schedule, relationship status, and social activities) on their Facebook profile.

Methods

Sample

We provided a self-administered survey to a nonrandom sample of college undergraduates at a southeastern university in the fall of 2007. Using methodology by Muthen and Muthen (1998), we included only those with Facebook pages. Our final sample of 224 undergraduates included 49.8% females and 50.2% males, most of whom lived off campus (73.2%). These characteristics closely represented the overall characteristics of that university.

Measures

Routine Activities—We provided respondents with a list of 25 items (e.g., name, e-mail address, physical address, phone number, school information, major, website, birth date, relationship status, interests, favorite books, music, movies, and personal statement) and asked them to identify which ones they included on their Facebook profile. The average was 18.4 items (sd = 4.6), indicating a vast amount of information provided on profile pages.

Privacy—The majority (90%) of respondents indicated that they used some of the privacy measures provided by Facebook. Although privacy settings are important in the implementation of the privacy options, this study did not assess this.

Fear—Using a measure adapted from Ferraro (1995), we asked respondents twelve questions to assess their fear of receiving threatening and harassing messages from three different entities with possible access to the Facebook account (i.e., someone barely known, one of the respondents' friends, and significant others). The questions used a 4-point Likert scale anchored by "not afraid at all" and "very afraid," with higher scores indicating being more afraid of these messages. The average was 12.8, indicating a low level of fear.

Perceived Risk—Per Ferraro (1995), we asked respondents to rate the likelihood of receiving threatening and harassing messages from those same three entities There were 12 items on a 4-point Likert scale anchored by "not likely at all" and "very likely." Higher scores indicated a greater perception of risk. The average score was 13.4, indicating a low perception of such risk.

Nonsocial Reinforcement (NSR)—We constructed an 8-item measure on a 5-point Likert scale anchored by "strongly disagree" and "strongly agree" to assess the amount of nonsocial reinforcement obtained from the use of Facebook. Respondents indicated if using Facebook was pleasurable, if Facebook provided satisfaction or a great feeling, and if they felt empowered after using Facebook. They also indicated how well friends treated them on Facebook, how much control they felt, and the extent to which they would feel guilty or out of control if they did not use Facebook. The reliability of the scale was high (r = .80). Higher scores demonstrated more nonsocial reinforcement (e.g., intrinsic rewards). The average score on the NSR measure was 21.5 (sd = 4.6), demonstrating a moderate level of nonsocial reinforcement.

Peer Association—Three items on a 4-point Likert scale anchored by "none or almost none" and "5 or more friends" assessed peer association. Respondents indicated how many of their Facebook friends were from the university, how many were not from the university, and how many of their friends they had actually met. The reliability was lower (r = .55) and may be due to only having a limited number of items for this measure. However, the questions asked were consistent with previous Internet use research (Higgins, 2005). Higher scores indicated more association with friends using Facebook. The average score was 9.75, indicating a high level of peer association on Facebook.

Analysis Plan

The first step in analyzing our data was the presentation of the bivariate correlations. Bivariate correlations assess the association between measures. For purposes of this study, we specifically examined fear, perceived risk, routine activities, nonsocial reinforcement, and peer association to determine if any of the variables were highly correlated and potentially redundant. The second step was ordinary least squares regression (i.e., OLS) analysis. This is a statistical technique for understanding the values of a dependent measure based on the values of one or more independent measures (Everitt, 2001; Freund & Wilson, 1998). We presented the unstandardized slope and the standard errors for analysis of statistical significance. To determine the effect of the measures on the perception of fear of victimization on Facebook, we compared the betas (i.e., standardized slopes) of the independent measures. Further, we used the tolerance and variance inflation factors (VIF) to determine the extent of multicollinearity of the measures (Freund & Wilson, 1998). Everitt (2001) wrote that tolerance measures had to be below .20 and variance inflation factors (VIFs) had to be above 4 before multicollinearity was an issue.

Results

Step 1

Table 5-1 presents the results of the bivariate correlations. The bivariate correlations show that perceived risk and fear (r = 0.36) had a significant correlation suggesting that as individuals perceived risk of victimization that fear increased. A similar correlation occurred between nonsocial reinforcement and routine activities (r = 0.36), suggesting that as individuals provided more information about themselves, they were more inclined to do so impulsively and without forethought of potentially adverse effects. As individuals had more friends on Facebook, they were more likely to have more nonsocial reinforcement (r = .21) and to put more information on Facebook (r = 0.27). For the students who used the privacy function on Facebook, they too had more routine activities on Facebook (r = 0.16), perceived more nonsocial reinforcement (r = 0.16), and associated with more peers (r = 0.18). However, users living at home were less likely to have as many friends on Facebook (r = -0.17). Overall, these results do not indicate excessively large correlations that would suggest that multicollinearity is an issue.

Table 5-1. Bivariate Correlation Matrix and Descriptive Statistics of Measures

Measures	1	2	3	4	5	6	7	8
1. Fear	1.00							
2. Perceived Risk	0.36**	1.00						
3. Routine Activities	0.14	0.07	1.00					
4. Nonsocial Reinforcement	0.06	0.01	0.36**	1.00				
5. Peer Association	-0.03	-0.00	0.27**	0.21**	1.00			
6. Gender	0.09	0.01	0.01	0.06	0.03	1.00		
7. Privacy	-0.03	-0.07	0.16*	0.16*	0.18*	0.01	1.00	
8. Residence	0.02	0.12	0.02	-0.06	-0.17*	0.12	-0.13	1.00
Mean	12.76	13.42	18.41	21.50	9.75	0.50	0.90	1.75
S.D.	3.35	3.93	4.60	4.58	1.39	0.50	0.30	0.44

Note: *p = .05, **p = .00

Step 2

Table 5-2 shows that two measures are important for understanding the amount of information that the students posted on Facebook. We show that nonsocial reinforcement (b = 0.30, S.E. = 0.07, Beta = 0.30) had a significant impact on the students' postings on Facebook. In addition, we show that peer association on Facebook (b = 0.66, S.E. = 0.24, Beta = 0.20) had a significant impact on Facebook postings. This indicates support for Akers's (1998) version of social learning theory that individuals are learning that posting personal information on Facebook is not that big of an issue. Further, we did not find evidence to suggest that multicollinearity was a problem with these results. That is, the tolerance and VIFs were not above their standards.

Table 5-2. Regression Analysis of the Measures—Routine Activities as DV

Measures	b	S.E.	Beta	Tolerance	VIF
Fear	0.02	0.10	0.02	0.85	1.18
Perceived Risk	-0.13	0.09	-0.11	0.84	1.19
Nonsocial Reinforcement	0.30***	0.07	0.30	0.94	1.07
Peer Association	0.66**	0.24	0.20	0.91	1.10
Gender	-0.09	0.62	-0.01	0.97	1.03
Privacy	1.72	1.09	0.11	0.95	1.06
Residence	1.02	0.73	0.10	0.93	1.08

R-square = .18
f-statistic = 5.78***
n = 225

Discussion

Facebook is an immense phenomenon, having grown to more than 500 million users since inception in 2004. What started as an online social networking site of and for college students now allows anyone to build a profile. Profiles can provide a multitude of personal information ranging from more routine data (e.g., name, birthdate, job, nicknames, school) to explicit details (e.g., updated profile status, relationship status, pictures, current location, and lists of "favorites"). The comments and messages received by the Facebook user from "friends" who view their profile information may elicit positive emotions and foster similar postings, pictures, and personal information. Due to the evolving nature of reinforcements, even nonsocial, the information provided by the user may actually increase the disclosure of more private details, whether written or pictorial, to attain the wanted gratifying emotions. Such disclosure might increase that person's risk of crime and victimization.

The exposure of personal information on a profile page could allow for the victimization of a user both online (e.g., identity theft, cyber-stalking) and off (e.g., stalking). With such incidents increasing, it is important to acknowledge the needed use of privacy options on Facebook to protect personal information and access to a user's profile. It is clear that undergraduates provide many types of information. Our research demonstrated that nonsocial reinforcement trumps privacy concerns. The intrinsic rewards of Facebook (i.e., positive feelings felt from the feedback from others) seem more vital than concerns over who may view a user's profile.

Previous research depicts college students as concerned with potential victimization due to profile information afforded to "friends," yet they still provide personal information. This research may help to understand why. Although there is concern over privacy and possible victimization, the gratification and personal boost received from others may reinforce views and feelings, and security features may limit those who could comment or agree with the user. Facebook users must accept invitations from others to become "friends," so perhaps those viewed as "friends" seem less threatening. Additionally, users can "unfriend" someone; and in doing so, they may believe access to their profile is limited, thus not requiring them to deploy additional privacy options. "Unfriending" someone does not eliminate access to all information. Shared friends, tagged photos, and blog postings may provide a "back-door" way to access information.

Our research is not without its limitations. Given the cross-sectional nature of the data, causality is an issue. It is unknown whether providing so much information on Facebook gives a sense of excitement and thrill to the user or if such nonsocial reinforcements allow for a lack of inhibition and as such, users place much information about themselves on their user profiles. Additionally, we used a convenience sample of undergraduates, which limits the generalizability of the findings. While future research should include a random and more diverse population of college students, our findings allow for some insight into the user profiles of many in the fast-growing phenomenon of Facebook. Since this study did not capture all the nuances of profiles, online applications, or the newest security features, future studies should encompass the new applications and security features (including the "unfriend" option) provided to Facebook users.

This research provides an initial look into the role of nonsocial reinforcements and profile information provided on Facebook. The findings should encourage college and university campuses to inform students of potential harms associated with not fully appreciating the privacy options provided on Facebook. Regardless of how Facebook may empower them, students need to be aware that sharing statuses and personal information to friends offline limits access to those who might want to use such information to harm them.

References

Acquisti, A. & Gross, R. (2006). Imagined communities: Awareness, information sharing and privacy on the Facebook. *Proceedings from the 6th Workshop on Privacy Enhancing Technologies.* Cambridge, UK, 2006.

Akers, R. L. (1998). *Social learning and social structure: A general theory of crime and deviance.* Boston: Northeastern University Press.

Akers. R. L., Krohn. M. D., Lanza-Kaduce, L., & Radosevich, M. (1979). Social learning and deviant behavior: A specific test of a general theory. *American Sociological Review, 44,* 636-655.

Alexy, E. M., Burgess, A. W., Baker, T., & Smoyak, S. A., (2005). Perceptions of cyberstalking among college students. *Brief Treatment and Crisis Intervention, 5,* 279-289.

Arnett, J. (1995). Developmental contributors to adolescent reckless behavior. Poster presented at the biennial meeting of the Society for Research on Child Development, Indianapolis, IN, March, 1995.

Baum, K., & Klaus, P. A. (2005). *Violent victimization of college students, 1995-2002* (No. NCJ 206836). Washington, DC: US Department of Justice Office of Justice Programs.

D'Ovidio, R., & James, J. (2003). *A study on cyberstalking: Understanding investigative hurdles.* Retrieved December 1, 2009 from <http://www.fbi.gov/publications/leb/2003/mar03leb.pdf>.

Ellison, N., Steinfield, C., & Lampe, C. (2006). *Spatially bounded online social networks and social capital: The role of Facebook.* Paper presented at the ICA conference, Dresden, Germany.

Everitt, B. S. (2001). *Statistics for psychologists: An intermediate course.* Mahwah, NJ: Lawrence Erlbaum Associates.

Facebook (2010). Press room: Statistics. Retrieved December 16, 2010 from http://www.facebook.com/editaccount.php?ads#!/press/info.php?statistics

Federal Trade Commission. (2003). *Federal Trade Commission: Identify theft survey report.* McLean, VA: Synovate. Retrieved December 1, 2009 from: http://www.ftc.gov/os/2003/09/synovatereport.pdf

Felson, M. (1998). *Crime and Everyday Life* (2nd ed.). Thousand Oaks, CA: Pine Forge Press.

Ferraro, K. F. (1995). *Fear of crime: Interpreting victimization risk.* Albany: State University of New York Press.

Ferraro, K. F., & LaGrange, R. L. (1992). Are older people most afraid of crime? Reconsidering age differences in fear of victimization. *Journal of Gerontology: Social Sciences,* 47: 233-244.

Ferraro, K., & LaGrange, R. L. (1987). The measurement of fear of crime. *Sociological Inquiry,* 57, 70-101.

Finkelhor, D.; Mitchell, K.; and Wolak, J. (2000). *Online Victimization: A Report on the Nation's Youth.* Arlington, VA: National Center for Missing and Exploited Children.

Fisher, B. S., & Sloan, J. J. (2003). Unraveling the fear of victimization among college women: Is the shadow of sexual assault hypothesis supported? *Justice Quarterly,* 20(3), 633-659.

Fox, S., Rainie, L., Horrigan, J., Lenhart, A, Spooner, T., & Carter, C. (2000). *Trust and privacy online: Why Americans want to rewrite the rules.* PEW Internet and American Life Project (August 20, 2000). Retrieved December 1, 2009 from: http://www.pewinternet.org/pdfs/PIP_Trust_Privacy_Report.pdf

Freund, R. J., and Wilson, W.J. (1998). *Regression analysis.* San Diego, CA: Academic Press.

Govani, T., & Pashley, H. (2005). *Student Awareness of the Privacy Implications while Using Facebook.* Unpublished manuscript retrieved from: http://lorrie.cranor.org/courses/fa05/tubzhlp.pdf.

Gross, R. & Acquisti, A. (November, 2005). *Information revelation and privacy in online social networks.* Paper presented at the Workshop on Privacy in the Electronic Society, Alexandria, VA

Higgins, G. E., Fell, B. D., & Wilson, A. L. (2006). Digital piracy: Assessing the contributions of an integrated self-control theory and social learning theory. *Criminal Justice Studies: A Critical Journal of Crime, Law, and Society,* 19, 3-22.

Higgins, G. E. & Makin, D. (2004). Self-control, deviant peers, and software piracy. *Psychological Reports,* 95, 921-931.

Jackson, A., Gilliland, K., & Veneziano, L. (2006). Routine activity theory and sexual deviance among male college students. *Journal of Family Violence,* 21, 449-460.

Lee, R. (1998, Spring). Romantic and electronic stalking in a college context. *The College of William and Mary Journal of Women and the Law,* 373-409.

Madrid, A. (2005, April 11, 2005). 'Offensive' facebook.com groups lead to Medill forum. *The Daily Northwestern,* 3, 9-10.

Marshall, M., & Tong, A. (August 29, 2005). Palo Alto, Calif.-based Facebook brings social networking online. *San Jose Mercury News,* 4, 3-4.

Martucci, B. (2005, December 9). As Facebook grows, more than just friends are watching. *The Mac Weekly,* 1, 13-15.

May, D. (2003). Nonsocial reinforcement and violence: Can juvenile justice policies be effective against intrinsic gratification, *Journal for Juvenile Justice and Detention Services,* 18(1), 9-32.

Mustaine, E., & Tewksbury, R., (1999). A routine activity theory explanation for women's stalking victimizations. *Violence Against Women,* 5, 43-62.

Muthen, L. K., & Muthen, B. O. (1998-2004). Mplus users' guide (3rd ed.). Los Angeles, CA: Muthen and Muthen.

Paquin, C. (November 21, 2005). Administrators advise caution in Facebook postings. *The Dartmouth.* Retrieved December 1, 2009 from: http://www.thedartmouth.com/article.php?aid=2005112101070.

Pathe, M. & Mullen, P. E. (1997). The impact of stalkers on their victims. *British Journal of Psychiatry,* 170, 12-17.

Ricketts, M. L. (2007). K-12 teachers' perceptions of school policy and fear of school violence. *The Journal of School Violence,* 6, 45-67.

Schreck, C. J., Wright, R. A., & Miller, J. M. (2002). A study of individual and situational antecedents of violent victimization. *Justice Quarterly,* 19, 159-180.

Sealy, W. (2005, December 14). What Facebook doesn't tell you. *The Flat Hat, student newspaper of The College of William and Mary,* 9, 11-13.

Skinner, W. F., & Fream, A. M. (1997). A social learning theory analysis of computer crime among college students. *Journal of Research in Crime and Delinquency,* 34, 495-518.

Spitzberg, B. H., & Hoobler, G. (2002). Cyberstalking and the technologies of interpersonal terrorism. *New Media & Society,* 4, 71–92.

Stutzman, F. (April, 2006). *An evaluation of identity-sharing behavior in social network \ communities.* Paper presented at the iDMAa and IMS Code Conference, Oxford, Ohio.

Tufekci, Z. (2008). Can you see me now?: Audience and disclosure regulation in online social network sites. *Bulletin of Science, Technology & Society,* 28(1), 20-36.

Viseu, A., Clement, A., & Aspinall, J. (2004). Situating privacy online: Complex perceptions and everyday practices. *Information, Communication & Society,* 7(1), 92–114.

Warr, M. (2002). Companions in crime: *The social aspects of criminal conduct.* Cambridge, UK: Cambridge University Press.

Woo, S. (2005, December 14). The Facebook: not just for students. *The Brown Daily Herald,* 10, 5-7.

Wood, P. W., Gove, W. R., Wilson, J., & Cochran, J. K. (1997). Non-social reinforcement and habitual criminal conduct: An extension of learning theory. *Criminology,* 35, 335-366.

Young, A. L., & Quan-Haase, A. (2009). Information revelation and Internet privacy concerns on social network sites: A case study of Facebook. *Proceedings from the Fourth International Conference on Communities and Technologies.* University Park, PA: ACM.

Zelkowitz, R. (November 22, 2005). Wasted: Facebook group causes controversy. *The Emory Wheel Online.* Retrieved December 1, 2009 from: http://www.emorywheel.com/vnews/display.v/ART/2005/11/22/48329c13eb4d8.

Discussion Questions

1. What features of Facebook might put users at risk for victimization.

2. Although many students express great concern over privacy issues on Facebook, many disclose personal information on the SNS. Why the disjunction?

3. Explain the concept of nonsocial reinforcement. Provide an example of a nonsocial reinforcer. Compare that to a social reinforcer.

4. If you were a member of the Institutional Review Board, what concerns would need to be addressed prior to approving replication of this study at your college or university?

5. What factors limit the generalizability of these findings?

6. How would you expect results to differ if the subject of the study were from different demographic groups?.

Chapter 6
CRIME AND THE GREAT RECESSION: AN ANALYSIS OF ECONOMIC AND CRIME VARIABLES FROM 2002 TO 2010

Krystal E. Noga-Styron, M.A., J.D. Central Washington University
Micheal Ruble, Ph.D., C.P.A. Central Washington University

Introduction

Many refer to the current state of the national economy as the "Great Recession." The recession began in the United States in December of 2007 and has since spread to much of the industrialized world. The financial crisis has reenergized the long-standing debate among criminal justice scholars, practitioners, and policy makers regarding the relationship, if any, between economic downturns and crime. Members of the media have joined the debate by disseminating news stories and anecdotal "evidence" depicting rising crime rates, implying a causal connection between the recession and increased crime.

Consequently, the consensus in public opinion is that criminal behavior increases during difficult economic times. The results of our six-month survey, which questioned nearly 1,000 subjects across the country, substantiated the mistaken belief that crime (mainly property crime) is on the rise. Media accounts and scholarly articles perpetuate this impression, particularly as it relates to high unemployment rates. However, our study of national and state level crime rates concluded that there is little, if any, correlation between rising crime and a struggling economy. In other words, our research indicates that crime rates do not necessarily rise as unemployment rates go up, and negative economic circumstances do not necessarily motivate criminal behavior.

Literature Review

Economists since 1968 have believed that crime responds to economic conditions and incentives. Becker (1968) asserted that as the economy slides downward, individuals will be more likely to commit income-generating crimes as long as the benefits of the crime outweigh the potential costs of getting caught. Becsi (1999) expanded on this theory in what he called the "supply-and-demand framework" of economics and crime: criminals supply crime, the public demands protection from crime, and the government provides public protections. Besci argued that crime represents a cost/benefit relationship: the net payoff of the criminal activity (the loot) is weighed against the costs. The costs include foregone wages from legitimate activities, direct costs of crime (supplies), and expected future penalties (fines, incarceration, etc.). According to Becsi (1999), the supply of crime is positively related to the net payoff from criminal activities, meaning that criminals will increase their activities when the net payoff rises.

Most early literature did in fact focus on individual decision making and rational choice models involving personal cost/benefit assessments (Gould, Weinberg, & Mustard, 2002). Such microeconomic theories dominated the research—and the debate—on the relationship between crime and the economy until they were supplemented with more quantitative and macroeconomic theories in the mid- to late-1970s (Yearwood & Koinis, 2009). In subsequent years, researchers studied the impact of unemployment on crime rates, often reaching conflicting conclusions. For example, Neustrom, Jamieson, Manual, and Gramlin (1988) found statistically significant correlations between unemployment rates and the crimes of larceny and assault. Allen (1996) reported a significant positive association between unemployment rate and the crimes of robbery and burglary, but not between unemployment rate and motor vehicle theft. However, research by Oster and Agell (2007) revealed statistical significance between unemployment rates and motor vehicle theft. Young's (1993) research focused outside the United States and found no significant correlation between unemployment and national theft rates. Most significantly, a definitive meta-analysis investigation of 60 research studies, all of which analyzed unemployment and crime (both general and specific), concluded that fewer than fifty-percent of these studies highlighted a statistically significant relationship between the two variables (Chiricos, 1987).

According to Yearwood and Koinis (2009), research findings on the relationship between unemployment rates and crime are mixed, inconclusive, and varied depending on the type of data used and the statistical analyses performed. In fact, they state that scholars have become skeptical and question the validity of using unemployment rates as predictive measures for changes in the crime rate (Yearwood & Koinis, 2009). As a result, criminal justice scholars have evolved to include other economic factors in their research on the relationship between crime and the economy.

Criminologist Richard Rosenfeld states that researchers should move away from using the unemployment rate as the key economic indicator, and encourages the use of what he regards as better indicators—gross domestic product per capita and consumer confidence—to show connections between economic downturns and increases in crime, which he believes do exist (Expert Says, 2009). Rosenfeld says crime rates rise in such times not because ordinary citizens become criminals, but because some consumers begin to enter the underground or black markets in which stolen goods are sold. According to Rosenfeld, "as that demand expands, the incentives for criminals to supply those markets will go up"; in other words, "it's not the case that downturns transform virtuous people into street criminals" (Expert Says, 2009).

Today, it is generally accepted that unemployment rates, alone, are not accurate predictors of crime. The research that has generated the most consistent findings has shown that unemployment is not the most effective economic variable with which to predict crime. More effective economic predictors of crime include, but are not limited to, inflation, salary data, the Gross Domestic Product (GDP), interest rates, the number of mortgage foreclosures, and public perceptions of the economy. For example, when inflation increases, property crimes also rise, and vice versa (Seals & Nunley, 2007). Bunge, Johnson, and Balde (2005) found inflation to be a reliable preditor of "breaking and entering" crimes such as motor vehicle theft, burglary, and robbery. Allen (1996) concluded that anti-inflation policies generally tended to decrease property crimes. Devine, Sheley, and Smith (1988) theorized that this may occur because inflation has the potential to reduce the wages of unskilled workers who, as a result, may seek out underground or black-market goods, thereby encouraging the rise of property crimes.

Other researchers found that unstable and declining wages also correlated with rises in youth crimes (Grogger, 1997) as well as violent and property crimes (Gould, Weinberg, & Mustard, 2002). Others found a significant relationship between increased GDP, per capita, and decreased robbery rates (Fajnzylber, Lederman, & Loayza, 2002). Jones & Kutan (2004) found that increased interest rates correlated with increased rates of theft and robberies involving knives. The U.S. Conference of Mayors and Police Chiefs, which sponsored a survey to identify key issues relating to crime in today's cities, found that 42% of surveyed cities reported increased crime as a result of current economic conditions. Likewise, 29% of the surveyed cities reported increased crime resulting from the mortgage foreclosure crisis and the increased number of vacant and abandoned properties (Cochran, 2008). Lastly, regarding public perception of the economy, improved consumer sentiment about existing economic climates tends to decrease the number of reported robbery and property crimes (Rosenfeld & Fornango, 2007).

Our Study

Despite the substantial work in the area, scholars still seem to be divided about whether economics, and its many variables, affect crime rates. The public seems largely unaware of the potential economic view of crime and its implications. In fact, by early 2010, the United States was in a severe economic recession—one felt worldwide—yet according to the Federal Bureau of Investigation's (FBI) Uniform Crime Report

(UCR), crime rates had decreased in nearly every measurable category. As such, Becker and Becsi's philosophies of the "supply-and-demand framework" of economics and crime may be the most valid. In essence, crime today may be too costly. Today's cost/benefit ratio regarding crime does not favor criminal behavior; there is less to steal in a downturned economy, and thanks to major media attention on increased gun and ammunition sales, would-be criminals are keenly aware that today's potential victim is better prepared than ever before to fight back. Additionally, deterrence measures, such as 3-strikes laws, remain in effect despite fewer police on the streets and decreasing incarceration rates.

To review, Becker (1968) and Becsi (1999) agree that crime represents a cost/benefit relationship in which individuals become more likely to engage in criminal behavior if the benefits of the crime outweigh the potential costs of the crime. Yet, the two diverge in their thinking in that Becker (1968) believes that such crimes would have the potential to increase when the economy spirals downward, whereas Becsi (1999) believes that individuals will increase their criminal activities in a more stable and upward economy when the potential net payoffs rise, i.e., when there is more to steal.

The substantial work in this area has focused on the relationship between crime and economics in the 1970s, '80s, and '90s. Our study focused on the years 2002/4-2008/9. We analyzed economic data from 2002-2008 and crime data from 2004-2009, allowing approximately one year for the economic downturn to affect crime. This period incorporated the most recent extreme economic highs and lows, but it did not incorporate the period surrounding the Enron scandal, the subsequent dissolution of the Arthur Andersen accounting firm, the stock market crash, and other economic calamities associated with the attacks of September 11, 2001, all of which affected the wider business world. This period also included the recent U.S. housing bubble, which began in 2002 and burst in 2008. Economic experts consider late-2008 and early-2009 to be the bottom of the economy; the Dow Jones Industrial Average hit bottom in March of 2009, although the unemployment rate did not begin to decrease until January 2010. As such, we examined how crime responded to a variety of demographic and economic factors. In total, we analyzed ten variables: population density, youth population, labor participation rate, unemployment/welfare, poverty rate, per capita personal/median income, education, state incarceration rates, police employment, and police expenditures.

Furthermore, to gather information regarding the public perception of crime during the current economic downturn, we conducted a national online survey during the first three months of 2010. To gather a random sample of responses, we advertised the survey on college and university campuses, in national and local media outlets, and on social networking cites such as Facebook and Twitter. In all, we surveyed nearly one thousand respondents and asked questions regarding the current state of the economy and current crime and victimization rates relating to both general and specific crimes, as well as questions about respondents' sources for obtaining news and information. We specifically asked questions about whether crime rates were up or down as compared to the previous five years. We only asked questions regarding the crimes for which the FBI collects incident data through its Uniform Crime Reporting system. We did not ask about white-collar crimes.

Population Density

Population density is an essential variable, as many believe crime is primarily an urban phenomenon (Becsi, 1999). As such, we narrowed our study to 14 states: Arizona, California, Florida, Illinois, Massachusetts, Michigan, Missouri, New Jersey, New York, North Carolina, Ohio, Pennsylvania, Texas, and Washington. These states are consistently ranked in the list of the top-20 most densely populated states and include some of nation's largest and most densely populated metropolitan areas (U.S. Census Bureau, 2010). This mix of states provided us with three to four states per FBI Uniform Crime Report region and representation from all but one region in the Bureau of Economic Analysis grouping (Rocky Mountain Region not included). Additionally, half of these states have habitual offender laws, which require state courts to hand down mandatory prison sentences of 25 years-to-life to individuals convicted of serious criminal offenses on at least three separate occasions.

Youth Population

Our second variable, youth population, represents the percentage of the state's population under the age of 25. Historically, nearly half of all arrestees are from the age group of 15-24, and they are disproportionately male (Marvell & Moody, 1991). In fact, according to FBI data from 2009, 15-24 year-olds made up 43.6% of all arrests and males accounted for 74.7% of total arrests (Uniform Crime Report, 2009). The young also tend to be less educated and have a lower legitimate earning potential than do their adult counterparts (Freeman, 1996). All of the states we analyzed had a greater percentage of youth residents than the national average of 29.7% (according to the 2000 U.S. Census), ranging from 1.3 % higher in Florida to 8.9 % higher in Texas.

Labor Participation Rate

The labor participation rate (LPR) is the percent of the population, age 16 and older, who are either employed or seeking employment. A decline in the LPR reflects workers leaving the workforce through retirement, or decreased expectation of finding work by those unemployed, faster than new workers are joining the workforce. Table 6-1 presents LPRs for 2002 through 2008. From the end of 2002 to the end of 2008, the U.S. LPR decreased slightly by 0.9%, while the LPR of the selected states varied from a decline of more than 4% in Michigan and Missouri to a 2% gain in Florida.

Table 6-1. Labor Participation Rates

	2002	2003	2004	2005	2006	2007	2008
Whole US	66.6	66.2	66.0	66.1	66.2	66.0	66.0
Arizona	65.8	65.4	64.8	64.3	64.2	63.8	64.2
California	66.8	66.1	65.5	65.5	65.4	65.6	65.9
Florida	62.6	62.1	62.0	62.3	62.9	63.5	63.9
Illinois	67.4	66.5	66.4	66.6	67.4	68.2	67.8
Massachusetts	68.4	67.8	67.1	66.8	67.1	66.8	66.5
Michigan	66.1	65.6	65.4	65.4	65.2	64.5	63.4
Missouri	69.3	68.6	68.3	67.8	67.4	67.0	66.3
New Jersey	66.8	66.2	65.8	66.3	66.9	66.4	66.6
New York	63.0	62.6	62.6	62.7	62.9	62.7	63.1
North Carolina	66.9	66.6	66.0	65.9	66.2	65.5	64.8
Ohio	67.1	67.0	66.8	66.9	67.2	67.3	67.1
Pennsylvania	65.2	64.2	64.5	64.7	64.7	64.5	65.2
Texas	68.4	68.2	67.6	67.0	66.5	65.8	65.7
Washington	67.5	67.4	67.5	67.6	67.6	67.8	68.4

Unemployment Rate/Welfare

The unemployment rate (UR) measures the subset of the labor force that is unemployed but actively seeking work. An increase in the UR could indicate that active workers are losing jobs, the workforce is shrinking through retirement, or the workforce is increasing in size but not enough employment opportunities are available to those entering the workforce. From 2002 through 2007, the employment rate for the United States dropped 1.4%, with the selected states experiencing a 1.5% drop. However, in 2008 and 2009, the national UR rose to 10.0%, with the selected states climbing to 10.4%. The rapid rise in the UR is the primary motivating factor for our study, as it is a common-held belief that rising unemployment leads to rising crime rates. Increases in unemployment rates imply diminished legitimate earnings expectations and potential increases in the net return from crime. Welfare expenditures, on the other hand, might reduce the pain from unemployment, thereby reducing the net return of crime (Becsi, 1999).

Poverty Rate

The U.S. Census Bureau calculates the official Poverty Rate (PR) based on annual surveys. We considered the percentage of families living below the 100% poverty level in each year. A rise in the PR demonstrates that family income is not keeping up with the rise in the poverty level income driven by increases in median income and cost-of-living. The national PR rose 0.5% from 2002 to 2004, declined by 0.4 % from 2004 to 2006, and rose by 0.9% by the end of 2008. This quick rise is also a concern with respect to a rise in crime rates.

Median Income

Median Income (MI) measures the midpoint of family income. As incomes rise, those on fixed or limited incomes fall behind on the ability to participate in the market for goods or services. Rising incomes put pressure on price-levels, as more dollars chase goods, which then cause prices on consumer goods to rise. Those on fixed, limited incomes might slide into poverty, and this might cause crime rates to rise. From 2002 through 2008, median incomes rose an average of 3.5% for both the U.S. ($42,409 to $52,029) and our 14 states. However, the increases among the selected states ranged from a low of 1.6% in Michigan to a high of 4.6% in New York, with 7 states within 0.3% of the 3.5% average.

Education

According to Becsi (1999), primary and secondary education equate to positive disincentives to commit crime. In the United States, this includes the compulsory education levels of elementary, middle, and high school. Becsi (1999) also argued that education expenditures increase opportunity costs of crime by keeping youth off the streets, by raising their earning potential from future legitimate sources, and by giving them tools necessary to realistically evaluate the costs of crime. Data from the 2000 Census indicated that 52% of the population had at least a high school education (U.S. Bureau of Census, 2000). Nine of our selected states–Illinois, Massachusetts, Michigan, Missouri, New Jersey, New York, Ohio, Pennsylvania, and Washington—were at or above the national average. Texas had the lowest education rate at only 46.4%, and Massachusetts had the highest at 57.0%.

State Incarceration Rates

Another variable of interest is the state incarceration rate. Studies suggest that imprisonment rates indicate that punishment has a strong effect on the ability to reduce crime (Becsi, 1999). For example, Becsi (1999) estimated that a 10% increase in the prison population produces a 0.5% to 1.9% reduction in crime (Becsi, 1999). As of January 2010, there were 1,403,091 persons under the jurisdiction of state prison authorities, 5,739 fewer than on December 31, 2008 (The Pew Center on the States, 2010). According to the results of a survey conducted by the Pew Center on the States, this marks the first year-to-year drop in the nation's state prison populations since 1972 (2009). Although the study showed an overall decline, it revealed great variation among jurisdictions. Nationally, the prison population declined in 27 states, but increased in 23 states and in the federal system (The Pew Center on the States, 2010). The incarceration rate increased in five of the states we studied (Arizona, Florida, Missouri, North Carolina, and Pennsylvania) and decreased in the other nine states. According to Becsi's theory, the decrease in the prison population would mean an increase in criminal activity (1999).

Police Employment/ Police Expenditures

Police employment and public expenditures on police and protection each measure the commitment of state and local governments to spend money to prevent crime through police presence. Per capita police expenditures and police employment are qualitatively very similar (Becsi, 1999). The FBI's UCR program defines law enforcement officers as individuals who ordinarily carry a firearm and a badge, have full arrest powers, and are paid from governmental funds set aside specifically for sworn law enforcement representatives (Uniform Crime Report, 2009).

Police expenditures per capita reflect both the rising prices and public efforts to reduce crime and raise expected cost to criminals. From 2002 through 2008, police expenditures increased by an average of 5.4% per year and expenditures per capita increased on average 4.5% per year, while at the same time inflation, as measured by the Consumer Price Index (CPI), only increased 2.8%. The data available for our selected states is consistent with this national trend. This seems to indicate that there was an increase in police expenditures over and above just the impact of rising prices. This would, in theory, decrease crime rates if increased policing was effective.

Yet, according to media accounts, police employment and expenditures decreased in 2009 due to police layoffs and department closures during increasingly difficult economic times. This information would lead the public to believe that crime would likely be rising, as criminals would equate the decrease in police presence as a decrease in the costs associated with crime. This logic, however, may be faulty. According to Becsi (1999), police are not necessarily an anti-crime variable; empirical data commonly find police to be positively associated with crime or find insignificant relationships. In other words, law enforcement officers are hired as part of crime-reduction efforts in reaction to increases in crime; when crime is on the rise, so are police hires.

Crime Data

We used crime data published in the FBI's annual Uniform Crime Report (UCR). We looked at crime rates, or number of reported offenses per 100,000 inhabitants, for the violent crimes of murder and non-negligent manslaughter, forcible rape, robbery, aggravated assault, as well as the number of officers feloniously killed on the state level. The crime rates, or number of reported offenses per 100,000 inhabitants, were obtained for the property crimes of burglary, larceny-theft, and motor vehicle theft. Before discussing the data, it is important to note some problems associated with UCR statistics. The UCR presents data only on crimes reported to the police. Because victims underreport certain crimes, such as hate crimes, domestic violence, and forcible rape, UCR numbers reflect less than the true amount of crimes committed. Furthermore, the FBI employs a hierarchical reporting system, which only counts the most serious crime when several crimes are committed together. Another concern is that the data collected by the UCR are voluntarily reported to the FBI by local and state agencies, without quality-assurance measures in place. Lastly, without standard and national quality-assurance measures in place, data collection may not be consistent among agencies.

The UCR data indicated decreases in both violent and property crime rates (measured as occurrences per 100,000 inhabitants). The percent change in volume and rate of violent crimes for 5 years (2004-2008) increased by 1.6%, peaking in 2006 (during good economic times) and steadily decreasing in 2007 and 2008 as the economy began to head into recession. For property crimes, the percent change in volume and rate for 5 years (2004-2008) decreased by 5.3%. Our survey results showed that people believed the opposite to be true; they thought violent crime was down and that property crime was up during those mentioned years.

The preliminary data that was available for 2009 was regional and represented only the first six months of the year (January to June 2009), so we compared the percentages with figures reported for the same time in 2008. The 2009 data indicated that crime was down nationally, in every category and in every region of the United States, except the South, which experienced an increase in its burglary rate of only 0.7% (see Table 6-2). Each region experienced decreases smaller than the national average in several categories: the Midwest in murder and non-negligent manslaughter, robbery, and aggravated assault; the Northeast in robbery and aggravated assault; the South in murder and non-negligent manslaughter, forcible rape, and larceny-theft; and the West in forcible rape, robbery, aggravated assault, and larceny-theft. Analysis of the 2009 data was particularly significant and informative because the recession is thought to have begun in late-2007 and early-2008, with the late-2008 and early-2009 period as the bottom of the economy, allowing some time for the economic downturn to show its effect on crime. In the end, the effect seems to be that both violent and property crimes increased during times of economic progress and decreased during difficult economic times.

Table 6-2. Percent by Region
Current data is only available for the first six months of 2009 (January to June 2009).

Percentages are compared with figures reported for the same time in 2008.

	Murder	Forcible Rape	Robbery	Aggra-vated Assault	Burglary	Larceny-Theft	Crimes Against L.E.
Whole U.S.	-10.0	-3.3	-6.5	-3.2	-2.5	-5.3	*
Northeast	-13.7	-6.1	-6.0	-0.8	-8.2	-5.3	
Midwest	-7.6	-7.5	-3.7	-2.6	-4.6	-7.8	
South	-7.8	-0.9	-9.0	-5.1	+0.7	-4.1	
West	-13.3	-1.4	-5.2	-2.2	-3.6	-5.0	

*These data are not yet available

Overall, compared with national data, the Northeast experienced a 9.3% larger decrease in crime, followed by the West, which experienced a 4.5% larger decrease in crime, and the Midwest, which experienced a 3% larger decrease in crime. The South, despite generally experiencing a decrease in crime in all areas except burglary (with a slight 0.7% increase), had a crime rate 7.4% higher than the national average. Regarding population density, the three Southern states in this analysis are among the top-ten of most populated states in the nation (Texas, [2], Florida [4], and North Carolina [10]). Of our selected states, the ones that ranked least populated were Northeastern states (New Jersey [11] and Massachusetts [15]), Western states (Washington [13] and Arizona [14]) and the Midwestern state of Missouri [18]. As mentioned previously, these three regions experienced larger decreases in crime than the national average. When comparing our crime data to the youth population data, the youth populations in our selected states was considerably higher than the national average, ranging from 1.3 %

higher in Florida to 8.9 % higher in Texas—both Southern states. At this point, there does not seem to be a correlation between youth population and recent crime statistics.

We analyzed changes in the Labor Participation Rate (LPR) of the selected states in relation to crime rates. The national LPR decreased 0.9% during our focus years. At the same time, Michigan and Missouri—both Midwestern states—experienced a decline of more than 4%, and the Southern state of Florida had an increased LPR of 2%. All three of these states had increases in crime rates, with Florida's crime rate being higher than the national average. Nevertheless, our data did not present a significant connection between decreased LPR and increased crime. In terms of the unemployment rate among our sampled states, Michigan noted the highest unemployment rate (8.4%), while Texas noted the lowest (4.9%). As Michigan is a Midwestern state, experiencing an overall decrease in crime, and Texas is a Southern state, experiencing an overall crime rate higher than the national average, there is no indication of a correlation between increased unemployment and crime rates.

The poverty rate was highest in Arizona (18%)—a Western state—and lowest in New Jersey (9.2%)—a Northeastern state—compared with the national average of 13.2%. The poverty rate for the Southern states was at or above the national average (Florida [13.1%], North Carolina [13.9%], and Texas [15.9%]). From 2002 through 2008, median incomes increased an average of 3.5% for both the United States and our 14 states, collectively. Individually, however, the selected states ranged from a low of 1.6% in Michigan to a high of 4.6% in New York, with seven states within 0.3% of the national average. The mixed poverty rate and median income results are inconclusive in establishing a correlation with crime.

In analyzing the variable of education and education expenditures, the largest discrepancies were between Texas, with an education rate at only 46.4%, and Massachusetts, with an education rate at 57.0%. The national education rate was 52%. Actually, all three of the Southern states (Florida, North Carolina, and Texas) had education levels below the national average. This variable is consistent with UCR data, showing a correlation between lack of education and an increase in criminal behavior. Conversely, the percent change in prison incarceration from December 31, 2008 to January 1, 2010 showed the largest increase in Pennsylvania (+4.3%) and the largest decrease in Michigan (-6.7%). These figures establish no definitive correlation between prison populations and crime.

Regarding police employment and expenditures, the states investing most in this security, per capita, were California, New Jersey, and New York. The states investing least in police were Pennsylvania, Texas, and Washington. Particularly interesting is the fact that California and

Texas are the nation's two most densely populated states, respectively.
The data from Texas—a Southern higher-crime state that invests
comparatively little in police protection—may suggest a correlation
between police employment and expenditure and a decrease or
deterrence in criminal behavior.

Survey Data

Again, UCR data revealed a national increase in violent crime by
1.6% and a decrease in property crime by 5.3% during the 2004-2009
period. In contrast, our survey results indicated that people believed that
the rate of murder, forcible rape, aggravated assault, and hate crimes
have either stayed the same or gone down in the last five years.
Likewise, of those surveyed, 69% thought robbery was on the rise, 69%
thought burglary was on the rise, and 72% thought theft was on the rise.
Another 77% believed that the number of police officers assaulted or
killed was up compared to the previous five years, when in reality, that
number has largely stayed the same. When asked whether weapons
were purchased because of the impression of increased crime, 14.2%
answered that they purchased a new weapon in the last two years;
22.8% of these people said that this was the first weapon they have ever
purchased. Of the weapons purchased in the last two years, 69% were
handguns or rifles.

Conclusion

We reviewed the relationship between 10 economic and social
variables as compared with the crime rates in 14 of the nation's most
densely populated states. Our data show no clear indication that a
negative change in the economy leads to an increase in crime. Despite
difficult economic times, desperate times may not call for desperate
measures. In employing a cost/benefit analysis, criminals seem to be
concluding that crime is too costly today, perhaps because there may be
less available to steal, suggesting that it takes a good economy to
motivate the criminal element. For example, consider the mass exodus
from the city of Detroit, Michigan—one of hardest hit cities by the
economic recession (Okrent, 2009). As the population of the city
dwindled, so did its murder rate, leading some to believe that the
decrease was significant only in that it meant that there was no one left
to kill. Regardless, deterrence measures remain in place despite fewer
police on the streets and decreasing incarceration rates. In fact, half the
states we analyzed enforced habitual offender laws. The media have
aggressively reported on the dramatic increases in both gun and
ammunition sales, which would lead most to believe that potential
victims are better prepared to fight back against would-be criminals.

As in nearly every economic climate, crime rates indicate that most of the nation's crime is perpetrated in the South, and the least occurs in the Northeast. The Northeast has some of the highest incomes and most educated residents in the nation, whereas the South, in particular the Southeast, has some of the lowest incomes and least-educated residents. In the end, despite the extensive research on the debate between crime and economics, there is no definitive correlation between a bad economy and an increase in crime. Even The Great Depression had the lowest crime rates for its era.

References

Allen, R. (1996). Socioeconomic conditions and property crime: A comprehensive review and test of the professional literature. *The American Journal of Economics and Sociology, 55* (3), 293-308.

Becker, G. (1968). Crime and punishment: An economic approach. *Journal of Political Economy, 76* (2), 169-217.

Becsi, Z. (1999). Economics and Crime in the States. *Economic Review, First Quarter,* 38-56.

Bunge, V., Johnson, H., & Balde, T. (2005, June 29). *Exploring crime patterns in Canada.* Retrieved December 21, 2009, from Statistics Canada: http://www.statcan.gc.ca/pub/85-561-m/85-561-m2005005-eng.htm

Chiricos, T. (1987). Rates of crime and unemployment: An analysis of aggregte research evidence. *Social Problems, 34* (2), 187-211.

Cochran, T. (2008, August 5). 2008 *Economic Downturn and Federal Inaction Impact on Crime.* Retrieved January 15, 2010, from The United States Conference of Mayors: http://usmayors.org/maf/CrimeReport_0808.pdf

Devine, J., Sheley, J., & Smith, M. (1988). Macroeconomic and social-control policy influences on crime rate changes, 1948-1985. *American Sociological Review, 53* (3), 407-420.

Fajnzylber, P., Lederman, D., & Loayza, N. (2002). What causes violent crime? *European Economic Review, 46,* 1323-1357.

Freeman, R. (1996). Why do so many young American men commit crimes and what might we do about it? *Journal of Economic Perspectives, 10* (Winter), 25-42.

Gould, E., Weinberg, B., & Mustard, D. (2002). Crime rates and local labor market opportunities in the United States: 1979-1997. *The Review of Economics and Statistics, 84* (1), 45-61.

Grogger, J. (1997). Market wages and youth crime. Cambridge, MA: National Bureau of Economic Research Working Paper Series, #5983.

Jones, G., & Kutan, A. (2004). *Volatile interest rates, volatile crime rates: A new argument for interest rates smoothing.* Ann Arbor: William Davidson Institute Working Paper Series, #694 – University of Michigan.

Marvell, T. B., & Moody, C. E. (1991). Age structure and crime rates. *Journal of Quantitative Criminology* 7, no. 3, 237-73.

Expert says economic woes may spur crime rate. (2009, February 24). All Things Considered [radio news program] Retrieved December 17, 2009 from http://www.npr.org/templates/story/story.php?storyId= 101106238

Neustrom, M., Jamieson, J., Manual, D., & Gramlin, B. (1988). Regional unemployment and crime trends: An empirical examination. *Journal of Criminal Justice,* 16 (5), 394-402.

Okrent, D. (2009, Oct. 5). Detroit: The Death—and Possible Life—of a Great City. *Time Magazine,* http://www.time.com/time/nation/article/ 0,8599,1925796,00.html#ixzz1HxJQek3X

Oster, A., & Agell, J. (2007). Crime and unemployment in turbulent times. *Journal of European Economic Associations,* 5 (4), 752-775.

Pew Center on the States. (2010, March 20). *Prison Count 2010: State Population Declines for the First Time in 38 Years.* Retrieved March 21, 2010, from The Pew Center on the States: http://www.pewcenter onthestates.org/report_detail.aspx?id=57653

Rosenfeld, R., & Fornango, R. (2007). The impact of economic conditions on robbery and property crime: The role of consumer sentiment. *Criminology,* 45 (4), 735-769.

Seals, A., & Nunley, J. (2007). *The effects of inflation and demographic change on property crime: A structural time series approach.* Murfreesboro, TN: The Department of Economics and Finance Working Paper Series—Middle Tennessee State University.

Uniform Crime Report (2010, September). *Arrests*—Retrieved April 29, 2011, from Department of Justice—Federal Bureau of Investigation: http://www2.fbi.gov/ucr/cius2009/data/table_42.html

Uniform Crime Report (2010, September). *Arrests—Persons Under 15, 18, 21, and 25 Years of Age, 2009.* Retrieved April 29, 2011, from Department of Justice—Federal Bureau of Investigation: http://www2.fbi.gov/ucr/cius2009/data/table_41.html

Uniform Crime Report (2009, September). *Police Employee Date.* Retrieved September 29, 2009, from Department of Justice—Federal Bureau of Investigation: http://www.fbi.gov/ucr/cius2008/police/index. html

U. S. Census Bureau. United States Population Estimates. Retrieved March 21, 2010, from U.S. Census Bureau: http://factfinder.census. gov/servlet/GCTTable?_bm=y&-geo_id=01000US&-_box_head_ nbr=GCT-T1-R&-ds_name=PEP_2009_EST&-_lang=en&-format= US-40S&-_sse=on

U.S. Department of Justice. Bureau of Justice Statistics. (1995). *Criminal Victimization.* Washington, D.C.: GPO.

Yearwood, D. L., & Koinis, G. (2009). *Revisiting Property Crime and Economic Conditions: An Exploratory Study to Identify Predictive Indicators beyond Unemployment Rates.* Munich, Germany: Munich Personal RePEc Archive.

Young, T. (1993). Unemployment and property crime. Not a simple relationship. *The American Journal of Economics and Sociology,* 52 (4), 413-415.

Discussion Questions

1. You are having lunch with your extended family, when your aunt brings up a string of crimes recently reported in the local newspaper. The group begins listing all of the local business that have laid off workers or closed altogether. They are convinced that there is a clear relationship between the economy and crime. Knowing you are studying criminal justice, they ask for your opinion. What do you tell them?

2. Noga-Styron and Ruble analyzed economic data from 2002 to 2008 and crime data from 2004 to 2009 in order to assess changes in crime and economy. Why didn't they just use data from the same period for both?

3. How did Noga-Styron and Ruble collect public opinion data? What techniques did they use to ensure a random sample of respondents? What limitations are there for relying on the chosen method of data collection? In other words, do you think soliciting information through other means would yield different groups of respondents and responses?

4. Why did the authors only ask respondents questions about crimes represented by the UCR? Does UCR data accurately reflect true crime rates? Explain.

5. What did the authors suggest was the impact of aggressive media reporting on gun and ammunition sales on crime and victimization?

6. According to Noga-Styron and Ruble, how did public perceptions of crime compare to actual crime during the period of economic downturn at the heart of this study? What did they conclude about the relationship between the economy and crime?

SECTION 3

POLICING ISSUES AND RESEARCH

Section 3
Policing Issues and Research

INTRODUCTION

In the early days of the twentieth century, legendary police chief and early criminal justice professor August Vollmer realized that police officers needed to be well educated. His subordinates and students became mentors to future generations of law enforcement officers. Today, Vollmer's successors are able to evaluate complex crime data and respond to the demands of their career with the critical thinking skills one can best develop while in college. The study of criminal justice for future practitioners provides them with the knowledge, writing skills and self-discipline to make difficult decisions, develop policy and serve the public in ways that were never possible in the days of the under-educated law enforcement officer. In the chapters that follow, pay close attention to the role that well-developed law enforcement research plays in the day-to-day management of U.S. police departments.

The Current State of Educational Requirements in Local Police Departments: Is the College Degree Important?

The President's Commission on Law Enforcement and the Administration of Justice (1967) reported that without higher educational requirements, quality police services could not be attained. However, over forty years later, in 2010, most police agencies (nonfederal) do not require anything more than a high school diploma or equivalent, although most agencies report a preference for college-degreed officers. Upon reviewing 36 departments that require a four-year degree, this exploratory analysis explores the reasoning behind the small number of police departments actually requiring the degree and describes police chiefs' opinions regarding why a college degree is important. Furthermore, the need for a college degree regarding community policing is discussed.

Traffic Suspects Encountered by the Police: A Social Ecological Analysis

Many explanations account for the observed variation in police behavior across physical space. Studies agree that the way a community setting shapes the exercise of discretion depends, partly, on that setting's actual levels of crime and disorder. Drawing on Klinger's (1997) theory of social ecology and data collected from the Project on Policing Neighborhood (POPN), this study examined whether police vigor varied inversely with district crime for citizens involved in traffic encounters. Bivariate results indicated that district crime had a significant and positive influence on police vigor. Multivariate results indicated that officer cynicism and workload did not mediate the vigor-crime relationship as hypothesized. Implications of these and other findings are discussed, along with suggestions for future research and theoretical development.

Leading and Managing Police Organizations

The police executive has a responsibility for setting expectations, vision, mission, and strategy. The executive has to pay attention to matters both inside and outside of the organization. Dependent on the size of the organizations, the chief will have several individuals of rank to help supervise and manage the organization. In this case, setting and articulating expectations, delegation, accountability, and trust are essential. This chapter allows readers to "peer behind the curtain" and better understand the complexities and inner workings of a law enforcement agency. It is intended to help students think about the many "balls in the air" that have to be considered by police executives. The chapter discusses and describes the differences of leading and managing and the elements of leadership, planning, leading organizing and controlling. The concepts of decision-making and the benefit of data analysis are included. The Human Capital factor in organizations will be included. This would include recruiting and retention, training, pay and benefits, labor issues, discipline, and motivation.

Assessing Police-Community Relations in a Changing Department

Using data collected from a Massachusetts police department, this chapter examines officers' perceptions of community-oriented policing services (COPS) during a time of administrative change and strained police-community relations. The literature suggests that many of the elements of COPS (e.g., crime prevention, intelligence gathering, community involvement, enhancement of residents' quality of life) remain important in the everyday lives of citizens and in the era of homeland security. However, the implementation and effectiveness of COPS may depend heavily on the leadership style, philosophy, and practices of the chief, and the "boots on the ground" commitment to carry out the COPS mission and goals. These issues were examined in this study by asking officers to relate their views of the previous and present chief, COPS, and the physical working environment. The results indicate that the leadership of the new chief improved officers' job satisfaction and police-community relations so much so that residents overwhelmingly voted to build a $4.65 million dollar state-of-the art police station to equip officers to better serve them in the twenty-first century.

Chapter 7
THE CURRENT STATE OF EDUCATIONAL REQUIREMENTS IN LOCAL POLICE DEPARTMENTS: IS THE COLLEGE DEGREE IMPORTANT?

Diana Bruns, Ph.D. Southeast Missouri State University

Introduction

Hiring college-educated candidates in the law enforcement field does not guarantee they will be good officers. Being a police officer is hard and to be successful, you have to want to be a police officer. Individuals who receive the required college degree have demonstrated their desire. Desire is something very hard to evaluate, but such an important trait. If all other qualities are equal—the college graduate with a four-year degree should be hired as a police officer before one who doesn't have the degree.

—Police Chief from a department
with mandatory degree requirement

The debate over the value of a college degree for police officers dates as far back as 1916, when August Vollmer, police chief and professor at the University of California at Berkeley, spurred the movement for college-educated officers. Decades of research followed regarding whether a college degree is an essential or important ingredient for police officers. From 1964 to 1974, the President's Commission on Law Enforcement and Administration of Justice, the National Advisory Commission on Criminal Justice Standards and Goals, and the American Bar Association Project on Standards for Criminal Justice advised that all police officers receive a four-year degree. However, over forty years later, most police departments have ignored such recommendations. Less than 1% of police departments require a four-year degree (Hickman & Reeves, 2006). Although leaders in law enforcement resist the implementation of educational requirements (Breci, 1997; Carlan, 2007; Remington, 1990; Roberg & Bonn, 2004), recruitment for college graduates continues to increase. This paradox needs to be studied.

Not enough is understood regarding why so few police departments require degrees despite many recommendations that a college degree is necessary. Furthermore, no studies have addressed the location of such departments requiring degrees or why those particular departments chose such requirements.

According to the U.S. Department of Justice (2004), there are 12,766 local police departments with 3,067 sheriff's offices, 49 primary state law enforcement agencies, 1,481 special jurisdiction agencies, and 513 "other" agencies, totaling 17,876 law enforcement agencies. A 2003 sample of 3,000 police departments revealed that 98% of local police departments had an educational requirement for recruits. Of those requiring college, 18% had "some type" of college requirement; 9% required a two-year degree, and less than 1% required a four-year degree (Hickman & Reaves, 2006). Scarce information exists as to the location of those few departments requiring bachelor's degrees.

As the literature suggests, although police administrators prefer officers with baccalaureate degrees, most do not require it. Verrill (2007) stressed the need to determine what factors led the select 1% of local police departments to do so. This study attempts to answer that question.

Background

The push toward having college-educated officers stems from two sources: the alleged importance of professionalism for police forces and the desire to change officer attitudes (Shernock, 1992). Contributing to the debate over the need for educated police officers is the contradictory evidence presented in research. Although many studies find support for the argument that officers need college educations, others do not. For example, Baro and Burlingame (1999) disputed recommendations that officers need a baccalaureate degree to increase levels of police professionalism, stating that officers need no more than a high school diploma or equivalency. Sherman and McLeod (1979) speculated that higher education for officers may be irrelevant because the education officers receive in higher educational institutions is similar to training officers receive in police academies. Critics of higher education believe "college-educated officers are more likely to become frustrated with their work, with restrictions imposed by supervisors, and with limited opportunities for advancement" (Worden, 1990, p. 567). Hudzick (1978) found that educated officers placed less value on obedience to supervisors and were less satisfied with their careers. Others were concerned that "college-educated officers will quickly tire of the irregular hours, constant pressures, and relative low pay of policing" (Varricchio, 1988, p. 11). Whetstone (2000) acknowledged, "hiring candidates with improved credentials also invites eventual problems such as greater job dissatisfaction and personnel turnover" (p. 247), and Kakar (1998) demonstrated that a college education might decrease officers' quality of service because police work does not offer opportunities to stimulate the college-educated mind. Further, because police performance measures differ in studies, no real consensus exists on exactly how police performance should be defined and measured.

On the other hand, countless studies have demonstrated several key differences between educated police officers and those without college education. For example, educated officers have better written and oral communication skills, display more professionalism and tolerance, and exhibit greater understanding of human behavior. They are more intellectually developed, independent, flexible, and well-rounded; they are better able to analyze problems and display increased self-confidence, morality and motivation. Educated officers place greater emphasis on the value of ethical conduct and are less authoritarian; they require fewer disciplinary actions, display better public relation skills, and receive fewer citizen complaints (Aamodt, 2004; Alpert & Dunham, 1988; Breci, 1997; Carlan & Byxbe, 2000; Carter, 2004; Cascio, 1977; Cunningham, 2006; Finckenauer, 1975; Kappeler, Sapp & Carter, 1992; Scott, 1986; Sherman et al., 1978; Shernock, 1992; Smith & Aamodt, 1998; Tyre & Braunstein, 1992; Varrichio, 1998; Worden, 1990).

Is the Type of Degree Important?

Verrill (2007) described the sparse amount of literature concerning the value of a bachelor's degree in criminal justice and whether employers prefer vocational over theoretical degrees. Verrill's study reviewed entry-level educational requirements for criminal justice agencies in Florida, where only two local police departments sampled required a bachelor's degree (N = 261). Realistically, Verrill's sample is indicative of local police departments nationwide, as less than 1% requires bachelor's degrees as prerequisites for employment. It is unclear at this point, however, whether that 1% of police departments requiring four-year degrees specify a preferred discipline. Bostrom (2005) addressed differences in levels of performance and work habits among officers who had Bachelor of Arts degrees versus Bachelor of Science degrees, finding that officers with Bachelor of Arts degrees had better work habits (measured by sick time usage, traffic collisions, discipline) than those with Bachelor of Science degrees. Although this was an exploratory study of just one large police department, Bostrom called for future research in this area.

Schafer and Castellano (2005) attempted to extricate the relationships that subsist among work experience, educational background, and attitudes toward criminal justice education, once again finding "the quality of police service will not significantly improve until higher educational requirements are established for its personnel" (p. 300). Carlan (2007) examined the worth of the criminal justice degree and found that "police officers (n = 299) with varying levels of experience and criminal justice education revealed positive attitudes concerning the degree's value with regard to conceptual development for employment purposes" (p. 616). Johnston, Cheurprakobkit, and McKenzie (2002) revealed that law enforcement administrators stressed that education should help police officers better understand the legal aspects of policing, as well as report writing, ethics, and procedures.

It is evident that leaders in law enforcement are hesitant to embrace the educational movement, considering the nearly nonexistent numbers of police departments requiring degrees (Roberg and Bonn 2004). Although leaders in law enforcement continue to hesitate the implementation of educational requirements (Carlan, 2007; Roberg and Bonn, 2004; Breci, 1997; Remington, 1990), recruitment for college graduates continues to increase—as today's police officers must be innovative, proactive, and involved in the community.

Fortunately, more than 150 years of research (Trojanowicz & Bucquoroux, 1990) helps identify successful police strategies and policies that serve to prevent crime and disorder and to improve the quality of life for all citizens in a community. This basic principle of quality policing is improving municipal/social services to people in communities, which will in turn develop trust between the police and the people they serve—a basic requirement for effective policing. The Office of Community Oriented Policing Services (COPS) describes the four most important components—community engagements and partnerships, crime prevention, organizational transformation, and problem-solving elements of community policing.

One of the tenets of community policing, which has transpired as the primary model to direct policing into the twenty-first century, is that officers are "better able to analyze problems and devise non-coercive solutions" (Worden, 1990, p. 571). Community policing is a concept that invites private citizens to act as their own problem solvers and to become involved with aspects of policing. Officers, therefore, must invite community support to help address social ills and crime via increased interpersonal skills with citizens (Trojanowicz & Bucquoroux, 1990). Furthermore, the U.S. Department of Justice (2000) stated that as of June 30, 1999:

> About 9 in 10 local police departments serving a population of 25,000 or more had full-time sworn personnel regularly engaged in community policing activities. State and local law enforcement agencies had an estimated 112,611 full-time sworn personnel serving as community policing officers or otherwise regularly engaged in community policing activities, compared to 21,239 in 1997.

Overall Estimates of College-Degreed Officers Regardless of Educational Mandates

Carter and Sapp (1990) indicated that regardless of departmental degree requirements, 23% of police officers had a four-year degree and 65% of police officers had at least one year of college. Peterson (2001) gave somewhat higher estimates: 30% of police officers sampled from ten medium-sized departments in the Midwest had four-year degrees. Mayo (2006) estimated between 25-30% of police officers have a four-year degree, which realistically nearly mirrors the percentage of U.S. population with bachelor's degrees. According to the U.S. Census Bureau (2005), 28% of the U.S. population over age 25 has a bachelor's degree, an all-time high. Those percentages of police officers with four-year degrees are representative of the education levels of the communities they serve. Nevertheless, people need to be aware that so few police departments require degrees, despite formal recommendations to do so.

Methods

Little is known about the location of the departments that require college education. Intensive Internet searches and e-mail and telephone contacts with multitudes of police recruiters and chiefs yielded 60 departments with four-year degree requirements, 37 of which had mandatory educational requirements resulting in no educational waivers. As it was unclear which departments had mandatory requirements at the outset, I mailed questionnaires to 45 police chiefs at departments believed to have mandatory requirements. Forty surveys were completed and returned—which was an excellent overall response rate of nearly 89%. Four of those surveys revealed that their departments actually did not require the four-year degree; therefore, we omitted their departments' information from analysis. The 36 remaining questionnaires revealed important and relevant information about departments with mandatory requirements and served as the subjects for this study.

To determine why police chiefs believed mandatory educational requirements were essential to their departments and why they believe only so few other departments have followed suit in mandating higher education, I asked two qualitative questions: 1) Why do their departments mandate a degree? 2) Why do these chiefs believe so few departments actually require the degree? My analysis focuses mainly on the chiefs' responses to those two questions.

This research enables further exploration into this important issue. Ultimately, the future professionalism of policing hinges on raising degree requirements across police departments in America. Although I surveyed only 36 police chiefs, their information speaks volumes on the need for other departments to follow their lead. As one respondent eloquently stated:

> *It is evident that society has become more complex. Problem solving skills along with communication skills are even more important today for police officers. A college education gives a foundation and more importantly legitimizes police work as a profession.*

Despite the fact that this instrument has no proven reliability, it provided a means to better understand issues regarding the importance of the college-degreed officer and possible future directions for college education mandates. At the outset, many officers are obtaining four-year degrees regardless of whether the degree is required.

Results

I used a qualitative approach to uncover themes predominant to this analysis. Thus far, few attempts have been taken to qualitatively explore the opinions of police chiefs from those departments with degree requirements. I surveyed police chiefs and asked them to explain why their departments mandated a degree and why they believed so few departments actually require the degree. The chiefs' responses to these questions should be held in high regard, as these people represent the select few who actually took concrete efforts to bring about professionalism to the policing field. Furthermore, of the 36 surveyed, 30 respondents (83%) replied that their departments had established formal community policing plans; whereas six respondents (16.7%) reported that their departments did not have community policing plans.

Why the Degree Is Required

Aside from stern recommendations encouraging police administrators and community leaders to adopt educational standards, six themes emerged from analyzing the data regarding why these departments actually have the degree requirement:

1. It is our tradition and part of our institutional, organizational, and community culture, and we are valued.

    > *"We are the only agency in the state that still requires a four-year degree. We have always required this and I believe we hire exemplary people with more maturity and a strong sense of direction than those without the degree. It's really a huge part of our culture."*

*"We hope to keep our four-year educational degree require-
ment forever. With the high percentage of college graduates in
today's society, I don't believe this requirement is unreasonable.
It's our goal to continue to pursue the 'most qualified' applicants
for our department."*

*"One of the best things I did 17 years ago was to convince the
governing body to pass the four-year degree requirement. Since
then the department has hired 140 of our 160 officers (bright,
educated and professional)."*

*"After becoming Chief in 1992, I felt strongly that this would
have a very positive impact on the department and it has. Very
well-respected, very few discipline problems or concerns."*

2. The degree carries with it a level of expertise, knowledge, and
    perseverance that represent us in our communities well.

*"The requirement for a bachelor's degree generally assures
that an applicant can read and write; has been exposed to
complex written materials requiring some level of analysis; has
developed some level of critical thinking and communication
skills, and has achieved at least some measurable relatively
long-term goal in their lifetime."*

*"A bachelor's degree limits the number of applicants who,
most probably, would not be selected anyway. It also increases
the quality of the applicant pool (education-level wise), which
makes for a better police officer and increases the minimum age
of the applicants, making them more experienced in life. It also
shows that you have people at the very least, had the
'stick-to-it-ivness' to persevere through four years of college. It
also eliminates the need for education reimbursement for officers
pursuing bachelor's degrees."*

*"We believe that it provides us with a more mature,
well-rounded and worldly candidate who has more experience
interacting with many different people from all walks of life."*

3. Education levels of the police force should mirror the education level
    of their communities.

*"To reflect the demographics of the community we serve.
According to the Census, Wilmette has one of the highest
education levels in America. We want to be representative of those*

we serve in race, gender, education level and foreign language. This is also a successful strategy for maintaining high salaries and benefits."

"We wanted to ensure our police officers' education level closely mirrored the education level and demographics of our community."

4. A belief in excellence and quality—the degree makes a difference in performance.

    "The department instituted this educational requirement in 1993 due to the belief that educated officers will be better decision makers and have better communication skills, both in oral and written form."

    "Department belief of excellence—higher quality of service to community, being leaders in profession."

    "Enhanced knowledge, skills and abilities as well as communications skills (oral and written); critical thinking and analytical skills; broader viewpoints; more tolerant; foundation of criminal justice concepts; self-discipline; and time management."

    "We believe that a better educated work-force is necessary in dealing with the public and are higher educated. We also believe that education enhances communication skills, which are necessary in police work."

    "A higher educated person is a more rounded individual, which leads to a better police officer."

5. A belief that the mandatory degree promotes professionalism both in their communities and for the entire police field.

    "We believe that this should be the standard if we are to continue to develop and promote a professional police organization."

    "Academics have pushed our department to a new level of professionalism and innovation."

    "To significantly improve the quality of police services via intelligent, articulate and professional personnel."

"We are located in a city with a university with a strong criminal justice program. We have several members of our police and fire commission who are affiliated with the university. The four-year degree requirement enhances our professionalism."

6. Officers with a college degree are more mature and have stronger goal-reaching abilities.

"I feel that a person demonstrates his/her desire to be a police officer by completing four year of study in criminal justice. They prove not only a strong desire to become a police officer, but possess the ability to set a goal and achieve it. It also demonstrates that ability to learn. That is why a four-year bachelor's degree in criminal justice, criminology or law enforcement exists. It is specific to those who set a goal for law enforcement and achieve it."

"Increases odds of mature/smart candidate."

"Maturity, dedication, experience and age of applicants are more suitable for employment."

Why So Few Agencies Require Degrees

Police leaders encounter two realities. First, most licensing boards do not mandate a college degree. Second, civil service regulations may prevent mandating college degrees. Beyond those explanations, comments from police chiefs revealed five additional themes:

1. It's all about money and overall job satisfaction that one perceives a college degree should bring.

"We have issues retaining officers and we frequently lose them to higher paying positions outside the field of policing. University instructors, technical school instructors, social work have all been attractive to our officers."

"Governments are reluctant to pay the higher wages for an applicant with a degree."

"Most agencies cannot pay adequate salaries for advanced degrees."

"Higher degreed people are not satisfied being a police officer."

"Money—most departments cannot afford to start out a patrol officer at what a college graduate could make."

"It certainly can hurt the applicant pool, depending on the salary."

"Possibly they believe their pay-rates are not high enough to attract college graduates."

"Lack of pay for many smaller agencies."

2. The degree requirement decreases applicant pools. Most respondents stated their department's degree requirement has reduced applicant pools.

    "It reduces the pool of potential applicants at a time when suitable applicants are hard to find. There remain a high percentage of law enforcement executives and government officials who believe a four-year degree is not a necessity in preparing an individual for a law enforcement career."

    "Because of the difficulty in finding a sufficient number of qualified candidates."

    "Reduction in applicant pool is significant."

3. Although the chiefs in this studied strongly valued education, education overall is under-valued in policing.

    "Most chiefs say they value education, but stop short of making it a requirement."

    "Education is under-valued in policing. The four-year degree requirement makes recruiting tougher and it creates challenges for retaining personnel."

    "I still believe that the majority of police leaders are, as a law-enforcement culture, anti-education for police officers."

4. Police leaders who do not have college degrees may not find one necessary. This presents itself as a great challenge, one of increasing overall education standards.

    "Administrators may not believe a college degree is necessary, especially if they have not earned one."

    "It is challenging to staff a police agency with a four-year college degree requirement and research indicates officers with experience may out perform those with only a college degree."

5. The other side of the debate that a college degree is not necessary for a police officer:

    "That long-standing belief—a more educated officer isn't necessary for effectiveness."

    "The traits required of a police officer are not learned at the college level. Character is forged long before that point in one's life and if not it is probably too late."

    "It is unnecessary. The qualities required of a police officer—maturity, judgment, discipline, is not attained by going to college. College can make a good person more educated, but it does not make a good person. We have been forced to bypass very qualified and exceptional people owing to the lack of a college degree. I have several officers I would gladly exchange for non-college graduates with a good work ethic."

Discussion and Implications

It would seem to signify that with only 1% of police departments requiring degrees that professionalism for policing is stalling. Despite current high unemployment rates, many may not apply for a police officer position due to the bad reputation of policing in general. Needless to say, if all police officers held a four-year degree, police officers would receive higher levels of esteem, thereby increasing the overall professionalism of the policing field.

Ultimately, there have been enormous improvements over the past 60 years. Bell (1979) found that in the 1950s, increasing numbers of local police departments began requiring at least some college as a prerequisite for entry-level hiring. By 1990, Carter and Sapp realized that 65% of police officers had at least one year of college and 23% attained a four-year degree. According to the Police Foundation (1979), approximately 25% of officers had at least one year of college. Whetstone (2000) added that, "every national consensus of police personnel shows the average educational level is on the rise, as is the proportion of officers holding degrees" (p. 247).

Whatever the case, police officers are becoming educated regardless of the educational mandates of their respective departments. Therefore, the degree does matter. It is unclear whether findings from this study can be generalized. One aspect is clear from this small population: the chiefs in this study do not intend to alter their degree requirement in the future—which may continue to separate them from others.

With regard to the community policing movement, major changes in any organization are difficult. There is a need for resources to comprehensively guide police officers and other personnel to understanding and implementing community policing. Future research should focus on whether community policing works more effectively if police officers have a college degree, with specific attention given to the relationship between community policing and higher education officer salaries, and population size. Essentially the following question presents itself—does a better-educated police force deliver higher-quality community policing services? Only 12% of "community policing departments" have even implemented one of the four critical elements of community policing (defined by COPS) (Connors & Webster, 2001). Could this be because such a small percentage of police departments require a college education?

Although glaring limitations to this analysis stem from the fact that little information exists regarding the reality of those 1% of police departments that mandate a four-year degree, this is an exploratory step enabling further exploration into these important issues as they relate to the progression toward professionalizing police forces. More important, does a college degree help officers better transition into community policing roles?

References

Aamodt, M. (2004). *Research in Law Enforcement Selection.* Boca Raton, FL: Brown Walker Press.

Alpert, G. & Dunham, R. (1988). *Policing in Urban America.* Prospect Heights, IL: Waveland Press.

Baro, A., & Burlingame, D. (1999). Law enforcement and higher education: Is there an impasse? *Journal of Criminal Justice Education,* 10 (1), 57-73.

Bell, D. (1979). The police role in higher education. *Journal of Police Science and Administration,* 7, 467-475.

Bostrom, M. (2005). The influence of higher education on police officer habits. *The Police Chief,* 72, (10), 12-19.

Breci, M. (1997). The transition to community policing: The department's role in upgrading officers' skills. *Policing: An International Journal of Police Strategy and Management,* 20, (4), 766-776.

Carlan, P. (2007). The criminal justice degree and policing: Conceptual development or occupational primer? *Policing: An International Journal of Police Strategies and Management,* 20 (4), 608-619.

Carlan, P. & Byxbe, F. (2000). The promise of humanistic policing: Is higher education living up to societal expectations? *American Journal of Criminal Justice,* 24, (2), 235-246.

Carter, D. & Sapp, A. (1990). The evolution of higher education in law enforcement: Preliminary findings from a national study. *Journal of Criminal Justice Education,* 7(1), 59-85.

Carter, D. (1989). *Methods and measures. In Trojanowicz and Bucqueroux, Community Policing.* Cincinnati, OH: Anderson, 165-194.

Cascio, W. (1977). Formal education and police officer performance. *Journal of Police Science and Administration,* 5, (1), 89-96.

Connors, E. & Webster, B. (2006). Transforming law enforcement organizations to community policing. Institute for Law and Justice. Retrieved on February 6, 2009 from http://www.ncjrs.gov.pdffiles1/nij/grants/200610.pdf.

Cunningham, S. (2006). The Florida research. *The Police Chief,* 73, (8), 6-7.

Finckenhauer, J. (1975). Higher education and police discretion. *Journal of Police Science and Administration,* 3, (4), 450-457.

Friedmann, R. (2006). University perspective: The policing profession in 2050. *The Police Chief,* 73 (8).

Hickman, M., & Reaves, B. (2006). Local police departments, 2003, (NCJ210118). Washington, D.C.: U.S. Department of Justice, Bureau of Justice Statistics.

Hudzick, J. (1978). College education for police: Problems in measuring component and extraneous variables. *Journal of Criminal Justice,* 6, 69-81.

Johnston, C., Cheurprakobkit, S., & McKenzie, I. (2002). Educating our police administrators regarding the utility of a college education, police academy training and preferences in our courses for officers. *International Journal of Police Science and Management,* 4, 182-197.

Kakar, S. (1998). Self-evaluation of police performance: An analysis of the relationship between police officers' education level and job performance. *Police Strategies and Management,* 21, (4), 632-647.

Kappeler, V., Sapp, A. & Carter, D. (1992). Police officer higher education, citizen complaints, and department rule violations. *American Journal of Police,* 11, (2), 37-52.

Maguire, E., Snipes, J., Uchida, C., & Townsend, M. (1998). Counting Cops: Estimating the number of police departments and police officers in the USA. Policing: *A Journal of Police Strategies and Management,* 21 (1), 97-120.

Mayo, L. (2006). College Education and Policing. *The Police Chief,* 73, (8), 20-38.

Office of Community Oriented Policing Services (COPS). (2008). U.S. Department of Justice. Retrieved on January 6, 2009 from http://www.cpos.usdoj/Default.aspItem=36.

Police Foundation. (1979). *Experiments In Police Improvement: A Progress Report.* Washington, D.C.

Peterson, D. (2001). The relationship between educational attainment and police performance. Unpublished doctoral dissertation, Illinois State University, Illinois.

President's Commission on Law Enforcement and the Administration of Justice, (1967). Task Force Report: The Police. Washington, D.C.: U.S. Government Printing Office.

Remington, F. (1990). American Bar Association, Standards Relating to the Urban Police Function. Chicago: Institute of Judicial Administration.

Roberg, R., & Bonn, S. (2004). Higher education and policing: Where are we now? *Policing: An International Journal of Police Strategies and Management,* 27, (4), 469-486.

Schafer, J., & Castellano, T. (2005). Academe versus academy; faculty views on awarding academic credit for police training. *Journal of Criminal Justice Education,* 16 (2), 300-371.

Scott, W. (1986). College education requirements for police entry level and promotion: A study. *Journal of Police and Criminal Psychology,* 2, (1), 10-28.

Sherman, L. & McLeod, M. (1979). Faculty characteristics and course content in college programs for police officers. *Journal of Criminal Justice,* 7, (3), 249-267.

Sherman, L. & the National Advisory Commission on Higher Education for Police Officers. (1978). *The Quality of Police Education.* San Francisco, CA: Jossey-Bass Publishers.

Shernock, S. (1992). The effects of college education on professional attitudes among police. *Journal of Criminal Justice Education,* 3, 71-92.

Smith, S. & Aamodt, M. (1998). *Empirical Studies of Higher Education and Police Performance.* Washington, D.C.: Police Foundation.

Sperling's Best Places to Live Online (2008). Retrieved February 2, 2009 from http://www.bestplaces.net.

Tyre, M., & Braunstein, S. (1992). Higher education and ethical policing. *FBI Law Enforcement Bulletin,* 61, (6), 6-11.

United States Census Bureau. (2005). *College degree nearly doubles annual earnings, Census Bureau Reports.* U.S. Department of Commerce, Washington, D.C. Retrieved on January 14, 2009 from

http://www.census.gov/Press-Release/archives/education/004214.h
tml.
Varricchio, D. (1994). Educational requirements for police recruits. *Law
and Order,* 43 (2), 91-94.
Varricchio, D. (1998). Continuing education: expanding opportunities for
officers. *Law Enforcement Bulletin,* 67, (4), 10-15.
Verrill, S. W. (2007). Criminal justice education and vocationally-
oriented students: An examination of agency college degree
requirements. *Southwest Journal of Criminal Justice,* 4, (1), 30-38.
Whetstone, T. (2000). Getting stripes: educational achievement and
study strategies used by Sergeant promotional candidates. *American
Journal of Criminal Justice,* 24, (2), 247-257.
Worden, R. (1990). A badge and a baccalaureate: Policies, hypotheses,
and further evidence. *Justice Quarterly,* 7, (3), 565-592.

Discussion Questions

1. The fact that you are reading this chapter means you are probably
    in a college-level courses in a criminal justice or related curriculum.
    Make the case that what you are doing makes you a better candidate
    for an entry-level job in (choose a criminal justice career) than a
    similar candidate who does not have a college degree.

2. Bruns had a response rate of almost 89%. What does that mean?
    What factors contribute to the likelihood that someone would
    participate in a research project?

3. Describe the themes that emerged from analyzing responses from
    chiefs of departments with 4-year degree requirements.

4. What factors have contributed to the push for college-educated
    officers?

5. What themes emerged as barriers to establishing an educational
    requirement for police officers?

6. How would you find out if the community supported an educational
    requirement?

Chapter 8
TRAFFIC SUSPECTS ENCOUNTERED BY THE POLICE: A SOCIAL ECOLOGICAL ANALYSIS

James J. Sobol, Ph.D. Buffalo State College
Scott W. Phillips, Ph.D. Buffalo State College

Introduction

Historians and social scientists alike have given much thought to the development and behavior of the police in America, and for very good reason. The discretionary decisions of these policy-makers—when ministering to people and their problems—can tell us a great deal about the quality and nature of policing, and to some degree, about the functioning of the rule of law in society.[1] For more than four decades, researchers have expended considerable effort attempting to identify factors that explain police behavior. The approaches used to explain variation in police behavior have been classified into five broad perspectives, based on level of explanation: situational, organizational, individual, neighborhood, and legal (for a full review, see Riksheim & Chermak, 1993; Sherman, 1980).

The situational approach focuses on such factors as citizen demographic characteristics, demeanor, the relationship between the citizen and the complainant, the number of officers and citizens present at the encounter, victim preference for arrest, and whether the encounter was citizen- or officer-initiated. The organizational approach explains variation in police behavior across or within police organizations, by examining characteristics such as department size, officer training, level of supervision, size of the primary assignment area, and organizational culture. The individual approach explains variation in behavior by examining officer characteristics, such as education, length of service, race, and gender, as well as officer attitudes and occupational outlooks. The neighborhood or community approach explains variation in police behavior across different contexts and has considered specific features of the neighborhoods where police work, such as neighborhood crime rates, demographic diversity, and economic characteristics. Finally, the

---

[1] Michael Brown (1981) provides a similar thesis, arguing that police decision making is tantamount to political decision making because police have significant policy-making powers "by virtue of their power to decide which laws to enforce and when" (1981:5-6). Lipsky (1980:1) also maintains that patrol officers "represent" government and at the same time, represent government social policy since their actions have far-reaching effects on citizens and their freedom.

legal approach explains variation in police behavior based on the seriousness of the offense and the strength of the available evidence.

Each level of explanation has been used to study many different aspects of police work (traffic encounters, non-traffic encounters, and interpersonal disputes). Significant relationships between a number of independent variables and different police outcomes such as arrest, use of force, and citation have been observed and cited in the literature (Sherman, 1980:93). Due to improvements in the rigor of statistical techniques used to analyze police-citizen encounters, researchers have been able to isolate the effects of situational and encounter variables with more precision. As a result of such advances, a number of studies have shifted focus away from decision-maker characteristics (i.e., individual—or officer-level correlates) to what was going on (i.e., situational-level correlates) and where it was occurring (i.e., organizational—and neighborhood-level correlates) (Brooks, 2001; Riksheim & Chermak, 1993). Our analysis continues this tradition by studying the impact of district crime on police decision making among a sample traffic suspects.

Neighborhood Context

The observation that police conduct in similar situations varies by type of residential area is not a new phenomenon, as early field researchers reported that police had different standards of what they considered "acceptable" and "unacceptable" conduct (Banton, 1964; Chambliss, 1973; Reiss & Bordua, 1967; Whyte, 1943). Banton (1964) speculated that police would be more formal (e.g., less assisting) in contexts where the social distance between them and the citizen was greatest. In this sense, different neighborhoods would receive different services because the police may be estranged or socially distant from the public in some neighborhoods and socially closer in others. Chambliss (1973) also noted that police enforced the law more strictly against juveniles who came from an underprivileged part of town and turned a blind-eye to misbehavior among juveniles from a more respected part of town.

Using observational data of 66 encounters between the police and juveniles, Werthman and Piliavin (1967) examined the effects of neighborhood context on police behavior. They hypothesized that police focus greater attention on juveniles known to reside in high crime areas because they associate these juveniles according to their group affiliation, including their age, race, dress, demeanor, and gang affiliation.[2]

---

[2]   Skolnick's (1966) research also points to such "cues" as being significant determinants of police action because in most encounters, little is known about the individual the officer is involved with. As a result, the officer develops a "working personality" that provides a framework upon which officers can make decisions in an uncertain environment.

Werthman and Piliavin (1967) reported that offense seriousness was an important decision premise for officer action, although additional cues from the encounter were significant predictors of police behavior. They reported police behavior was motivated by normative expectations about appropriate forms of citizen behavior within particular communities, stating, "residence in a *neighborhood* is the most general indicator used by the police to select a sample of potential law violators" (1967, p. 76). As a result, "tough looking" juveniles would be found in particular areas of the city and thus be subject to strict enforcement. In this sense, the officer labeled residents according to distribution in physical space, and those labeled as more likely to be deviant in their eyes received greater scrutiny than those presumed to be less deviant. This categorization of workplaces in turn provides officers with a perceptual short hand for making decisions. This early work informs our understanding that police perceptions and decision making may depend on where citizens reside and where encounters occurred.

A more systematic study of neighborhood context has shown how neighborhood economic and social power influences police behavior. Sung (2002) posited that police would be less coercive and more informal in their operational style in neighborhoods that had greater affluence. He reported that police were more coercive and inclined to use their formal legal authority in marginal and peripheral neighborhoods where the police seemed uninterested and, generally, disconnected. He concluded that citizens living in affluent areas are cherished allies of the police, given their wealth and social power, whereas residents in peripheral areas are alienated from the police and are perceived to be in need of control. As a result, such areas attract more police attention, not less.

Using the same data as Sung, three earlier studies examined a variety of neighborhood-level variables on different forms of police behavior (Smith, 1986; Smith & Klein, 1984; Smith, Visher & Davidson, 1984). Smith et al. (1984) analyzed 611 encounters involving contact with suspects and used neighborhood contextual variables to assess the independent effects of neighborhood racial composition on arrest decisions, as well as on how officers handled victims in racially heterogeneous neighborhoods. Their bivariate analysis showed arrests moderately correlated with the poverty level of the neighborhood where the encounters occurred, yet their multivariate analyses reported that both black and white suspects were more likely to be arrested in low SES (socio-economic status) neighborhoods. However, because their data only included and considered the SES of neighborhoods where the suspects were encountered, and not the income or occupational status of the individual suspects, their results might be spurious.[3] They reached the tentative conclusion that since neighborhood effects are independent of suspects race, all suspects confronted in poorer neighborhoods share an increased probability of arrest (Smith, 1984, pp. 247-248).

In a more comprehensive analysis of neighborhood effects, Smith (1986) studied the effects of eleven neighborhood variables on five measures of police behavior.[4] His findings revealed several neighborhood characteristics that were statistically significant determinants of police decisions of arrest, their use of coercive tactics, report writing, and investigating and assistance behaviors. He reported that the police were more likely to initiate contacts with suspected persons in racially heterogeneous neighborhoods and neighborhoods with a greater proportion of single-parent households. He also found that neighborhood SES had a direct negative effect on the probability of arrest, even after controlling for encounter-level factors. Police were three times more likely to arrest suspects encountered in lower-class neighborhoods than those encountered in higher-status neighborhoods, regardless of the seriousness of the immediate offense, race, offender demeanor, and victim's preference for arrest.

Smith (1986) also reported that police were more likely to use or to threaten to use force against suspects encountered in primarily black or racially heterogeneous neighborhoods. He observed a significant interaction effect between a suspect's race and racial composition of the neighborhood. He reported that police acted more coercively toward African-American suspects encountered in African-American neighborhoods than African-American suspects in predominantly white neighborhoods. The probability of coercive authority directed against whites was relatively stable across all neighborhoods in the study (Smith, 1986, p. 336).

Although Smith's (1986) findings identified some significant neighborhood effects on a range of officer behaviors, he did not control for the type and seriousness of the offense; therefore, his results must be cautiously interpreted. Because it is probably accurate to note that officers' arrest, use force, and take reports when the offense is serious and there is evidence of wrongdoing, Smith's conclusions might be spurious.

Absent from the research reviewed above is any systematic theoretical framework from which we might begin to explain observed neighborhood effects on police behavior. David Klinger's (1997) theory of

---

[3]   In other words, their study is really showing neighborhood effects at the individual level.

[4]   The police behavior variables included proactive investigation, proactive assistance, arrest, coercive authority, and report writing. The neighborhood variables included a crime scale, SES scale, residential mobility, interaction of single parents with children, percentage of nonwhite, racial instability, percent living alone, percent over 65 years of age (see Smith, 1986 p. 320) for a full description of each.

social ecology may fill this theoretical gap by providing a framework on which others might begin to empirically examine ecological determinants of police behavior. He hypothesized that district crime and deviance levels are vital precursors to explain a form of police behavior he called "vigor." Klinger used the terms vigor and leniency to represent opposite ends of the formal authority continuum such that an arrest is more vigorous than no arrest, a report represents more vigor than no report, and a citation more vigor than taking no action (Klinger, 1997, p. 280). Controlling for the seriousness of the offense, he hypothesized that vigor would vary inversely with district crime levels because officers assigned to high crime districts would be more cynical of residents, view crime as "normal," perceive victims as less deserving and have less time to devote to all calls compared to their colleagues assigned to low crime districts (Klinger, 1997).

Research testing Klinger's (1997) theoretical arguments is limited. Results have been mixed and in some cases, contradictory to the theory. For example, one study (Johnson & Olschansky, 2010) found that district crime rates were inversely related to the number of vehicle stops, were positively associated with the number of arrests, and were weakly connected to the number of vehicle searches, traffic tickets, and misdemeanor arrests. A second study (Lawton, 2007) showed that district violent crime rates were not significantly related to the use of non-lethal force. Still, a third research study (Sobol, 2010) reported positive bivariate relationships among district crime, police vigor, and cynicism on a sample of non-traffic suspects. However, a multivariate analysis showed that the effect of district crime on vigor was not mediated by officer cynicism and district workload as the theory predicted. As such, the validity of Klinger's (1997) theory is apparently unsettled and more empirical assessment is warranted.

Our Study

Researchers have studied the behavior of the police after a stop has occurred in order to shed light on the complex nature of patrol work and the many discretionary choices that officers have at their disposal during such an encounter (Engel, Sobol & Worden, 2000; Whitaker, 1982; Worden, 1989). Findings from this body of research demonstrate that traffic stops afford the opportunity for the officer to use considerable discretion because traffic enforcement occurs at a low level of visibility.

In this study, we examined the effects of district crime on police vigor for citizens involved in traffic encounters. Consistent with Klinger's (1997) theory, we attempted to answer two research questions.

1. Are police less vigorous with traffic suspects encountered in high crime districts?

2. Is the hypothesized relationship between police vigor and district crime rate mediated by officer cynicism and workload, controlling for seriousness of the traffic infraction?

Data and Methods

To answer these research questions, we used four sources of data originally collected by the Project on Policing Neighborhoods (POPN): systematic social observation (SSO), in-person interviews with officers, census data, and police crime records. The Project on Policing Neighborhoods (POPN) was a multi-method study conducted in two cities (Indianapolis, Indiana and St. Petersburg, Florida) in the summer of 1996 and 1997, respectively (for details of methodology used by POPN, see Mastrofski, Parks, Reiss, Worden, DeJong, and Snipes, 1998).

In-person interviews with patrol officers provided data on officer characteristics, district assignment, and attitudes. POPN representatives asked officers about their views on problem-solving, community-policing, and perceived neighborhood problems, as well as their views of citizens, training, and perceived priorities of the department. The original survey data set included information from 601 of the 638 officers or 94 percent of the sample population (373 in Indianapolis and 228 in St Petersburg). Cases with any missing attitudinal data were dropped from the current analysis, as were those cases in which an officer's primary assignment area (e.g., patrol district) could not be identified.

POPN field researchers also conducted systematic observation of a minimum of 28 shifts in each of the 24 study beats across both cities. They observed 322 different patrol officers (194 in Indianapolis and 128 in St. Petersburg) for nearly 6,000 hours with nearly 12,000 police-citizen encounters. Researchers identified citizens as crime victims, witnesses, service recipients, or suspects. We based our analysis of police on officers who were both interviewed and observed by POPN researchers. The selection criterion for our study included all encounters with suspects resulting from proactive traffic encounters. We also selected out data from officers who were assigned to their district for less than one year. After list-wise deletion of cases with missing data, we ended up with 534 traffic encounters in which observed officers had contact with a suspect.

Dependent Variables

Five mutually exclusive categories of behavior formed the police vigor measure (e.g., see Sobol, 2010). Behaviors included in the measure sufficiently discriminated among various courses of police action to allow examination of the amount of formal legal authority officers applied to situations where each decision they made ranged from more (vigorous) to less (lenient). The categories included: (1) no action/release; (2) suggest, persuade, request, and negotiate; (3) command and threaten the suspect to do something; (4) interrogation and search; and (5) arrest. Higher categories of vigor were likely to bring suspects and their conduct to the attention of other agencies or institutions, which often resulted in greater legal consequences. The percentage of traffic encounters in which each action represented the highest level of vigor used by officers was as follows: no action (28.4); suggest/persuade (8.2); command and threaten (9.0); interrogate and search (27.9); and citation/arrest (26.5). (For more detail on this measure, see Sobol [2010, pp. 483-484]).

Independent Variables

District Crime Levels—We used Uniform Crime Report data for the violent crimes of murder and non-negligent manslaughter, forcible rape, robbery, and aggravated assault for 1996 in Indianapolis and 1997 in St. Petersburg to create a violent crime rate measure for each district based on census data population estimates for Indianapolis and St. Petersburg, standardized by 1,000 residents.

Police Officer Cynicism—Data from the POPN structured interviews with officers provided the basis for the measure of police cynicism used in our analysis. We utilized three Likert items to measure patrol officer attitudes toward residents as proxy measures to capture their level of cynicism towards residents in their assigned district. This cynicism scale summed three responses to these three interview items: 1) How many of the citizens in your beat would call the police if they saw something suspicious? 2) How many of the citizens in your beat would provide information about a crime if they knew something and were asked about it by the police? 3) How many of the citizens in your beat are willing to work with the police to try to solve neighborhood problems? For each of these questions, responses ranged from most (1) to none (4). High scores reflect officers who perceive citizens as uncooperative—thereby representing a more cynical outlook towards citizens in their assigned district.

Workload—For our analysis, workload measures the amount of time officers have available during their observed shifts by assessing the percentage of their time that was a directed activity (e.g., assigned time) versus a non-directed activity (e.g., unassigned time). Workload is another deviance-driven indicator of behavior because patrol district workgroup rules prioritize calls for service as levels of deviance rise and resources become scarce.[5] The workload measure reflects the percentage of unassigned time that officers had during their observed shifts. A higher percentage of unassigned time is indicative of less work.

---

[5]   In other words, greater workload is theorized to lead to limited resources, which in turn may compel officers to find ways to allocate and prioritize their time more efficiently.

Control Variables

Prior research in this area has consistently found several variables to be predictors of various forms of police behavior; therefore, we had several control variables. First, we controlled for suspect characteristics such as gender, race, approximate age, approximate wealth, whether the suspect was under the influence of drugs or alcohol, suspect's emotional state, and whether the suspect was disrespectful to the responding officer were all included in the analysis.

Second, we controlled for the level of concentrated disadvantage in the districts where the encounter occurred because of the likely influence neighborhood structural characteristics might have on police behavior. Concentrated disadvantage was the sum of the percentage of labor force that was unemployed, the percentage of population that was very poor, and the percentage of families headed by single women. A scale of higher concentrated disadvantage thus indicated higher levels of unemployment, poverty, and female-headed households. The city in which the incident occurred was also controlled because Indianapolis' officers stressed aggressiveness and a get-tough policy, whereas St. Petersburg emphasized solving problems and community organizing. The seriousness of the traffic infraction was included to control for its impact on police vigor. Table 8-1 provides an overview of each of the study variables, showing how those variables were coded and their hypothesized relationship to vigor (+, -, +/- signs denote positive, negative and underdetermined directions of influence, respectively). Table 8-2 provides descriptive statistics for each of the variables used in our analysis.

Table 8-1. Overview of Descriptive Study Variables

Variable	Hypothesized Effect	Definition
Vigor		Level of Vigor: 1 = no action; 2 = suggest, persuade, negotiate; 3 = command and threaten; 4 = interrogate and search; 5 = cite and arrest.
District Crime	-	Violent crime rate per 1,000 district residents
Discretionary Time (Workload)	+	Time free of assignments from dispatch or supervisors (percentage)
Police Cynicism	-	Scale ranging between 3-12. Created by summing 3 separate items (1 = most; 2 = some; 3 = few; 4 = none) How many of the citizens in beat would call the police if they saw something suspicious? How many of the citizens in beat would provide information about a crime if they knew something and were asked about it by the police? How many of the citizens in beat are willing to work with the police to try to solve neighborhood problems?

Table 8-1. Overview of Descriptive Study Variables

Variable	Hypothesized Effect	Definition
Concentrated Disadvantage	+/-	Percentage unemployed plus percentage below 50 percent poverty plus percent female-headed households plus percent Black
Site	+	1 = Indianapolis; 0 = St. Petersburg
Night Encounter	+	1 = yes; 0 = no
Suspect Characteristics		
Gender	+	1 = male, 0 = female
Race	+	1 = non-White, 0 = White
Age	-	0 = not elderly, below 60, 1 = elderly, 60 and above
Wealth	-	1 = chronic poverty, 2 = low, 3 = middle, 4 = above middle
Determined by the citizen's appearance and dress, property and possessions, as well as the information provided by the citizen about his or her possessions (e.g., job, home, other resources)
Drug/Alcohol	+	1 = yes, 0 = no
Citizen displays indication of alcohol or drug use, including the smell of alcohol on the breath, slurred speech, impaired motor skills, or unconsciousness
Disrespect	+	1 = yes, 0 = no
Citizen displays disrespect to the individual or authority of the police officer
Seriousness	+	1 = no observed violation, 2 = vehicle violation, equipment/inspection lacking, missing/improper license plate, routine check/vehicle violation, 3 = Moving violation, 4 = Driving under the Influence/speeding.

Table 8-2. Descriptive Statistics of Study Variables

Variable	Range	Mean	Standard Deviation
District Crime	12.50-25.68	20.41	3.04
Discretionary Time	0.10-0.44	0.23	0.08
Police Cynicism	3-12	6.43	1.79
Concentrated Disadvantage	-1.19-2.17	0.32	0.89
Site (1=Indianapolis)	0-1	0.73	0.44
Night Encounter	0-1	0.57	0.49
Gender	0-1	0.75	0.43
Race	0-1	0.66	0.47
Age	0-1	0.74	0.43
Wealth	1-4	2.59	0.52
Drug/Alcohol	0-1	0.09	0.29
Disrespect	0-1	0.07	0.24
Seriousness	1-4	2.53	0.75

Analysis and Results

We conducted both bivariate and multivariate analyses. The former focused on the relationships between officer cynicism, workload, district violent crime rate, and the vigor with which police used their formal authority. Although not shown in tabular form, bivariate analyses revealed that vigor significantly correlated with district violent crime rate $(r = .12)$ and officer cynicism $(r = .34)$. Other significant correlations showed that officers were more vigorous in Indianapolis $(r = .20)$ with non-white suspects $(r = .12)$, suspects who were disrespectful $(r = .15)$, and with those suspects perceived as being under the influence of alcohol or drugs $(r = .10)$.

We performed multivariate analyses following Baron and Kenny's (1986, p. 1177) recommendation to test for mediation, a way to measure the impact of any intervening variables (e.g., see also Murphy & Tyler, 2008, for use of this strategy). Baron and Kenny suggested that four conditions should be met in order to have perfect mediation. First, the independent variable (here, district violent crime rate) should be related to the mediating variables (cynicism and district workload). Second, the independent variable (district violent crime) should be related to the dependent variable (vigor). Third, there should be a relationship between the mediators (police cynicism and workload) and the dependent variable. Fourth, the significant relationship observed between the independent variable and the dependent variable under study should disappear after controlling for the mediator, if in fact there is a mediating effect.

The dependent variable was a five-level ordinal measure of police behavior ranging from no action to arrest. Ordered logistic regression is appropriate when the dependent variable is ordinal and the effects of the independent variable are constant across all levels of the dependent variable (Long & Freese, 2006). Table 8-3 presents results from the multivariate analyses. The findings show little support for the mediating effect of cynicism and district workload on the crime-vigor relationship with traffic suspects. As displayed, Step 1 shows a significant relationship between violent crime rate and vigor, while Step 2 shows that this direct effect was not mediated by officer cynicism and district workload because district crime still had a significant and positive effect on vigor. Interestingly, this finding directly contrasts to the theory tested. Whereas the theory predicts an inverse relationship between district crime and vigor (district crime goes up and vigor goes down), these findings indicated that the relationship was positive and significant (police are more vigorous in high crime areas, not less). Once we entered the seriousness of the offense and other controls into the model, however, the significant district crime effect on vigor disappears. One interpretation is that the effect on district violent crime may be mediated by other variables (other than officer cynicism and district workload) or the relationship between district crime and vigor is spurious.

Table 8-3. Ordered Logistic Regression Predicting Vigor and Testing Mediating Effects of Cynicism and District Workload (n = 534)

	Step 1	Step 2	Step 3
Variable	Coef.	Coef.	Coef.
District Crime	0.08*** (0.03)	0.06** (0.032)	-0.03 (0.04)
Discretionary Time		0.13 (1.25)	0.24 (1.54)
Police Cynicism		0.06 (0.06)	0.09 (0.07)
Concentrated Disadvantage			-0.15 (0.14)
Site			-1.05*** (0.23)
Night Encounter			-0.03 (0.21)
Gender			0.13 (0.19)
Race			0.60** (0.24)
Age			-0.36* (0.19)
Wealth			0.21 (0.13)
Drug/Alcohol			0.56 (0.35)
Disrespect			1.84*** (0.36)
Seriousness			0.05 (0.13)
Chi-Square	8.54***	9.07***	64.32***
Pseudo R^2	0.005	0.006	0.052
*p < .10 **p < .05 *** p < .01			
Note: Table entries include ordered logistic regression coefficients and standard errors in parentheses. Robust standard errors were computed for Step 2 and Step 3 so as to adjust for the non-independence within groups (in this case, individual officers).			

While not central to the theory we tested, an interesting finding emerged in the multivariate model: officers were more vigorous with non-white suspects compared to white suspects even after controlling for the seriousness of the traffic infraction and other individual and situational covariates. As previous research would lead us to believe, suspect demeanor was significantly related to vigor, as was suspect age (Engel et al., 2000).

Discussion and Conclusion

Do officers working in different communities perceive residents differently? Are levels of crime and deviance likely to shape police cynicism toward citizens and ultimately their decision making? Do officers assigned to high crime districts perceive that residents "deserve" less attention than those citizens who reside in low crime districts? And, does exposure to constant crime deviance (more victims, offenders, and unsavory individuals) make officers view crime in that area as "normal"? Using data collected as part of the Project on Policing Neighborhoods (POPN), we attempted to examine some of these questions. While clearly not exhaustive or definitive, our study sought to examine whether district-level crime, police cynicism, and district workload influenced police decision making in traffic encounters.

Bivariate findings revealed that police vigor significantly correlated with district-level crime, suspect race, demeanor, city, and whether the suspect was under the influence of alcohol or drugs. Additionally, vigor significantly correlated with police cynicism, suggesting that officers with higher cynicism scores were more vigorous with the traffic suspects that they encountered.

We hypothesized that vigor would decline with increasing district crime rates because officers would be more cynical and have more work to do as measured by less discretionary time available during their shift. In order to test the mediating effects of these two variables, we analyzed a series of regression models using a procedure outlined by Baron and Kenny (1986). Controlling for the seriousness of the offense and other predictor variables, the findings showed no support for Klinger's (1997) theory. Interestingly, the findings showed that police were more vigorous with suspects who were non-white, disrespectful, and younger, respectively.

We wish to acknowledge several limitations to our analysis. The patrol district was the centerpiece for police cynicism levels, workload, and level of crime and deviance. The null findings might be due to the large district ecological measures and the fact that some districts might be so large that intra-district variation in crime levels may mask the district crime impact on policing. Future research might wish to explore patrol beats, census tract areas, or block levels where the traffic stopped occurred. Disaggregating ecological level correlates to the smaller spatial unit may provide information on whether those locations differentially influence officer attitudes (i.e., about normal crime and victim deservedness, and their degree of cynicism) and police vigor.

Second, these findings may be a product of the way in which key theoretical variables were operationalized. The cynicism variable might be considered less than optimal for a test of Klinger's theory because the items used to construct this measure were adapted from the POPN survey data set that asked general questions about officer perceptions of residents' willingness to work with them to solve neighborhood problems, to call them if they saw something suspicious, or to provide them any known information about a crime if asked. A more precise measure of the concept might yield different results.

A third limitation is the problem of unmeasured mediating variables associated with Klinger's theory (victim deservedness, normal crime). Measures of officer perceptions of victim deservedness and normal crime could not be constructed from information in the POPN data set, thereby making this a partial test of Klinger's theory.

The findings presented here represent a first step in using Klinger's theory to study police decision making with traffic suspects. It is important to note that this study did not seek to directly examine suspect race or examine the decision to stop drivers, like many recent analyses focusing on racial profiling (e.g., for an excellent review see Tillyer, Engel & Wooldredge, 2008; pp. 139-140; Meehan & Ponder, 2002). Nevertheless, our study found that once stopped, suspect race was indeed a significant predictor of police vigor. More research is needed to study the complex nature of police decision making in traffic encounters that takes into consideration the effect of police officer attitudes, driver race, and neighborhood context on police vigor. Such an inquiry might enhance our understanding of the impact of crime levels on police behavior and extend Klinger's theory to the decision to stop.

References

Banton, M. (1964). *The Policeman and the Community.* London: Tavistock.

Baron, R. M., & Kenny, D. A. (1986). The moderator-mediator variable distinction in social psychological research: Conceptual, strategic, and statistical considerations. *Journal of Personality and Social Psychology,* 51, 1173–1182.

Brooks, L. W. (2010). Police Discretionary Behavior. In R. G. Dunham and G. P. Alpert (Eds.), *Critical Issues in Policing,* (pp. 71-90). Long Grove, Illinois: Waveland Press Inc.

Brown, M. K. (1981). *Working the street: Police discretion and the dilemmas of reform.* New York: Russell Sage Foundation.

Chambliss, W. (1973). The saints and the roughnecks. In J. M. Henslin (Ed.), *Down to earth sociology* (pp.180-194). New York: The Free Press/Macmillan.

Engle, R. S., Sobol, J. J., & Worden, R. E. (2000). Further exploration of the demeanor hypothesis: The interaction effects of suspects' characteristics and demeanor on police behavior. *Justice Quarterly,* 17, 235-258.

Johnson, R., & Olschansky, E. (2010). The ecological theory of police response: A state police agency test. *Criminal Justice Studies,* 23, 119-131.

Klinger, D. A. (1997). Negotiating order in patrol work: An ecological theory of police response to deviance. *Criminology,* 35, 277-306.

Lawton, B. (2007). Level of non-lethal force: An examination of individual, situational, and contextual factors. *Journal of Research in Crime and Delinquency,* 44, 163-184.

Lipsky, M. (1980). *Street-level bureaucracy: Dilemmas of the individual in public services.* New York: Russell Sage Foundation.

Long, J. S., & Freese, J. (2006). *Regression models for categorical dependent variables using STATA.* College Station, TX: STATA Press.

Mastrofski, S. D., Reisig, M. D., & McCluskey, J. D. (2002). Police disrespect toward the public: An encounter-based analysis. *Criminology,* 40, 519-552.

Mastrofski, S. D., Parks, R. B., Reiss, A. J., Jr., Worden, R. E., DeJong,
C. D., & Snipes, J. B. (1998). *Systematic observation of public police:
Applying field research methods to policy issues.* Washington, DC:
National Institute of Justice.

Meehan, A. J. & Ponder, M. C. (2002). Race and place: The ecology of
racial profiling African American motorists. *Justice Quarterly,* 19(3),
399-430.

Murphy, K., & Tyler, T. (2008). Procedural justice and compliance
behavior: The mediating role of emotions. *European Journal of
Social Psychology,* 38, 652–68.

Reiss, A. J., & Bordua, D. (1967). Environment and organization: A
Perspective on the police. In D. Bordua (Ed.), *The police: Six
sociological essays,* (pp. 25-55). New York: Wiley.

Riksheim, E. & Chermak, S. M. (1993). Causes of Police Behavior
Revisited. *Journal of Criminal Justice.* 21: 353-382.

Sampson, R. J., Raudenbush, S.W., & Earls, F. (1997). Neighborhoods
and Violent Crime: A Multilevel Study of Collective Efficacy, *Science,*
277, 918-924.

Sherman, L. W. (1980). Causes of Police Behavior: The Current State of
Quantitative Research. *Journal of Research in Crime and Delinquency,* 17, 69-100.

Skolnick, Jerome H. (1966). *Justice without trial.* John Wiley & Sons Inc.

Smith, D. A (1986). The neighborhood context of police behavior. In A. J.
Reiss, and M. Tonry (Eds.), *Communities and crime* (pp. 313-341).
Chicago: University of Chicago Press.

Smith, D., & Klein, J. (1984). Police control of interpersonal disputes.
Social Problems, 31, 468, 481.

Smith, D., & Visher, C.A. (1981). Street-Level Justice: Situational Determinants of Police Arrest Decisions. *Social Problems,* 29, 167-178.

Smith, D. A., Visher, C.A., & Davidson, L. (1984). Equity and discretionary justice: The influence of race on police arrest decisions.
Journal of Criminal Law and Criminology, 75, 234-249.

Sobol, J. J. (2008). *Social ecology and the vigor of police response—An
empirical study of work norms, context, and patrol officer behavior.*
Germany. VDM Verlag Publishers.

Sobol, J. J. (2010). Social ecology and police discretion: The influence
of district crime, cynicism, and workload on the vigor of police
response. *Journal of Criminal Justice.*

Sobol, J. J. (2010). The social ecology of police attitudes. *Policing: An
International Journal of Police Strategies and Management,* 33,
253-269.

Sun, I. Y., Payne, B. K., & Wu, Y. (2008). The impact of situational
factors, officer characteristics and neighborhood context on police

behavior: A multilevel analysis. *Journal of Criminal Justice,* 36, 22-32.

Sun, I. Y., & Payne, B. K., (2004). Racial differences in resolving conflicts: A comparison between Black and White police officers. *Crime and Delinquency,* 50, 516 541.

Sung, H.E. (2002). The fragmentation of policing in American cities: Toward and ecological theory of police-citizen relations. Westport, CT: Praeger Publishers.

Terrill, W., & Reisig, M.D. (2003). Neighborhood context and police use of force. *Journal of Research in Crime and Delinquency,* 40, 291-321.

Werthman, C., & Piliavin, I. (1967). Gang members and the police. In D. Bordua (Ed.), *The police: Six sociological essays,* (pp. 56-98). New York: John Wiley and Sons.

Whitaker, G. P. (1982). What is patrol work? *Police Studies,* 4, 13-22.

Whyte, W. F. (1943). *Street Corner Society.* Chicago, IL. University of Chicago Press,

Worden, R. E. (1989). Situational and attitudinal explanations of police behavior: A theoretical reappraisal and empirical assessment. *Law & Society Review,* 23, 667-711.

Discussion Questions

1. Summarize the five approaches used to explain variation in police behavior.

2. What sources of data did Sobol and Phillips use to answer their research questions?

3. Describe the benefits of using tables to present data in a research report.

4. Based on the results of Sobol and Phillip's research, what, if any, action might police administrators take to help guide discretionary police actions in future traffic encounters?

5. What did Sobol and Phillips identify as limitations of this study? Why is it important for researchers to acknowledge their limitations?

6. How well does this study support Klinger's theory of social ecology?

Chapter 9
FROM FOLLOWERS TO LEADERS: PRINCIPLED DECISION MAKING IN POLICING

Jeffrey S. Magers, Ed.D. California University of Pennsylvania

Introduction

Upholding the highest ideals of ethical behavior in police agencies remains a top goal of police, government officials, and community leaders. Although this may seem to be a required element of policing, law enforcement both in America and worldwide, continue to face ethical issues and suffer instances where officials have behaved inappropriately and sometimes illegally. As long as humans occupy positions as police officers and police leaders, maintaining highly ethical police behavior will continue to require great effort, as there are many temptations, opportunities, and even rationalizations for unscrupulous and sometimes even illegal acts. This seems like a fatalistic viewpoint; however, it is a prelude to a positive perspective for identifying a constant forward movement for improving the ethical landscape of American policing. This chapter will focus on what is arguably the most crucial element of police ethical behavior: the daily process of ethical decision making.

The core of police ethical behavior is the proper use of discretionary police power. Police officers, leaders, and administrators make critical decisions every time they go to work, often quickly and independently. These decisions greatly affect the quality of police services for the community. When flawed decision making lead law enforcement officials to unethical behavior, consequences can be vast, beyond undermining the respect, support, and high public expectations. Unethical decisions can end what are otherwise promising police careers. It takes only one really bad decision or following an unethical path to produce disastrous results for everyone involved, not the least of whom is the police officer who makes the critical, unethical decision.

This examination of police ethical decision making will consider elements of accountability and the process decision making plays in the role of producing ethical behavior in policing. A crucial note needs to be established early. This chapter in no way implies that all police officers are dishonest or unethical people. That is not my intent or belief. Most police officers at all levels of organizations spend their careers trying to do the right thing, making good, ethical decisions, and working honorably in a difficult profession where they face not only physical danger, but also the danger of having their character and integrity impugned. It takes strength of character to navigate the perils of an ethical police career. Despite the perils, many officers navigate the straight and narrow path of ethical behavior and provide a sound example of professional integrity for younger officers to follow.

What Is Ethics in the Context of Policing?

Michael Josephson (1993) offers an excellent definition of ethics in the policing context, "Ethics is a code of values which guide our choices and actions and determine the purpose and course of our lives" (p. 5). This definition provides a poignant focus for ethical decision making. Decisions made by police officers throughout America are based on values and beliefs held by each individual officer and, more important, the officially sanctioned and internally held organizational value, as defined in rules, regulations, customs, law, and leadership directives. A key point is that one cannot direct someone to be ethical or give them ethics (Brown, 1990).

> *Ethics does not produce a product but engages one in a process—a decision making process of discovering what should be done ...The best guides do not tell people what they should do; rather, they show people how to discover the best course of action for themselves* (Brown, 1990, p. xi).

This is especially important for police officers who operate independently of their supervisors. Leaders set the tone for the ethical climate of an organization, but ultimately it is the responsibility of each individual officer to be accountable for making proper decisions. It is a responsibility of both leaders and supervisors to focus on ethical conduct in the everyday decisions made by officers. Without this mutual commitment, unethical conduct will creep into decision making at every level of the organization. Often poor, unethical decisions are made by officers based on emotions of the moment. As Covey (1990) noted, "Reactive people are driven by feelings, by circumstances, by conditions, by their environment. Proactive people are driven by values—carefully thought about, selected and internalized values" (p. 72). This proactive approach serves officers well because without the emotionally driven decisions, officers can focus on what is right, what is expected in accordance with organizational values, and what is highest ethical expectations of modern policing.

Ethical Issues in Policing

The ethical pitfalls in policing are numerous. They are covered routinely in initial policing training and codified in police regulations, standard operating procedures, and codes of ethics. Ethical misconduct ranges from minor infractions of rules to more serious issues of excessive force, brutality, economic corruption, unlawful arrests, sexual misconduct on-duty, abuse of power, violations of public trust, alcohol or drug abuse, and criminal violations. This list provides only small examples of the depth and breadth of potential unethical conduct. Probably one of the more insidious ethical behaviors prone to occur in policing is lying. Lying, or any untruthfulness including withholding of information, is at the core of all unethical behavior and provides the most problematic issue for maintaining the character and integrity of police agencies. With lying as the center of unethical behavior, principled decision making becomes an imperative for avoidance of such unethical behavior (Magers, 1997; Magers, 2004).

Closely associated with lying is a concept identified as "noble cause corruption" (Delattre, 2002; Crank & Caldero, 2004). The concept of noble cause assumes that unethical decisions are acceptable if the ultimate result provides for an acceptable end. In other words, justifying the means if the ends are noble (Delattre, 2002). In the context of policing, that may mean doing something otherwise considered unethical, such as lying to obtain a conviction of a criminal, in order to achieve a desirable result. Unlike economic corruption, the officer who engages in noble cause corruption receives no monetary or tangible reward. The result is what is perceived by the officer as a justifiable result or noble cause result (Crank & Caldero, 2004). Noble cause ethics creates a sense of entitlement for an officer to do whatever is necessary to achieve the desired ends as defined by the officer. The discretionary power to do so can be seductive and ultimately destructive to the cause of justice, resulting in potential discovery and the end to what might have been an otherwise productive police career. "Ends justifying the means" as a method for ethical decision making has serious flaws, all leading to unethical decision making. Informal police officer culture often values justifying unethical behavior based on the noble cause. Police leaders and police officers must work to eradicate the ends-means focus on justifying the unethical behavior for perceived good ends (Caldero & Crank, 2004).

Another major ethical issue is what Gilmartin (1998) called the continuum of compromise. He describes this "path of ethical compromise" as the compromising of ethical principles when officers face the stresses of police work. Specifically, he defines the continuum of com-promise as "A perceived sense of victimization [that] can lead to the rationalization and justification of: Acts of omission, acts of commission-administrative, acts of commission-criminal, entitlement versus account-ability, loyalty versus integrity" (Gilmartin, 1998, p. 26). He further explains that victimization develops over time as motivated, enthusiastic young officers become over-invested and over-identify with the police role and with other officers, leading to an eventual resentment of their role as police officers. This creates a "victim mentality" that leads to the rationalization or justification for shortcuts that often include unethical actions, violations of rules and regulations, or even crimes.

Acts of omission can include overlooking criminal acts, avoiding paperwork, not taking reports that should be completed. Administrative acts of commission primarily involve actions that violate administrative departmental rules and regulations, such as drinking on duty, on-duty sexual activity, or other activity lacking personal accountability or inte-grity. Criminal acts of commission devolve into activities by officers where a total respect for the law pervades the thinking of an officer and the principles of ethical policing are ignored in favor of rationalized criminal behavior (Gilmartin, 1998). Some of these types of behavior emanate from attitudes that develop where the special role of police officers become an entitlement for special status where the rules do not apply to the police, resulting in the loss of personal and professional accountability for actions as a police officer. Loyalty issues sometimes will erode professional integrity of officers when they value loyalty to back up fellow officers to the exclusion of all other professional values, resulting in lying to cover up unethical, unprofessional, or even crimes by other officers. These feelings of loyalty over everything else are some-times unwittingly fostered by police unions or fraternal organizations such as the Fraternal Order of Police (FOP) (Jones & Carlson, 2001).

Ethical Organizational Imperatives

Significant to the building of an organizational culture that supports ethical police behavior and strengthens an ethical organizational climate are ethical organizational imperatives. One such imperative is leader-ship integrity. Police leaders who exhibit ethical behavior and who value ethical behavior in their organizations create an environment where ethical behavior thrives and unethical behavior results in discipline. Equally important are the challenges by fellow officers toward their colleagues who chose to make unethical choices. Developing and maintaining such an ethical environment can be difficult, if not impossible, without the support of leaders throughout the organization. A corollary to this imperative involves the integrity and ethical environment of the governments in which police agencies operate. Some police agencies in the United States have nearly an impossible task of improving ethical culture in their police organizations because corruption and unethical behavior is widely accepted at the city, county, or state level or practiced by political leaders in those governments. Ethical police leadership depends on a reasonably ethical culture in the overall government environment in which police operate. An ethical leader has a difficult course to navigate when political leaders fail to support initiatives to improve police ethical culture (Magers, 1997; Magers, 2004; Walker, 2005).

Another ethical imperative involves the development of an organizational strategic plan. Strategic plans identify the police mission, organizational values, and a specific plan for addressing organizational needs, which might include organizational development policies that address police integrity and accountability. Specific plans can produce specific, positive results. A lacking of detailed planning produces little but status quo, thus not proactively addressing improvement of police ethical behavior (Covey, 1992). A significant corollary to this imperative focuses on the institutional support provided for improving and sustaining efforts to show that the organization values, ethical conduct, and especially effective ethical decision making can occur in the absence of direct supervision. This support is required from internal and external leadership and from peer support (Magers, 1997; Magers, 2004). Police leaders must define and exemplify explicitly-stated organizational values that support an organizational culture that encourages and sustains leadership efforts to enhance ethical conduct (Walker, 2005; Caldero & Crank, 2004).

Ethical decision making determines ethical climate in an organization. This imperative uniquely recognizes police officers often making critical decisions in the absence of supervisors, under stressful circumstances, with lasting effects. Often peers have greater influence on police officer decision making because they are in immediate contact with fellow officers at the particular time when critical decisions are made. Consequently, police leaders must exert their influence through the development of a peer culture that supports ethical behavior. The harnessing of peer support for ethical decision making creates an environment where an ethical climate will flourish (Kouzes & Posner, 2007).

Organizational Culture Supporting an Ethical Climate

Edgar Schein (1992) described organizational culture as the shared beliefs and assumptions that characterize how organizations conduct business and how the members of the organizations view themselves and their environment. Some police organizations produce better results than others in the pursuit of an organizational culture that supports these shared beliefs that ethical behavior is honored and revered. Some police organizations have a history of a culture that values destructive beliefs of less than honorable conduct; these attitudes have a divisive, corrosive, and destructive effect on the entire organization, even though there may be just a small number of officers who engage in unethical behavior. Often an important determining factor for the ethical climate of a police organization is the ethical climate of the government in which the police operate. A climate of unethical city government infests the organizational culture of a police organization because city policing operates within the organizational structure of city government and is subject to supervision and oversight by city government leaders, and managers (Delattre, 2002).

For police organizational culture to have a supportive environment for ethical behavior, there must be a focus by agency leaders to have a set of organizational values that are both explicitly stated and followed by everyone. Covey (1990) described values as road maps that guide our behavior. Josephson (1993) described organizational values as core beliefs that guide or motivate actions. People have personal values that are freely chosen and arrived at in various ways (Lewis, 1990). Organizational belief systems comprise what collectively are the organizational values. Organizational values that support ethical conduct by police officers include: honesty, integrity, truthfulness, compassion, justice, courage, dedication, professionalism, fairness, service, and teamwork, to name just a few (Delattre, 2002; Gaffigan & McDonald, 1997; Kleinig, 1996). Organizational values are based on these enduring principles. "Principles are proven, enduring guidelines for human conduct" (Covey, 1990, p. 35).

Values can be defined as either good or bad, whereas, principles reflect natural laws universally accepted as acceptable or proper human conduct. A well-defined set of organizational values based on these enduring principles provide a basis for effective principled decision making by officers, but only if accepted by the people in an organization. Police leaders must expect adherence and hold officers accountable for conduct consistent with these organizational values, particularly leader behavior that sets the example for ethical conduct (Gaffigan, & McDonald, 1997). Organizational values based on enduring principles provide the basis for professional, ethical policing and police leadership. Souryal (2003) succinctly described this concept by stating, "The first step toward incorporating a principle-based management system is to publicly commit the agency to the practices of ethics and integrity and to always act in accordance with moral principles" (p.203). He further said that principled management required "...vision, enlightened reasoning, moral responsibility, and good faith" (Souryal, 2003, p. 203). In the business context, Tom Morris (1997) indicated ethical organizations depended on the people within, their wisdom, and virtue that collectively provide corporate strength. This applies to law enforcement as well.

Comprehensive Ethics Strategy

A focal leadership action for improving police ethical behavior at all levels of the organization can be encompassed in the development of a comprehensive ethics strategy (Magers, 1997; Gilmartin, 1998). Comprehensive ethics strategies can be instrumental for police leaders in their efforts to address organizational integrity issues and focus on the development of a systematic approach for the improvement of ethical decision making by officers. Developing a leadership plan for sustained improvement of ethical behavior is one such approach that provides a specific strategy. First, chiefs of police and their staffs must answer the question: What is the ethical status of the organization? It is imperative to have a complete understanding of the current situation. Quite often police chiefs fail in the improvement of the ethical behavior of their departments because they overlook or underestimate the sustained ethical conduct of their officers. Second, police administrators must ask who the stakeholders are. This question requires the close examination of key people who are capable of developing a unified effort to comprehensively address the key ethical issues at the level required to effect change. Some key stakeholders might include people outside the organization that have a specific stake in ethical police behavior and can exert some external influence, such as the prosecutor's office, or even police unions. The third question for introspective examination of the agency involves the identification of key issues in the department undermining ethical behavior. Simply stated, what are the critical ethical issues? It is imperative that the identification of these ethical issues focuses on particular activities that have led to problematic areas of concern.

Reflections on those questions should lead the police leader to ask the fourth question: What steps can provide specific actions for change

leading to improved ethical behavior and decision making? These
courses of action must be tied directly to specific goals, objectives, and
plans of action, including identifying the people responsible for implementing change and assessing accountability for results. Often police
leaders will try to address unethical behavior in their organizations with
simplistic responses that do not really address the systemic problems
that lead to the resolution of organizational ethical issues. To fully
address ethical issues multiple approaches usually are required. Simply
addressing the problem as a training issue is insufficient. Training can
be helpful, but as a single strategy, it is not a comprehensive approach
to corrective actions for an improved organizational ethical climate. One
approach to addressing ethical issues as part of a comprehensive
strategic approach is to revisit the organizational vision mission
statements as a means of clarifying organizational values supporting
ethical policing. These clarified values can be used as the guideposts for
implementing changes required to improve organizational ethical
climate (Magers, 1997; Magers, 2004).

An effective method for the organizational analysis necessary for
development of strategies for improved ethical include: 1) an organizational review of disciplinary records, 2) review of citizen complaints,
3) close examination of the attitudes of leaders, managers, and
supervisors towards police misconduct and unethical behavior, 4) an
examination of departmental policies to determine whether there are
sufficient safeguards against unethical behavior and other misconduct,
5) training policies on ethics, ethical decision making, and other issues
related to personal responsibility for both officers' and supervisors'
ethical conduct, 6) an examination of accountability for officer decision
making and supervisory oversight, 7) clear focus on developing a
comprehensive understanding of police officer attitudes regarding issues
of accountability for ethical decision making with special emphasis on
integrity issues such as the avoidance of an ends justifies the means
perspective (Office of Community Policing Services, 2006).

Ethical Decision Making

A critical component of improving ethical decision making includes
providing police officers with a method for considering how to make
good, ethical decisions in difficult circumstances where ethical dilemmas
develop. Often difficult ethical dilemmas are resolved with emotion-
based decision making, which frequently creates flawed decisions where
critical thinking skills would better serve the officer in resolving a
difficult issue. Laying the groundwork for good ethical decisions starts
with the development of organizational values based on the enduring

principles of ethical policing. When organizational leaders explicitly define these values, express them accurately, and exemplify them in their actions, officers can better articulate these values and incorporate them into daily decision making. It is not enough to merely publish a list of the organizational values; those values must become part of the fiber of organizational life, at levels, whether administratively, operationally, or technologically. The decision making process of the entire agency must use the organizational values as the foundation for decision making. This Values Model of decision making provides a solid basis for a mental framework to make ethically challenging decisions (Magers, 1997).

The first step in the Values Model decision-making process is to clearly consider the ethical situation. An understanding of the ethical dilemma is necessary to fully understand what potential ethical issues might arise from whatever decision is made. Second, there must be an understanding of who the stakeholders are in the decision to be made. In other words, who will be affected by this decision? In considering potential stakeholders, the officers obtain a full realization of the many people that might be adversely affected by an unethical decision. The third step is a critical element in the decision making process. The decision maker must determine the various potential courses of action. Some of these may be readily dismissed as unacceptable, but when each is adequately considered, there likely will be several potential avenues to take in making the decision. The decision maker must then in step four select the course of action that is most consistent with the organizational values (Magers, 1997).

Remembering that personal values can be either good or bad, so ethical decision making in policing must rely more on organizational values based on the enduring principles of ethical policing. Substituting personal values that are contrary to the organizational values may result in a flawed, unethical decision based on emotion rather than effective reasoning (Covey, 1990).

One example of these enduring principles of ethical policing is the International Association of Chiefs of Police Code of Ethics, 1991 (see Figure 9-1), later replaced with the Oath of Honor (see Figure 9-2). Although these documents are not ethical decision-making models, they exemplify the highest ideals of ethical policing (Delattre, 2002; Kleinig & Zhang, 1993). If a police agency's organizational values are consistent with the ethical principles within these documents, then they will provide a firm foundation for ethical decision making.

Figure 9-1.   IACP Code of Ethics (1991)

As a law enforcement officer, my fundamental duty is to serve the community; to safeguard lives and property; to protect the innocent against deception, the weak against oppression or intimidation, and the peaceful against violence and disorder, and to respect the constitutional rights of all to liberty, equality, and justice.

I will keep my private life unsullied as an example to all and behave in a manner that does not bring discredit to me or my agency. I will maintain courageous calm in the face of danger and, scorn, or ridicule; develop self-restraint; and be constantly mindful of the welfare of others. Honest in thought and deed both in my personal and official life, I will be exemplary in obeying the law and the regulations of my department. Whatever I hear or see of a confidential nature or that is confided to me in my official capacity will be kept secret unless revelation is necessary in the performance of my duty.

I will never act officiously or permit personal feelings, prejudices, political beliefs, aspirations, animosities or friendships to influence my decisions. With no compromise for crime and with relentless prosecutions of criminals, I will enforce the law courageously and appropriately without fear or favor, malice or ill will, ever employing unnecessary force or violence and never accepting gratuities.

I recognize the badge of my office as a symbol of public faith, and I accept it as a public trust to be held as long as I am true to ethics of police service. I will never engage in acts of corruption or bribery, nor will I condone such acts by other police officers. I will cooperate with all legally authorized agencies and their representatives in the pursuit of justice.

I know that I alone am responsible for my own standard of professional performance and will take every reasonable opportunity to enhance and improve my level of knowledge and competence.

I will constantly strive to achieve these objectives and ideals, dedicating myself before God to my chosen profession ... law enforcement.

Source: Kleinig & Zhang (1993)

Figure 9-2.   IACP Oath of Honor

IACP Oath of Honor

On my honor,
I will never betray my badge[1],
my integrity, my character,
or the public trust.
I will always have
the courage to hold myself
and others accountable for our actions.
I will always uphold the constitution[2]
my community[3] and the agency I serve.
Before any officer takes the Law Enforcement Oath of Honor, it is important that he/she understands what it means. An oath is a solemn pledge someone makes when he/she sincerely intends to do what he/she says.

Honor means that one's word is given as a guarantee.
Betray is defined as breaking faith with the public trust.
Badge is the symbol of your office.
Integrity is being the same person in both private and public life.
Character means the qualities that distinguish an individual.
Public trust is a charge of duty imposed in faith toward those you serve.
Courage is having the strength to withstand unethical pressure, fear or danger.
Accountability means that you are answerable and responsible to your oath of office.
Community is the jurisdiction and citizens served.

[1] Insert appropriate term such as: badge; profession; country
[2] Insert appropriate term such as: constitution, laws; monarch
[3] Insert appropriate term such as: community; country; land; nation

Source: International Association of Chiefs of Police, 2011

Proactive Accountability

Ethical police organizations must have ethical leadership with the courage to hold themselves and their employee accountable for their actions. The chief executive of an organization sets the ethical tone for the organization but supervisors are the backbone for holding employees accountable. These supervisors need the unwavering support of the chief executive for an exceptional level of accountability to exist. An ethical climate can flourish when leaders take proactive steps to establish and maintain ethical accountability the public wants and deserves.

First, proactive accountability requires proactive leaders willing to take the necessary steps to identify ethical concerns and take the appropriate steps to effectively address ethical issues. It is not enough to assume that ethical issues can be addressed without intentional, proactive leadership actions. Leaders must effectively communicate the expectations for ethical conduct and live up to those expectations themselves. Leadership actions must be clearly stated, publicly endorsed, effectively enforced, and visibly reinforced through the actions of all supervisors, managers, and executive leadership (Magers, 2010).

Second, there must be an effective citizen complaint system. The system must be explicitly stated in policy and rigorously adhered to throughout the organization. The complaint process must have the support and confidence of the citizens in the community. There are many formats for citizen complaint processes; however, it is not so much the particular process that is most important, but it is the integrity of the process that produces support and confidence of a community. This is the exclusive domain for organizational leaders to develop (Walker, 2001; Walker 2005; Office of Community Police Services 2006).

Third, early interventions systems must be in place to identify officer behavior that may lead to future misconduct (Office of Community Policing Services, 2006). The idea behind early intervention is to identify actions and behaviors of police officers that can be collected and reported in order to identify developing patterns that might indicate a behavioral trend of behavior that predicts potential current or future misconduct. Early intervention programs focus on four areas of concern: 1) performance indicators, 2) the identification and selection process, 3) intervention, and 4) post-intervention monitoring (Walker, 2005). Performance indicators include issues such as use of force reports filed by an officer, high-speed pursuits, vehicle accidents, civil suits filed against an officer, disciplinary actions of all types including supervisor reprimands, and citizen complaints. Performance indicators can involve more factors, but in early intervention programs, the agency determines the indicators and captures the information necessary to determine the presence of any problematic patterns. When an officer is identified for intervention, further individualized scrutiny of the officer's performance determines if the early intervention measures are needed. Intervention actions might include counseling, retraining, and additional supervision. The intent is to prevent these potentially problematic patterns from developing into actions that would require severe internal consequences, such as suspension or termination. Early identification helps hold the officer accountable to higher expectations consistent with organizational standards (Walker, 2005).

Fourth, police leaders must develop and sustain an effective system of discipline that identifies misconduct and implements fair and equitable discipline while upholding officers' due process rights. Police leaders must have rules, regulations, policies, and standard operating procedures that establish standards to hold officers accountable for accomplishing their work in compliance with these standards. Disciplinary procedures must be applied with fairness, lacking any indication of favoritism. These standards must apply to police leaders as well as employees at all levels in the organization. Disciplinary procedures often fail because police leaders do not wholly enforce written standards. Lack of enforcement of certain rules degrades the respect for the rest of the standards. Police leaders must clearly state the expectations of employees and hold them accountable for their actions in accordance with the rules (Delattre, 2002).

Fifth, police leaders must take positive actions toward effectively communicating that honesty is one of the most important organizational values in a police organization. This message must be effectively communicated throughout the organizations. Police leaders must proactively support honesty, integrity, and virtue in an organization, while denouncing lying as unacceptable behavior. Lying is a destructive police behavior. Lying takes many forms, but its most destructive qualities always involve deception to cover up unethical behavior. Leaders must practice honesty in all their actions as an example of the importance of honesty. Leaders must hold officers accountable for lying. It is important that leaders send a message against lying that is clear, unambiguous, and universally known to be unacceptable behavior (Magers, 2010).

Sixth, police leaders must have an effective training program to support ethical decision making and adherence to ethical standards. Ethics training provides opportunities to discuss ethical quandaries, and to address the expectation of the highest ethical performance. This training begins with recruits and is reinforced through yearly training programs that realistically address the ethical issues most critical to particular organizations (Caldero & Crank, 2004; Delattre, 2002). Police leaders must play prominent roles in this training and no one should be exempt from the training (Davis, 1996).

Seventh, it is important for police organizations to have a commitment to community involvement using many of the principles identified as part of a community policing philosophy. Greater community involvement and police interaction with the community tend to build a level of trust and mutual respect that reinforces ethical behavior by police officers. These police-community partnerships establish a level of transparency within the police agency that develops expectations of honesty and integrity that have a greater opportunity to develop.

Eighth, police organizations must hire people of character. Flawed hiring practices make having an ethical organizational environment difficult. There can be little expectation that police recruits of questionable character will improve when they become police officers, when working independently, with considerable discretion and power, and when tempted by the many influences that provide opportunity for misconduct. Many pressures sometimes lead to poor recruiting procedures, reduction of standards, and the acceptance of the attitude that recruiting people of good character is nearly impossible. Police leaders must not accept mediocrity when it comes to good character (Delattre, 2002). While screening recruits takes time and money, placing effort in the process pays great dividends. Police leaders must hold police recruits accountable for their actions early in their careers, during training and during the probationary period. Misconduct that occurs during this period of time, when the recruit knows they are under great scrutiny, is a reliable indicator of poor performance and misconduct throughout the officer's career. Police leaders must take swift action to terminate recruit officers who do not live up to organizational values, mission, and ethical standards. Terminating an unethical recruit is much easier than terminating an unethical veteran officer, and the damage to the organization (and community) is far less the earlier such misconduct is uncovered (Delattre, 2002).

Enemies of Accountability

While accountability should be a given factor in any police agency, there often are organizational elements that can unwittingly, yet effectively, make organizational accountability difficult. Appellate review organizations, such citizen review boards, civil service boards, or merit boards, often impede accountability (Walker, 2001). This seems counterintuitive because these boards provide not only an additional level of organizational review, but dually they provide another step in officer due process rights in the disciplinary. This due process guarantee function should not be—and largely it is not—a detriment to accountability, but there are times when it can be, as when well-meaning members routinely rule that disciplinary actions should be reduced, often reversing severe suspensions or termination for egregious officer misconduct. It is not unusual for a chief of police to severely discipline an officer following a sustained complaint only to have the decision overruled in the review process by a citizen board. This would be understandable if these results were based on procedural errors in due process, but often the reduced penalty seems only to be giving another chance to an officer. Second chances are acceptable where the offenses are less serious, but when penalties are reduced for serious offenses, the result is an unnecessary undermining of discipline and accountability. It seems that in some communities police leaders cannot rely on citizen boards to reliably support harsh penalties for deserving misconduct.

Other enemies to accountability are police fraternal organizations and unions. Fraternal organizations with collective bargaining power are not unlike unions when engaging in the function of protecting job rights of police officers. Both provide legal aid for police officers accused of misconduct. The proper position for this support is to ensure the accused officer's due process rights are provided in the disciplinary process. This has morphed beyond protection of rights to the unwavering attempt to exonerate the accused officer of all wrongdoing or to mitigate the charges and penalties. The latter sends the message that it matters little what the charges are, but of utmost importance to the union or fraternal organization is the protection of the officer's job, to the exclusion of all other considerations. Often this includes providing legal assistance in the defense against criminal charges. Legal support for protection of officer rights is well understood as a function of such organizations, but the explicit protection against the charges, despite the depth of evidence of wrongdoing, sends the subtle message that such behavior is acceptable or at least tolerated (Kleinig, 1996).

Police fraternal organizations and unions spend considerable amounts of money on legal defense of police officer misconduct, whether it is administrative or criminal charges. It would seem in these organizations' self-interest to promote ethical conduct rather than implicitly condoning unethical behavior or blatant administrative or criminal misconduct. If a fraternal organization were about supporting fellow officers, providing assistance for a quality workplace, and furthering a police career, then it would seem to indicate the focus should be on working together to hold one another accountable for proper conduct. This is not to imply that unions or fraternal organizations should not provide assistance to police officers accused of wrongdoing. Certainly, that is one of their expected functions, but there is a significant difference between supporting an officer's right of due process and reducing accountability for misconduct (Kleinig, 1996).

A third enemy of accountability are police chief executives who take a low profile in holding officers accountable for misconduct. Some police leaders avoid their responsibilities to have a proper citizen complaint process, an effective internal investigative process, and accountability at all leadership levels in the police agency. This hands-off approach to leadership accountability systems provides fertile ground for misconduct and other unethical behavior.

Conclusion

Who is responsible for ethical behavior? Ethical behavior is the individual responsibility of every police officer, regardless of rank or position. Each police officer makes the decision to abide by the rules, regulations, laws, and the U.S. Constitution. It is an individual decision to honor the ethical obligations of their position as police officers. No one can force another officer to make an unethical decision. Despite all that has been presented in this chapter about the ethical (unethical) influence of police leaders, managers, and supervisors, there can never be any question that the ultimate responsibility for ethical action and proper conduct lies solely with individual officers. That can be a heavy burden for police officers who may face many temptations or pressures to do otherwise. It is incumbent on police leaders to provide the organizational climate that supports ethical decision making. If police officers see supervisors exhibiting unethical behavior, this reinforces the implicit value that they can do the same (Magers, 1997; Magers, 2004). If police leaders or supervisors look the other way, ignoring unethical behavior of subordinates, they send the message that such behavior is acceptable. Police leaders set the tone and climate for the ethical conduct within an organization. They can make officers neither ethical nor unethical, but through leadership, they can shape the expectations of subordinates and either support ethical or unethical behavior with their own actions and ethical perspectives. Who is responsible? Police officers, police leaders, governmental leaders, and citizens all have a role in the ethical conduct of a police agency. Without the support for ethical behavior from any one of these groups makes it more difficult for individual officers to make ethical decisions throughout the course of their careers.

References

Brown, M. T. (1990). *Working ethics: Strategies for decision making and organizational responsibility.* San Francisco, CA: Jossey-Bass.

Caldero, M.A. & Crank, J. P. (2004). *Police Ethics: The corruption of noble cause* (2nd ed.). Cincinnati, OH: Anderson Publishing Co.

Covey, S. R. (1990). *The 7 habits of highly effective people: Restoring the character ethic.* New York, NY: Simon & Schuster.

Covey, S. R. (1992). *Principled-centered leadership.* New York, NY: Simon & Schuster

Davis, M. (1996). Police discretion, and professions. In J. Kleinig (Ed.) *Handled with discretion: Ethical Issues in police decision making.* (13-35). London: Rowman & Littlefield.

Delattre, E. J. (2002). *Character and cops: Ethics in policing* (4th ed.). Washington, DC: The AEI Press.

Gaffigan, S. J. & McDonald, P. P. (1997). *Police integrity: Public service with honor* (NCJ 163811). Washington, DC: National Institute of Justice.

Gilmartin, K. M. (1998). Law enforcement ethics: The continuum of compromise. *Police Chief*, 65(1), 25-28.

International Association of Chiefs of Police (2011). *What is the law enforcement Oath of Honor?* Retrieved February 20, 2011, from http://www.theiacp.org/PoliceServices/ProfessionalAssistance/Eth ics/WhatistheLawEnforcementOathofHonor/tabid/150/Default.aspx.

Jones, J. R. & Carlson, D. P. (2001). *Reputable conduct: Ethical issues in policing and corrections.* Upper Saddle River, NJ: Prentice Hall.

Josephson, M. (1993). *Making ethical decisions* (2nd ed.). Marina del Rey, CA: The Josephson Institute of Ethics.

Kleinig, J. & Zhang, Y. (1993). *Professional law enforcement codes: A documentary collection.* Westport, CT: Greenwood Press.

Kleinig, J. (1996). *The ethics of policing.* New York, NY: Cambridge, University Press.

Kouzes, J. M. & Posner, B. Z. (2007). *The leadership challenge* (4th ed.). San Francisco, CA: John Wiley & Sons, Inc.

Lewis, H. (1991). *A question of values: Six ways we make the personal choices that shape our lives.* New York, NY: Harper Collins Publishers.

Magers, J. S. (1997). Police supervisors and ethical behavior in police organizations. UMI Dissertation Services (UMI No. 9721195).

Magers, J. S. (2004). Ethical practice for police leaders: Critical issues for organizational integrity. *Law Enforcement Executive Forum*, 4(2) 55-70.

Magers, J. S. (2010). The Message. In J. Dempsey, L. Forst, *An Intro-duction to Policing* (5th ed.), Clifton, Park, NY: Delmar/Cengage Learning.

Morris, T. (1997). *If Aristotle ran General Motors: The new soul of business.* New York, NY: Henry Holt and Company.

Office of Community Policing Services (2006). *Protecting civil rights: A leadership guide for state, local, and tribal law enforcement* (NCJ 215876). Washington, DC: OCPS.

Souryal, S. S. (2003). *Ethics in criminal justice* (3rd ed.). Cincinnati, OH: Anderson.

Walker, S. (2001). *Police Accountability: The role of citizen oversight.* Belmont, CA: Wadsworth/Thomson Learning.

Walker, S. (2005). *The new world of police accountability.* Thousand Oaks, CA: Sage.

Discussion Questions

1. What realities of the job of police officer make managing officer behavior difficult?

2. Which of the features of proactive accountability do you think is most important? Explain.

3. Which of the features of proactive accountability do you think is least important? Explain.

4. List the barriers to accountability identified by Magers. Do you agree with his conclusion?

5. Who, ultimately, is responsible for the behavior of police officers?

6. What is at stake when officers make unethical decisions?

Chapter 10
ASSESSING POLICE-COMMUNITY RELATIONS IN A CHANGING ENVIRONMENT

Yolanda Scott, Ph.D. Roger Williams University

Introduction

Communities expect their law enforcement officers to be highly competent, well trained, and professional in the performance of their basic functions: order maintenance, public service, and law enforcement (Gaines, Worrall, Southerland & Angell, 2003). For various reasons, some officers do not meet this expectation, straining relationships among community members and police departments, making it even more difficult to fulfill those purposes. To reduce such tensions, many departments adopt a community-policing paradigm (Peak, 2012).

In 1994, President Clinton signed the Violent Crime Control and Law Enforcement Act (S. 10003. H.R. 3355 103d). Title I of that Act established the Community Oriented Policing Services (COPS) grant program to assist departments with development of community policing initiatives by funding a number of programs, personnel, and services (James, 2011). With community policing, law enforcement officials partner with public agencies, elected officials, businesses, non-profit service providers, media, and community members to take proactive, problem-oriented measures to reduce fear, to decrease crime, and to address underlying social issues. Title 1 funding was aimed, in part, at placing 100,000 American police officers in community policing programs (U.S. Department of Justice, 1994).

Researchers have studied police-community dynamics for many years, placing much emphasis on citizen satisfaction with police services. However, officer perception is an equally important matter to consider, as job satisfaction and delivery of quality policing may depend on their working environment (Dantzker & Surrette, 1996; Greene, 1989). Dissatisfied, disgruntled employees uninterested in the COPS philosophy are unlikely to perform up to community expectations and gain community support—something the department so desperately needs and desires.

Turning difficult police-community relations around to meet twenty-first century challenges and community demands rests largely with police administrators, who set the overall mission and goals of the organization. This first requires that police chiefs be able to recognize any problems with the police-public relationship. Then, they must work with officers to change how they view their role and function and to insist upon community involvement. As evidenced by the evolution of American policing from the mid-nineteenth century political era to the homeland security era of today, resistance from officers and community members entrenched in hurt feelings and old ways of thinking and practice often complicates such transitions. It is in this larger context of police-community relations that I present the recent history of the Seaside Police Department and describe how police personnel, led by a new chief, worked to regain the support and trust of their Massachusetts community.

Eras of Policing

Every organization experiences change of some kind or risks becoming stagnant and unable to meet the needs of its constituents. The institution of policing in American society is no different. Researchers (Gaines et al., 2003; Oliver, 2006; Thurman, Zhao & Giacomazzi, 2001; Williams & Murphy, 1990) have charted a number of profound historical shifts in formalized policing: the political era, the reform era, and the community era. Given the events of September 11, 2001, Oliver (2006) suggests that police agencies have begun shifting directions again, to the homeland security era. Each change in police focus was a response to socio-cultural crises that redefined the police mission, role and function and alters how they serve their communities (DeLone, 2007).

The Political Era
From about the 1840s to 1919, police agencies were underdeveloped, decentralized, and disorganized in their mission, role, and function. Local politics had great influence over them. Police administrators understood that they were to direct resources and power toward the majority political party's interests. Politicians used their influence to become self-made stakeholders in matters both internal and external to police departments; they authorized what policing style departments should adopt, how officers would be deployed, when to arrest, and who was most suitable for hiring and for promoting within the particular precincts over which they held power. To sustain this politically based policing and to preserve public trust and the confidence needed to ensure votes for the next election cycle, politicians were most concerned with having police officers primarily focus on maintaining order and serving the public. This meant they had to make the majority group of the time (the most influential community members) believe that their neighborhood and their livelihood was safe, secure, and orderly and that they would face little negative attention from police personnel. Aside from this, there was little input expected or solicited from residents.

Officers routinely patrolled the community on foot and exercised little discretion in performing their duties; they were generalists providing an array of social services, including organizing meals for the homeless, checking on citizens with disease during widespread outbreaks, keeping disorderliness to a minimum, and ensuring the subjection of non-whites and immigrants. Discouraged from arresting voting and voting-age majority group members, officers spent much of their time idle until their immediate supervisors provided direct orders for action. The corrupt nature of this type of early formalized policing often resulted in inequitable application of laws and acts of brutality and, overall, did not serve the community well. Police organizations nationwide were exposed for their inability to maintain order, to control crime, or to fairly provide appropriate services. This eventually prompted some to question the purpose and authority of police and to call for considerable reform.

The Reform Era

The Reform Era, thought to occur between 1920s and 1970s, removed police from the political arena and established them more as members of a centralized, professional organization formed for the public good. Criminal law provided the foundation for the case that the function of the police is rooted in crime control, so officers were released from social services-type activities (Oliver, 2006). Police were now viewed as "crime-fighters," capable of detecting and investigating crimes and bringing law violators to justice. To meet the specialized, complex demands of the job and presumably to resist the brutality endemic of the previous era, reformists proposed greater professionalization and higher levels of education among officers. Policing became more organized through the adoption of a paramilitary structure and the hiring of military veterans who helped develop a top-down management approach that required strict adherence to a hierarchical chain of command.

With this organizational philosophy came a closed system that placed police as the only ones responsible for fighting crime, with limited input from the public. Police managers, in particular, dictated departmental priorities and set out the rationale for the agency's mission. Police were largely accountable only to themselves and justified their decision making by claiming domain expertise of community problems, law enforcement strategies, and crime-control tactics. Improvements in technology, science, and data collection, as well as the elimination of police participation in social services' activities, helped push police managers and officers forward into this new era.

The various legal battles and crises that occurred during this era (e.g., prohibition; the Great Depression; struggle for civil rights; assassinations of high profile social and political leaders; war protests), however, proved too much for policing. Although reform strategies were partially successful in extracting departments and police personnel from former types of abuse and political corruption, an "us" against "them" mentality had calcified. Although police could answer calls for service faster, pulling them from foot beats to motor patrol created a distance between the police and the communities they served. National and local crime statistics were often used to manipulate the community's perception of departmental need or effectiveness. Police intermingling with criminal elements involved in prostitution, gambling, separatism, and drug and alcohol activities increased, as did crime rates. Promoting the image of police as "crime-fighters" became hard to sell to a public faced with economic challenges and intent on demanding their rights. During this era, two presidential commissions called for new perspectives on policing. These commissions acknowledged that the primary role of police of this era had actually contributed to these problems creating negative police-community relations. Their recommendations for improvement sought to close these gaps through strengthening ties between the police and community.

The Community Era

The 1980s-2000 was the era of community-oriented policing services (COPS). The focus was on public relations—improving the image of police agencies among the general public—and community relations, which involved developing administrative strategies geared toward improving relations between the public and the police. During this era, emphasis was placed on a more open systems approach to policing where citizen input and feedback would be valued. Rather than viewing all residents as potential criminals in need of a watchful eye, police chiefs would prioritize the philosophy and practice of treating citizens as stakeholders in partnership with the police for the betterment of their community. Officers were more proactive than reactive during this era and strived to improve the quality of life among community residents. The 40-year development of a police culture that supported the role of "crime fighters" would have to change to "community/organizers" and "crime preventers." Police administrators were to adopt and promote an understanding that police should focus less on the quantifiable measures of police performance, such as "... number of arrests, changes in crime rates, volume of recovered property, numbers of citations issued, and a rapid response to calls" (Gaines et al., 2003, p. 81).

The new primary functions of police would be to engage in activities with residents that would solve community problems (problem-oriented policing, or POPS) by reducing fear of crime and working to resolve actual and perceived neighborhood disorders. The mode of policing would also change; rather than providing police services exclusively in patrol cars with the windows up, community members saw officers on foot, on bicycles, or on horses. These patrol techniques increased interaction and allowed community members greater opportunity to relate their concerns or make suggestions for improvement.

A special element of this era was the sharing of authority as management agreed to flatten the traditional police hierarchy to allow greater freedom for officers to problem-solve with community members and actively participate in identifying the direction of police services in the geographic areas for which they are most familiar. Under the community policing approach, the familiarity and social bonding of police and the community was expected to significantly increase, creating a trust that would open lines of communication and improve the public's overall sense of satisfaction with services and safety. Nurtured over time, a reciprocal relationship may develop as residents come to believe officers are professional and that they "have their back," so they must support their department with necessary resources to maintain a high level of police services.

The numerous studies on the effectiveness and efficiency of policing in the community era suggest mixed results. Implementation problems, costs, and resistance by police officials and officers have been cited as the major barriers (Skogan, 1994; Skogan, 1990). The promise of COPS and all of its elements seems to have met a premature demise, or at least a temporary one since the terror attacks on September 11, 2001 brought forth what some believe is a new era in American policing: homeland security.

The Homeland Security Era
Although the groundwork for defining the mission, role, and function of police personnel in a homeland security era are still under way (DeLone, 2007), Oliver (2006) provides an analysis of several COPS elements that arguably remain significant in police organizations today. At the local level, police departments' shift in focus is a result of the threat of domestic and international terrorism. The government, as well as community residents, authorizes police to develop a homeland security philosophy, strategies, tactics, and organizational structures capable of intervening to prevent and to combat the threat. For officers, who are the "boots on the ground," interaction and closeness with the community is necessary to both reduce fear of a terror attack and to gather intelligence; however, information sharing is largely one-way and held within the confines of law enforcement agencies. Officers are expected to return to their "crime-fighter" role, to receive direct orders, to address identified problems from central command, and to relate information to superiors about problems community members reported to them. To maintain professional and respectable police-community relations, the police agency emphasizes the need to balance civil liberties with officers' discretionary decision making to stop, detain, and arrest individuals. Because it is understood that police will need the necessary resources, personnel, training, and academic and practical knowledge to fulfill their duties in this new era, community support is vital. Despite

department size, police personnel—especially patrol officers—are expected to remain vigilant to the challenges brought by this new era, which are compounded by the persistence of common crime problems and social issues communities faced pre-9/11.

Officers' willingness and ability to engage in developing strong police-community relations in general and through COPS principles seems an important matter to consider. Police officers' perceptions of how conducive the work environment is to a COPS approach may play a significant role in nurturing these relationships. If the previous and current eras of policing have taught us anything thus far, it is that sustained change must begin at the top of the organizational level. The purpose of this chapter is to describe an independent needs assessment conducted of a police department in the early stages of transition to a COPS framework.

The Assessment

In 2003, the new police chief of the Seaside Police Department asked me to assist with an external needs assessment to examine several issues; of primary concern was the state of relations between the public and the department. On the job for only a short time, the chief became concerned that although police personnel were dedicated to their job, there was tension within police-community relations. Officer morale was low, resources were scarce, and the police station was ill-suited for the work of a professional police force, yet the community seemed largely apathetic to the whole situation. The chief was clear that the department needed the community's help and that an open-systems approach—requiring transparency about issues of strengths, weaknesses, and promise—might be the best way to gain trust and confidence in the department's mission and vision. In this chapter, I will present portions of the needs assessment and describe factors that led this department to adopt a community-oriented policing strategy as a way to improve police-community relations, concluding with one major indicator of success in this effort.

General Community and Department Characteristics

During the time of the needs assessment, the town of Seaside spanned about 22.12 square miles, consisting of a business district, which had a large mall and shopping center, and residential and mixed zone areas. The police department served a population of 15,901 residents, 9,181 of whom were registered voters (57.73% of total population). A large transitory population regularly visited the town through easily accessible interstate highway. Police addressed both legitimate and illegitimate activities, including a large number of traffic incidents. Although the overall crime rate was relatively low, the department and community experienced increasing problems with drug offenses, thefts, vandalism, traffic violations, and accidents. At the beginning of the assessment, the Seaside Police Department employed thirty-one people: a chief, a deputy chief, six sergeants, seventeen patrol officers, five dispatchers (three full-time), and one administrative assistant. By the end of the assessment, the total increased to thirty-five, after the department hired four additional patrol officers.

Collecting the Data

I used two primary methods to gather data for this needs assessment: face-to-face interviews and a survey questionnaire. I conducted ride-along interviews with seven of the seventeen patrol officers and in-house interviews with the chief, three of the six sergeants, two of the five dispatchers, and several members of the media. Each interview averaged 2.5 hours. I asked three open-ended questions that dealt with the police department's interaction with the community. The first question assessed how the police department was involved in any dimensions indicative of COPS. The second examined the degree of perceived community support, and the third questioned whether they thought the community was aware of departmental and officers' concerns (i.e., funding, physical condition of the department, previous mistreatment by management). Several months after the interviews, I presented these themes again, in the form of a self-administered questionnaire offered to all police personnel, except for the chief and deputy chief. A departmental union representative distributed and collected the questionnaire from all respondents and gave them to me in a sealed envelope.

Of these thirty-three police personnel, twenty-nine completed the questionnaire, resulting in an 87.8% response rate. Using a three-point scale of 1 (Low), 2 (Medium), and 3 (High), I asked respondents to rate the chief's contributions to twelve items that assessed leadership philosophy, style, and practices identified as important for COPS implementation and practice. Additionally, I asked police personnel ten questions concerning the existence of and their experience with COPS within the department. These questions used a three-point scale: 1 (Strongly Agree), 2 (Somewhat Agree), and 3 (Strongly Disagree). Finally, I asked respondents to assess the level of disruption their police station had in completing their duties and in maintaining the privacy and safety of the public using a three-point scale: 1 (No/Little Disruption), 2 (Somewhat Disruptive), 3 (Very Disruptive).

Results

The findings of the needs assessment are best viewed from the perspective of the officers and other police personnel and along a continuum spanning three distinct phases of administrative change, as shown in Figure 10-1.

Figure 10-1.   Seaside Police Department's Administrative Phases

Phase I represents the 10-year tenure of a chief whom most officers described as a "miserable human being," whose management skills erred on the side of "favoritism" and a "divide and conquer" style. Phase II marks the one-year tenure of an interim chief who took over after the chief left the department under a highly publicized no confidence vote by the police union. Having worked under the first chief, the interim chief's approach was described as "hands-off," in an attempt to "make up for the horrible treatment we received." Finally, Phase III is the early tenure of the current chief (hired April 1, 2003) whose management style seems in the middle of the previous chiefs: he "demands professionalism and is fair to everybody." It was important to assess how officers viewed their chief's leadership because of its possible impact on the community; the chief's decision to make creating a mutually respectful and supportive relationship a top priority may heavily influence the department's philosophy on police-community relations.

Chief Ratings

Because respondents routinely made past/present comparisons, these data reflect their perceptions of the chiefs during Phases I and III and thus excludes the brief leadership provided by the interim chief during the second phase. As displayed in Table 10-1, police personnel presented a picture of a department that for ten years largely operated on an unprofessional level; employees viewed the department as mainly disorganized, unstable, unfair, non-participatory, and weak in effectiveness and efficiency.

Table 10-1. Chief Ratings: Past and Present (n = 29)†

VARIABLES	Past				Present			
	Low*	Some	High	New Hire/NA	Low*	Some	High	New Hire/NA
Morale	21 (72.4)	4 (13.8)	0 (0.0)	4 (13.8)	9 (31.0)	11 (38.0)	9 (31.0)	0 (0.0)
Department Stability	11 (38.0)	9 (31.0)	5 (17.2)	4 (13.8)	5 (17.2)	11 (38.0)	13 (44.8)	0 (0.0)
Department Organization	13 (44.8)	8 (27.6)	4 (13.8)	4 (13.8)	9 (31.0)	8 (27.6)	12 (41.4)	0 (0.0)
Department Pride	16 (55.2)	5 (17.2)	4 (13.8)	4 (13.8)	5 (17.2)	7 (24.1)	17 (58.6)	0 (0.0)
Professionalism	15 (51.7)	7 (24.1)	3 (10.3)	4 (13.8)	2 (6.9)	8 (27.6)	19 (65.5)	0 (0.0)
Mutual Respect	20 (69.0)	3 (10.3)	2 (6.9)	4 (13.8)	7 (24.1)	8 (27.6)	14 (48.3)	0 (0.0)
Department Effectiveness	8 (27.6)	9 (31.0)	8 (27.6)	4 (13.8)	3 (10.3)	6 (20.6)	20 (69.0)	0 (0.0)
Department Efficiency	8 (27.6)	11 (38.0)	6 (20.6)	4 (13.8)	3 (10.3)	8 (27.6)	18 (62.1)	0 (0.0)
Department Fairness	18 (62.1)	4 (13.8)	3 (10.3)	4 (13.8)	11 (38.0)	4 (13.8)	14 (48.3)	0 (0.0)
Optimism/Hope for the Future	17 (58.6)	3 (10.3)	5 (17.2)	4 (13.8)	7 (24.1)	8 (27.6)	14 (48.3)	0 (0.0)
Own Sense of Job Security	6 (20.6)	5 (17.2)	14 (48.3)	4 (13.8)	1 (3.5)	5 (17.2)	23 (79.3)	0 (0.0)
Encourage Participation	17 (58.6)	3 (10.3)	5 (17.2)	4 (13.8)	7 (24.1)	5 (17.2)	17 (58.6)	0 (0.0)

† Listwise Deletion of Cases; * Percentages in Parentheses

Although nearly half of police personnel may not have thought that their job security was threatened, the length of time enduring this type of working environment negatively impacted morale, pride in the department, optimism, hope for the future, and mutual respect for one another. Clearly, hiring a new chief who brought a different type of leadership to the department had an immediate positive impact, but as one officer explained:

> If you talk to some officers, they'll say the only changes made are that we have to wear our hats—it was a miracle that no one got laid off given budget problems. Some guys are taking a wait and see attitude, officers will say he [new Chief] hasn't done anything and this is just not fair to him—they [officers] expect too much. We were such a depressed department for so long, you can't blame people for still being bitter—there is such low morale here.

Although internal struggles among personnel in this department were clear, previous eras of policing demonstrated that working under such conditions can spill over, creating a barrier that thickens over time, isolating and alienating the police from the very people it has been entrusted to serve and protect.

Police-Community Relations

When asked about the existence, type, and level of COPS within the department, many respondents related what one officer experienced as a matter of routine: "If asked, we do ... I have to, well, we do reactive policing." Table 10-2 displays in more detail police personnel's long-term experiences with COPS in this department. Of the five citizen-specific items (input, quality of life, stakeholders, enhance lives, and initiate solutions), a large percent of police employees strongly agreed there is an emphasis on one—enhancing the lives of citizens—while the other four items resulted in a greater proportion of somewhat agree or strongly disagree responses. As for the police role in COPS, responses to the remaining five items (discretion, officer input, continued education, education rewarded, and seniority) revealed about a one-third split across all categories regarding the exercise of discretion. Although continued education seemed encouraged within this department, as about 40% of the employees strongly agreed or somewhat agreed (7.1%) with this item, a large proportion strongly disagreed (53.6%) that this was the case. The other three items central to COPS (i.e., initiate solutions, officer input, and seniority recognized more) resulted in a strongly disagree perspective. Only the results of the last item—"seniority recognized more"—seemed consistent with a COPS framework, as opportunities for promotion, advanced training, and the like were to be based on merit rather than length of service on the job.

Table 10-2. Community-Oriented Policing Services (*n* = 28)†

Variable	Strongly Disagree*	Somewhat Agree	Strongly Agree
Citizen Input	12 (42.8)	11 (39.3)	5 (17.9)
Quality of Life	16 (57.1)	10 (35.6)	2 (7.1)
Encourages Discretion	10 (35.6)	9 (32.1)	9 (32.1)
Citizens As Stakeholders	12 (42.8)	8 (28.6)	8 (28.6)
Enhance Lives	8 (28.6)	9 (32.1)	11 (39.3)
Initiate Solutions	11 (39.3)	9 (32.1)	8 (28.6)
Officer Input	18 (64.3)	6 (21.4)	4 (14.3)
Continued Education	15 (53.6)	2 (7.1)	11 (39.3)
College Education Rewarded	14 (50.0)	7 (25.0)	7 (25.0)
†Listwise Deletion of Cases; * Percentages in Parentheses			

Despite the virtual absence of the philosophy and practices necessary to establish and maintain COPS previously within this department, many respondents perceived that the public supports or wants to show support for them, but that residents are either unaware of their working conditions or distrustful of how the town government will spend their funds. Reflecting on the situation, one respondent stated:

I think the public is supportive of the department as a whole; they like their police department, our efforts but towns people are very distrustful of government. Have not done enough to stand up for us. The police department needs to be a priority in our community as opposed to a necessary evil.

Respondents believed that the community was largely unaware of their concerns for three reasons: lack of intimate knowledge of officers' physical work environment, lack of participation in town government, and lack of understanding of the demands of modern police work. Several members of the media confirmed these points. One reporter stated:

I have talked with some officers—appointed as liaisons and have been in the detective's office. It is hard to find a place to sit down and have a confidential conversation with them or some victim. For example, if there was another reporter there it is hard to talk, it seems crowded and cramped. Could you imagine a victim telling a story of what happened? I wouldn't feel comfortable doing that!

Police personnel worked daily in a dilapidated building erected in 1970, ill-suited for modern police services. As shown in Table 10-3 and Table 10-4, police employees overwhelmingly agreed that the police station lacked necessary privacy to conduct police business and that it was quite dangerous for both the police and the public. These realities contributed to the barriers of effective police work in the twenty-first century and further threatened any strides toward better relations with the community.

Table 10-3. Physical Condition of Department—Danger (*n* = 29)†

Variable	Level of Assessed Disruption*			
	Not/Little	Somewhat	Very	New Hire/NA
Danger in Dealing with Suspects	3 (10.3)	4 (13.8)	21 (72.4)	1 (3.4)
Physical Health (hygiene)	5 (17.2)	1 (3.4)	22 (75.9)	1 (3.4)
Booking Suspects	2 (6.9)	1 (3.4)	25 (86.2)	1 (3.4)
Jailing Suspects	2 (6.9)	4 (13.8)	22 (75.9)	1 (3.4)
Danger in Dealing with Suspects	3 (10.3)	4 (13.8)	21 (72.4)	1 (3.4)
† Listwise Deletion of Cases; * Percentages in Parentheses				

Table 10-4. Physical Condition of Department—Privacy (*n* = 29)†

Variable	Level of Assessed Disruption*			
	Not/Little	Somewhat	Very	New Hire/NA
Personal Privacy	4 (13.8)	4 (13.8)	20 (69.0)	1 (3.4)
Privacy with Suspects	2 (6.9)	1 (3.4)	25 (86.2)	1 (3.4)
Privacy with Witnesses	2 (6.9)	1 (3.4)	25 (86.2)	1 (3.4)
Privacy with Victims	1 (3.4)	3 (10.3)	24 (82.8)	1 (3.4)
Supervision	10 (34.5)	4 (13.8)	14 (48.3)	1 (3.4)
† Listwise Deletion of Cases; * Percentages in Parentheses				

Overall, respondents' impressions indicate a closed system—a completely top-down, "take calls" approach to policing that is counter to the benefits of COPS (Gaines et al., 2003). When combined with the lack of participative management encouraged by the former chief and the physical work environment, the circle of involvement and interoperability of police-community relations becomes smaller, rendering it inoperable and non-communicative. In short, police do not talk much to the community, and the community does not reach out in any significant way to the police. During the period of this assessment, remnants of past leadership philosophy, style, and practices persisted in the minds of police personnel in this department, creating resistance and making the transition from "what was" to "what should be" difficult. The hope of what a change at the top of the police hierarchy might bring was coupled with even more adaptation to the new administrator's belief that police-community relations were central to effective policing. This meant that officers would need to adopt such a view as they carried out their daily activities in interacting with the public. An officer explained that this organization:

> ...was never a COP department. We would not [engage in COPS] before because the hierarchy would not encourage citizens' ideas. Right now, relations are a lot stronger because the new Chief is among them and he projects an image of professionalism—I think it's filtering to patrol.

I delivered the final needs assessment report to the chief in 2005. The chief could use it purely as an internal document to address stated concerns of police personnel and to work to heal wounds inflicted by previous administration, but he took a different, more transparent approach. One of the main reasons for requesting the needs assessment initially was to improve police-community relations. He was most concerned about creating an organizational atmosphere within and outside of the agency that would result in mutual respect, trust, and support of the community. Emphasizing safety concerns, professionalization of the police force, and enhanced quality of life for citizens, the chief opened the department up to the public to try to achieve these goals. He and his officers presented the needs assessment to the Board of Selectmen during town council meetings, posted it on the department's website, and regularly interviewed with media. This further showed that the department is progressing in a decidedly new direction. Given the challenges that remain from previous eras and the new ones posed in the homeland security era, this was a significant first step. Inviting community involvement was an attempt to garner their support and confidence in the police department. Officers worked daily on the action recommendations proposed in the report to fulfill their new philosophy, mission, role, and functions. The consistency of their professionalism and effectiveness forced the community to take notice. It was a five-year journey of transition that ultimately resulted in the community voting 81% in favor of contributing higher taxes to authorize the construction of a $4.65 million state-of-the art station for their police personnel. With the community's emotional blessings and financial support, the Seaside Police Department moved into the facility in November 2010.

Conclusion

The history of American policing has demonstrated the need for police agencies to keep pace with, if not ahead of, community needs. The various crises that have occurred brought particular challenges and thus new eras—political era, reform era, community era, and now the homeland security era—that resulted pronounced shifts in police organization, structure, role, function, and technology. Although aspects of COPS may show promise as a policing philosophy, officers' perceptions of their working environment is also an important matter to consider. The delivery of services goes beyond officers' willingness to provide such services; job satisfaction, professionalism, and the style of leadership exposed to daily within the department can influence morale, job performance, and connection to the community. Today's challenges demand that officers be in a strong position to effectively discharge their duties and function as a twenty-first century professional agency. Police need to be equipped to work with residents to detect and control crime, to intervene and prevent terrorist attacks, to reduce fear of crime, and to enhance citizens' overall quality of life. Although individual officers may cultivate healthy one-on-one professional relationships with residents, to ensure the outcomes of effective policing, such efforts must also occur organizationally.

References

Dantzker, M. L. & Surrette, M. A. (1996). The perceived levels of job satisfaction among police officers: A descriptive review. *Journal of Police and Criminal Psychology,* 11 (2): 7-12.

DeLone, G. J. (2007). Law enforcement mission statements post-September 11. *Police Quarterly,* 10 (2): 218-235.

Gaines, L. K., J. L. Worrall, M. D. Southerland & J. E. Angell. (2003). *Police administration* (2nd ed.). New York: McGraw Hill.

Greene, J. R. (1989). Police officer job satisfaction and community perceptions: Implications for community-oriented policing. *Journal of Research in Crime and Delinquency,* 26 (2): 168-183.

James, N. (2011). *Community Oriented Policing Services (COPS): Background, Legislation, and Funding* (Order Code No. RL3308). Washington, D.C.: Congressional Research Service—The Library of Congress.

Oliver, W. M. (2006). The fourth era of policing: Homeland security. *International Review of Law Computers & Technology,* 20 (1 & 2): 49-62.

Peak, K. J. (2012). *Policing America: Challenges and best practices* (7th ed.). Boston, MA: Prentice Hall.

Scott, Y. M. (2005). *Assessing the needs of small-town police departments: Final report.* Retrieved April 2, 2011 from: http://www.swan seapolice.com/forms/assessment.pdf

Skogan, W. G. (1994). The impact of community policing on neighborhood residents: A cross-site analysis. In D. P. Rosenbaum (ed.), *The challenge of community policing: Testing the promises* (pp. 167-181). Thousand Oaks, CA: Sage.

Skogan, W. G. (1990). *Disorder and decline: Crime and the spiral of decay in American neighborhoods.* New York: The Free Press.

Thurman, Q., J. Zhao, & A. L. Giacomazzi. (2001). *Community policing in a community era.* Los Angeles: Roxbury.

U.S. Department of Justice. Office of Justice Programs. National Institute of Justice. (1990, January). *Perspectives on policing: The evolving strategy of police: A minority view,* 13, 1-16. by H. Williams & P. V. Murphy. Washington, DC: U.S. Department of Justice. (NCJ 121019)

U.S. Department of Justice. (1994). *Violent Crime Control and Law Enforcement Act of 1994: Fact sheet.* Retrieved April 17, 2011, from http://www.ncjrs.gov/txtfiles/billfs.txt

Discussion Questions

1. Under what conditions might police be inherently distrustful of citizens?

2. What role does community policing have in the Homeland Security era?

3. Describe how organizational structure and dynamics can affect police behavior.

4. Describe the barriers to effective community policing posed by the physical condition of the Seaside Police Department? Can you think of any community-based organizations or government offices in your community whose physical appearance hinders fulfillment of its goals and mission?

5. What did the Seaside police chief do with the completed needs assessment? Do you think that the Seaside Police Department would be in a different position today if the police chief handled it differently?

6. What benefit would a follow-up study have? Who would you solicit information from and what would you hope to learn?

SECTION 4

RESEARCHING LEGAL ISSUES IN THE CRIMINAL JUSTICE SYSTEM

Section 4
Researching Legal Issues in the Criminal Justice System

INTRODUCTION

This section contains chapters on what happens in courts. As in previous sections, these chapters discuss topics that we think would interest most students and in the process, provide information on how this part of the criminal justice system works.

The first chapter, by Smith and Moore, is on domestic violence shelters. At many colleges and universities, there is substantial student interest in the plight of the victim instead of or in addition to the offender. This chapter may provide the reader with some ideas of how their interest in criminal justice can translate into careers helping others. It is an approach to careers in criminal justice that often does not immediately come to mind but one worthy of consideration. Smith and Moore study nationwide data on shelters and the services they provide. They also study backgrounds of the clients who use these shelters. This gives a reasonable snapshot of the resources and needs that still remain for victim services.

Balboni's chapter is on sexting, the practice of sending sexually explicit text messages. Balboni examines trends in processing sexting cases and points out some of the long-lasting legal ramifications of sexting. She makes clear that in the eyes of the criminal justice system, sexting is not an innocent act and should not be undertaken casually. She also makes policy recommendations.

Mauck's chapter is on what she refers to as the "*CSI* Effect." She shows how the prevalence of crime dramas have affected the court system and jury deliberations and how it has become more difficult to reach guilty verdicts when jurors believe that they should be provided with the kinds of evidence that television shows suggest is available. Her research is based on a survey on potential jurors and shows that there is correlation between television viewing habits and perceptions of forensic evidence.

Floss and Bernstein's chapter illustrates the benefits of pre-program evaluation design. Their involvement in the planning, establishment, and evaluation process of a juvenile youth drug court illustrates how one community sought a solution to a major problem. Specialty courts (sometimes called problem-solving courts) like the one described in this chapter are becoming more prevalent throughout the United States. These courts focus only on select cases. Juvenile drug courts deal with qualifying juvenile offenders whose behavior was determined to have been influenced by underlying drug use or addiction. Juvenile drug use has a well-known connection with juvenile crime and the victimization of our youth. What has not been well documented is the effectiveness of programs such as a well-managed juvenile drug treatment court. Floss and Bernstein have shared their findings and have demonstrated the importance of strong methodical research and the careful interpretation of all sorts of data influencing policy in the area of juvenile offending.

"They Didn't Even Dust the Lawn for Fingerprints:" How *CSI* and Other Crime Dramas Have Affected the Court System and Jury Deliberations

Prior to the development of *CSI: Crime Scene Investigation* and other forensic-based crime dramas, jurors knew little about forensic evidence or how a crime scene was processed. The intense popularity of these programs indicates a fascination with the subject matter—one that continues to expose viewers to criminalistics and forensic science. Many cases presented and scientific techniques practices on *CSI* are fiction, though presented with great realism. These programs could mislead potential jurors on how crime scenes are processed and forensic evidence is analyzed. Consequently, real-life cases might be dismissed by jurors who believed that not enough forensic evidence was presented or properly analyzed. Does this *CSI effect* really exist? Results from questionnaires completed by 177 potential jurors from the Conroe, Texas area revealed an association between television viewing habits and individual perceptions of forensic evidence. The television drama *CSI* did not show a marked difference in viewing habits and perceptions. Further research needs to be conducted to discover the extent to which television plays a part in public perceptions and to better understand what impact forensic-based crime dramas like *CSI* has on juror expectations and case outcomes.

After Teens Click and Press Send: Sexting and the Law

The phenomenon of *sexting*, the transmission of nude or semi-nude photos via digital communication, has exploded in frequency among young people in the United States over the last several years. Police and prosecutors have responded using existing tools, including invoking child pornography statutes, which can involve serious social and financial consequences. Legislatures have contemplated how to address the issue, with varying responses. Some carved out minor-to-minor exceptions or tried to effectively minimize legal consequences for minors; other states have made it easier to prosecute these youth by modifying existing child pornography statutes to include more explicit language regarding online and digital communication. This chapter will examine trends in processing sexting cases through existing statutes and designing new legislation to more succinctly deal with this behavior. Policy recommendations will be proposed.

Domestic Violence Shelters: Services Provided, Requested, and Received

Domestic violence shelter networks have grown substantially over the last several decades and are considered a critical element in responding to domestic violence. However, additional research is needed before definitive conclusions are made regarding the effectiveness of shelter-based services. This study uses data collected from shelter programs in eight states to examine those shelters' volume, accessibility, and diversity of services provided. In addition, we used data collected from shelter clients to examine demographic information, the types of help clients requested upon entrance to a shelter, and the degree to which they received each type of help during their shelter stay. This study found that programs offered a variety of services to meet the complex needs of their clients, including specialized and culturally sensitive services, but offered very few child-related services. Clients requested an average of 16 services when they entered a shelter, but the types varied according to the race and age of the client. Client education, race, and the number of children with them influenced the extent to which their needs were met while in a shelter. These findings demonstrate the substantial diversity existing among clients and services offered in domestic violence shelters. Future research should further delineate the types of services needed for different populations and explore how programs can best tailor their services to meet the needs of clients represented.

Examining the Quality and Effectiveness of a County Juvenile Treatment (Drug) Court

Concerns about the health and well-being of the youth in one Upstate New York community led local criminal justice leaders, health professionals, and academics to form a team that would proactively seek out a plan to reduce teenage pregnancy, high school drop-out rates, and an increased drug usage. A key element of what would become a highly successful juvenile drug court treatment plan was the careful planning and multi-method research design and evaluation that would track the successes and weaknesses of the program. The assessment of these data contributed to this community's ability to understand the role of substance abuse in leading some juvenile toward criminal activity. Juvenile drug court treatment plans need to be able to accurately determine the outcomes of their efforts and this chapter provides a classic example of how that can be done.

Chapter 11
"THEY DIDN'T EVEN DUST THE LAWN FOR FINGERPRINTS": HOW *CSI* AND OTHER CRIME DRAMAS HAVE AFFECTED THE COURT SYSTEM AND JURY DELIBERATIONS

Melissa J. Mauck, M.A., Sam Houston State University

Introduction

When that memorable song starts to play and the kaleidoscope of scenes race by the screen, the room falls silent and all turn their attention to the large box in the center of the room. Millions of homes in America tune in to watch the crime scene investigators of *CSI: Crime Scene Investigation* (Bruckheimer, 2000-2009) perform whimsical forensic techniques, collecting seemingly impossible amounts of forensic evidence and dodging suspects' bullets, all while keeping their hair and makeup intact. The hit television show *CSI: Crime Scene Investigation* has sparked a keen interest in forensic chemistry and crime scene investigation; but according to recent studies, it might have gone too far. The scenes that fill the television screen are those of drama-filled moments when forensic evidence is found in pristine condition, leading the crime scene investigators straight to the correct suspect. What many people do not realize is that some of the techniques, analytical approaches, collection methods, and general happenings in the depicted crime lab are simply impossible to perform or complete.

The forensics-based crime drama *CSI: Crime Scene Investigation* created nationwide interest in forensics that has remained unsurpassed by any other crime-based drama of recent years. The stir created by this series has opened many generations' eyes to the world of forensic chemistry and the field of criminal justice. This new sense of alertness has both hindered and helped the field of criminal justice and forensic study. The typical person watching the series might believe most forensic work and proceedings of the criminal justice system are real and correctly portrayed. In fact, many techniques and proceedings shown in the series are impossible in the real world due to lack of funding, time, and staff. Further, some portrayals on the series have perpetuated stereotypes and false perceptions, such as the thought that crime scene technicians work a crime scene then go into the lab to process the evidence they collected. In actuality, the crime scene technicians who locate and collect evidence from crime scenes hand the evidence over to the forensic scientists in a laboratory to analyze. Many people are also

151

misinformed about the process of analyzing forensic evidence collected. It takes much more time than portrayed in the series. For example, the average DNA test can take months, leaving police agencies in limbo while they wait for results. Fingerprints are not always apparently visible on different surfaces as the drama shows; in fact, some crime scenes yield no prints at all. Although common for television's *CSI* investigators, partial prints are incredibly hard to match to a known fingerprint. This depiction of fingerprint analysis is not consistent with reality.

The computer system named Combined DNA Index System (CODIS) that identifies and matches fingerprints entered into the system can take days and even months to find a match, if it finds one at all. On *CSI*, investigators never wait that long.

The question that arises out of these discrepancies is how it affects the real-life court and criminal justice systems. If potential jury members are watching *CSI*, their viewing habits might transfer into an expectation that physical evidence must be presented at trial. This hypothesized phenomenon is known as the *CSI effect*: it results in amplification of an individual's expectation of forensic evidence and interest in the field itself because of the program. Does this phenomenon really exist and to what extent? Does watching *CSI* and other forensic-based crime dramas influence an individual's opinions of forensic science and evidence collection? If so, does that then influence their decisions as jurors? Does the viewing of these crime dramas increase the burden of proof placed on the prosecution, leaving juries wanting more forensic evidence? If the *CSI effect* exists, prosecutors need to consider how this could impact trial proceedings and juror deliberations, and if the *CSI effect* is shown to create an unfair advantage for either the prosecution or defense, the justice system would need to devise a plan to combat these effects.

Review of the Literature

Before the study of the relationship between crime dramas and the criminal justice system became popular, researchers, prosecutors, and defense counsel saw the benefit of studying jury behaviors and decisions. Prosecutors and defense attorneys could potentially use such information to choose jurors who might give them the outcome they desire. Voir dire, the practice of questioning potential jurors for selection in a trial, is very important and has evolved to include opinions about race, gender, occupation, and even television viewing habits. Jurors are asked these questions to see if they are biased in any way that might sway their judgment in a case, giving one side an unfair advantage (Vidmar & Hans, 2007). Either lawyer can have a potentially biased prospective juror removed through use of a challenge for cause. Additionally, each lawyer may remove a certain number of potential jurors using peremptory challenges, which allow them to eliminate an individual from the pool without needing to state a reason. Prosecutors and defense attorneys may use "juror consultants," focused on the art of reading potential jury members or other scientific jury selection (SJS) tools, to help them decide whom to pick for their individual cases (and whom to eliminate via peremptory challenge).

Research has shown that social climate on crime issues and the gender of trial counsel significantly affects the way jury members decide cases, especially criminal cases (Devine et al., 2001). Only in recent years has television viewing habits been assessed when questioning potential jury members. Television dramas such as *CSI: Crime Scene Investigation* changed the way the public views not only the criminal justice system, but also the role of forensic evidence and court proceedings. The type of television programs the prospective juror watches occasionally affects jury selection. Defense attorneys choose jurors who watch these programs because they are more likely to notice the absence of forensic evidence (Mopas, 2007). Research suggests that compared with those who do not watch such dramas, jurors who are tuning in hold different thoughts and opinions concerning evidence in criminal cases and believe these shows portray the real inner workings of a crime lab and criminal investigations. A survey of 500 potential jury members in a pool found that 70 percent watched crime shows (Hughes & Magers, 2007). Knowing the possible effect of crime shows, prosecutors and defense attorneys heavily consider these factors when choosing potential jury members for trial.

Crime dramas have been around for decades: from the murder mysteries of *Perry Mason* and *Murder She Wrote* to more recent dramas, such as *Law and Order*, forensic-based *CSI: Crime Scene Investigation*, and *Without a Trace*. Through the development of this genre of programs, mainly the introduction of *CSI: Crime Scene Investigation* and its many spinoffs, the focus on forensics and crime labs is more popular than ever. With this growing fan base comes a belief that the techniques and machines utilized are real and infallible; a dangerous confidence accompanies a false understanding. Are jurors believing everything they see on *CSI: Crime Scene Investigation* and related crime dramas and basing their judgments in court on them? The U.S. Supreme Court and the American Bar Association have recognized that television shapes an individual's thoughts and opinions of the criminal justice system (Anderson, 1999). With crime dramas shaping the public's mind concerning investigations, the criminal justice system must work even harder to maintain integrity through assuring the accuracy of jurors' beliefs.

The *CSI effect* may be defined as the interest created for the field of forensic science from the hit TV series *CSI: Crime Scene Investigation*. Various definitions are associated with the term *CSI effect*, but most commonly it refers to:

> *The phenomenon in which jurors hold unrealistic expec-*
> *tations of forensic evidence and investigation techniques, and*
> *have an increased interest in the discipline of forensic science*
> *because of the influence of CSI-type television shows. This effect*
> *includes raising the state's burden of proof because of jury*
> *expectations that forensic evidence should always be discussed at*
> *trial, and the belief that forensic evidence is never wrong.*
> (Robbers, 2008, p. 86)

Other definitions refer to the effect of these crime-based television programs on prosecution, scientific evidence, and juror knowledge (Podlas, 2006). The misconceptions that arise concerning funding, available resources, and time management can prevent the courts from conducting a fair trial. For example, one juror eloquently demonstrated how little the public really understands fingerprinting by criticizing crime scene investigators because, "They didn't even dust the lawn for fingerprints" (Shelton, 2007, p. 2). This statement was made by a juror when asked why the jury did not find the defendant guilty in a criminal trial and shows that the juror's grasp of forensic evidence was not as sophisticated as they might have thought.

Another misconception presented in crime dramas relates to the databases technicians use. For example, *CSI* investigators use fingerprint databases that turn up 'hits' or matches in a matter of minutes. Realistically, it may take days, sometimes months, in these databases to sift through the thousands to millions of fingerprints on file. Also, the different databases that technicians are accessing are only available to a select group of people, and in some cases, do not even exist or work in the same capacity in real life. Similarly, software programs that place fingerprint fragments together electronically or that look up paint colors of cars and match them to an individual car either do not exist or do not work in the same capacity as portrayed on television. In all criminal cases, the burden of proving guilt rests on the prosecution. Prosecutors must prove beyond a reasonable doubt that the individual committed the crime. Beyond a reasonable doubt was defined by the courts in *People v. Bennett* in 1872 and expanded in *People v. Smith* in 1900 (Podlas, 2006). It can be defined as: the evidence excludes to a moral certainty every hypothesis but guilt (*People v. Bennett*); the inference of guilt is the only one that can be drawn from the facts; or the evidence excludes every hypothesis of innocence (*People v. Smith*). Many legal commentators put the percentage of certainty associated with reasonable doubt around 90%. However, many jurors apparently require only approximately 70% certainty when deciding cases (Lillquist, 2002). If the *CSI effect* exists, the state's burden of proof would effectively be increased, and *beyond a reasonable doubt* in essence becomes *any and all doubt*, effectively increasing certainty to 100% (Podlas, 2006, p. 452).

A competing definition of the *CSI effect* focuses on the misleading characteristics that can lead a juror to believe scientific or forensic evidence blindly. Evidence can be compromised in different ways, and, in some cases, without the scientists' awareness. With the knowledge obtained from various crime and forensic television dramas, the public may be led to believe forensic science is infallible (Podlas, 2006, p.437). On television, forensic evidence is always portrayed in a positive light and is always accurate and imparts the truth. Many courts have warned that scientific or forensic evidence can have a persuasive effect on the jury (*U.S. v. Addison*, 1974). Thus, a *CSI effect* could create a potent combination of infallibility and blind trust. On crime dramas, evidence leads the examiners to the person(s) responsible for the crime and seldom shows how evidence can lead an examiner to the wrong individual. Moreover, DNA testing is only as good as the technician who is performing the test because it can be "interpreted differently by different technicians" (Thompson, 1997, p. 405). Many techniques used by crime labs nationwide have not been empirically tested and may not be accepted in the scientific community, yet they are still used to present evidence in court. Fingerprinting has been used for decades for identification purposes but does not have an existing empirical literature that verifies its accuracy. Also affecting forensic evidence credibility is that crime labs do not have to be accredited, and there exists no professional standard for forensic experts to follow in the labs and testify in court (Podlas, 2006, p. 440).

Another competing definition of the *CSI effect* focuses on the increased awareness of the public toward the field of forensic study. This idea states that the increase in interest in the field of forensic science has created more funding and can even make people look forward to jury duty, a once dreaded task (Podlas, 2006, p. 442). This definition holds that the *CSI effect* actually creates better-educated individuals who can more properly assess the situations and forensic testimony. This, in effect, states that *CSI*-like shows are educational to the public and provide viewers with an inside look into the workings of forensics and police work (Podlas, 2006, p. 442). Although this may be true, if the lessons being taught to the public are plagued with inaccuracies, they can transfer into courtroom proceedings and decisions.

Current research on the *CSI effect* strives to discover the real thoughts and opinions of potential jurors and the public. Does the public really believe that prosecutors should present scientific or forensic evidence in every case in order to reach a guilty verdict? Podlas (2006) examined how the viewing of *CSI* and other related shows changed students' perceptions and decisions in relation to criminal cases. She found that the most common types of crimes investigated on the television show were murders and rapes (Podlas, 2006, p. 454). In her analysis of viewing habits and decisions on a hypothetical criminal case, Podlas (2006) found no link between *CSI* viewing and an anti-prosecution type of attitude.

Robbers (2008) conducted a survey of prosecutors, public defenders, and judges from all over the United States. Most respondents, 85%, believed that their responsibilities changed after the development of *CSI*, mostly in the form of spending more time at trial explaining and discussing forensic and scientific evidence. In addition, 79% believed that television programming focusing on forensic and scientific evidence influenced verdicts and outcomes at trial. They noted that with the presence of any scientific or forensic evidence, guilty verdicts were easier to achieve, while cases without forensic evidence were almost impossible to convict (Robbers, 2008). According to Shelton et al. (2006), the most common *CSI* viewers were female and politically moderate, and those with less education were more likely to watch *CSI* than more highly educated people. Shelton (2007) tested juror perception of *CSI* programming reality. The more an individual watched *CSI*, the more likely they were to perceive the television drama to be true to life. Some potential jurors expected to see forensic evidence presented at a trial. Shelton's (2007) interviews of potential jurors found that 46% believed they needed to see some kind of scientific evidence in every criminal case.

Shelton et al. (2006) found that expectations concerning types of forensic evidence correlated with the different types of crimes committed. In the case of murders or attempted murders, 46% of respondents believed there needed to be DNA evidence presented, whereas 73% of respondents expected DNA evidence in rape cases. For breaking and entering cases, 71% of respondents expected fingerprint evidence, with 59 percent believing it needed to be present in all theft cases. About two-thirds, 66%, expected fingerprints in cases involving a gun (Shelton et al., 2006).

In relation to the differences between *CSI* and non-*CSI* viewers, *CSI* viewers in the Shelton et al. (2006) study generally expected more evidence to be present in criminal cases, but there was a marked difference in the types of evidence that was expected by the different groups. *CSI* viewers did not expect evidence to be presented if it were not relevant to the case at hand. The authors note that the most important question answered by the study was whether or not viewing these television programs affected the viewer's likelihood of handing down a guilty verdict. The study showed that even though high percentages of the *CSI* respondents expected forensic evidence to be present in certain cases, it did not translate into a breakdown in guilty verdicts. Although

"They Didn't Even Dust the Lawn for Fingerprints": How CSI and   **157**
    Other Crime Dramas Have Affected the Court System and
    Jury Deliberations

forensic evidence may not be presented, respondents were more likely to find a defendant guilty, whether they watched crime dramas or not, except for in rape cases (Shelton et al., 2006).

Methods

In order to assess the relationship between juror decisions and forensic-based television viewing, I distributed a survey questionnaire to prospective jury members. These were people summoned for jury duty in Conroe, Texas but who ultimately were not selected. This approach maximized the external validity advantages discussed above related to Shelton's et al. (2006) research. Using the Shelton approach as a guide, the questionnaire contained four parts, which related not only to television programming, but also to the infallibility of forensic evidence, the perceived reality of different types of programming (drama, reality, and comedy programming), and the types of evidence required for conviction in different types of criminals cases. The survey requested demographic questions relating to political orientation, sex, age, income, education, children, ethnicity, and occupation.

Choosing prospective jury members as participants allowed me to gauge the impact crime-based television shows might have on those members of the public who actually could be deciding the outcomes of real cases. After members of the jury pool were selected for the various court proceedings of the day, I invited the remaining jury-eligible individuals to participate anonymously in the study. In all, 177 potential jurors returned completed questionnaires. This approach ensured that potential jury members who were chosen to serve on juries would not have their deliberations affected by questions listed in the survey.

I hypothesized that there would be a positive correlation between time spent viewing crime dramas and expectations relative to forensic evidence. I analyzed responses from questionnaires to assess possible correlations among viewing habits, perceived reality of crime dramas, and types of evidence believed necessary for different types of convictions. (I also performed analyses on demographic variables.) Survey questions asked participants about their beliefs about the realism in the different types of programming, knowledge of forensic science, and opinions about forensic evidence required. Respondents indicated the different types of evidence they thought should be required for convictions in various cases. Respondents described their television viewing habits, including the types of programming watched and duration of viewing. These data were included to control for the other dependent variables in the questionnaire and to determine whether a correlation exists between types of programming viewed on opinions of forensics and evidence.

Results

I performed several descriptive tests on the demographic variables. Most respondents (65.3%) were from ages 41 to 60, with only 5% of respondents being from 18 to 30. Respondents were closely distributed between the sexes (52.8% male). In the case of household income, the respondents were closely matched, with 30.4% having a household income of $100,000 or more. The majority of respondents attended at least some college (85.9%), with 39.4% holding a college degree, reflecting the demographics of the community from which the sample was drawn. Respondents were predominantly white—88% Caucasian, 3.6% African American, 4.2% Hispanic, and 4.2% other. Only 26.7% of respondents described themselves as single, and most had children (79.8%). As far as political orientation is concerned, 1.9% claimed they were liberal, 63.7% conservative, and the remaining 34.4% did not identify themselves as liberal or conservative. Only 8.8% of respondents had taken some kind of forensic-based class. Despite the low level of formal training in the subject, only 32.1% claimed to have no knowledge of forensic science or evidence.

Discussion

When respondents were asked whether or not forensic evidence should be present at every criminal trial, the majority of those surveyed (50.6%) responded that they agreed or strongly agreed that it must be present to convict. This imposes a significant burden of proof for the prosecution in the eyes of the majority of the public, as jurors expect some kind of forensic evidence presented in every criminal trial. In many cases, however, there is no forensic evidence, for a variety of legitimate reasons. Because of this unsatisfied expectation, juries may be less likely to convict at criminal trials where prosecutors do not present forensic evidence, possibly leading to the release of factually guilty offenders into society.

Respondents were also asked viewpoints concerning whether or not forensic evidence is foolproof. More than 50% of respondents (59.1%) disagreed or strongly disagreed with the statement that forensic evidence is foolproof. This might mean that respondents understand that there is a level of error associated with forensic evidence, but researchers do not know by how much or what their level of understanding really is when it comes to the fallibility of forensic science. Even though the majority of those surveyed stated that they would require forensic evidence to be present in order to convict in a criminal case, they did not believe forensic evidence is foolproof.

This phenomenon of expecting, but not fully trusting, forensic evidence is perplexing and may present some difficulty when it comes to combating the issue of increased burden of proof. The only age group that strongly agreed that forensic evidence is foolproof was the 61 to 70 age range. Older generations might have less knowledge of forensics and the ongoing operations of the criminal justice system, affecting their perceptions of forensic evidence presented at trial. Also, they may think that if the scientific community has stated that these techniques are credible, then they are in no position to question it.

A rather large disparity was evidenced in respondents' viewpoints concerning convicting without forensic evidence if other evidence was present in relation to burglary cases. The majority of those surveyed (82.5%) agreed or strongly agreed that they could convict at a burglary trial as long as other evidence was present, even if no forensic evidence existed. Also, in the case of victimless crimes, 68.2% of respondents could also convict an offender even if no forensic evidence was presented, as long as other evidence existed. Responses to both murder and rape cases remained evenly distributed on this variable. What is it about victimless and burglary crimes that make them easier to convict without forensic evidence? One thing that is missing in these crimes is personal contact with the victims. Murder and rape cases are extremely personal crimes and can have a significant impact on both the physical and mental state of the victim. Although this might be true of burglary offenses in rare cases, the majority of burglary offenses are very impersonal, and victimless crime effects can be quite abstract. This may account for the variation in viewpoints concerning the different types of cases. However, the majority of the responses to questions concerning forensic evidence at trial reveal that potential jury members view forensic evidence as an extremely important part of a court case, regardless of the charges.

The survey asked respondents to identify their perceptions on the reality of different types of television programming; 36.1% of respondents stated that they strongly agreed or agreed that crime drama programming portrayed reality. This type of programming received the highest number of respondents agreeing that it portrayed reality. This could be due to its relatively new appeal or personal dealings with the criminal justice system. If an individual has no idea about the criminal justice system and how it operates, he or she may take these television programs at face value, believing that they portray reality. In the cases of comedy, drama, and reality programming, individuals have experience with the different types of situations portrayed, as these types of programming generally address everyday life events and tribulations.

However, crime programming incorporates processes and ideas that individuals may never have experienced.

The portrayal of reality is a topic that fascinates many who study public perceptions. Do individuals blindly believe what they view on television, or is there a screening process involved that parcels out good information from the bad? Of those surveyed, only 36.1% agreed or strongly agreed that crime drama programming portrayed reality. Respondents agreed that crime dramas portrayed reality to a greater extent than any other type of programming. It seems that the public believes, at least in part, that crime dramas accurately portray reality. This could account for the increase in potential jurors' expectations of forensic or scientific evidence in court. The criminal justice system has seen a change in the average citizen due in part to their exposure to the inner-workings of the system. Moreover, these changes have resulted in attitudes and beliefs that vary systematically with certain variables.

The relationship among education level and other variables demonstrated an interesting pattern. On the one hand, persons with higher education levels were less likely to report a belief in the infallibility of forensic evidence. One the other hand, they expressed a willingness to convict, at least in burglary cases, even without such evidence. Perhaps more highly educated people approach evidence more objectively than those with lower education levels. That is, they will neither be over-persuaded by the presence of nor under-persuaded by the absence of forensic evidence. Indeed, that their willingness to convict in the absence of forensic evidence seemed to be confined to burglary cases may reveal that they are particularly discerning. Because of the relationship between income level and education, it is not surprising that the income variable showed a similar pattern of correlations. Both education level and income were negatively correlated with the variable associated with other television viewing habits (those shows that were not explicitly listed, such as *Law and Order* or *CSI*). The total amount of television viewed in a single week was significantly higher for persons of lower income and education. Like education, as respondents' income levels rose, so too did the expressed confidence in their ability to convict someone of rape or murder based on the absence of forensic evidence.

Analysis of the variable associated with the perceptions of how foolproof television shows showed significance with the amount of television subjects viewed and the types of television shows watched, including *CSI* and *Law and Order*. This illustrates that there is an association between the two variables, meaning that how participants feel about the infallibility of forensic science is associated with how much television they watch. After accounting for controls, such as age, gender, and education level, the significance increased. This is surprising because generally when controls are added to an ordinal regression equation, significance level decreases between variables. This phenomenon also occurred when subject responses concerning evidence needed in murder trials were compared with how much *Law & Order* they viewed. Here, participants' perceptions of whether or not forensic evidence is required to convict in a murder trial is associated with the viewing of all *Law & Order* programs.

Subject responses concerning evidence at rape trials demonstrated significance before controls were added with the amount of *Law & Order* they watched, meaning that an association exists between respondents' perceptions of forensic evidence needed at rape cases and their viewing habits of the television show *Law & Order* and its affiliates. The *Law & Order* variable's significance level decreased slightly when controls were added to the aggression, showing that the covariates did not affect the association between the variables substantially. Subject responses concerning evidence at rape trials were also associated with the amount of television respondent's watched after controls were introduced. This shows that there is an association between the amount of television respondents' watched and their requirement of forensic evidence in a rape case. The fact that these two variables changed significance levels only after controls were introduced illustrates that the controls actually negated some outside influences that were present in the original ordinal regression.

Subject responses concerning evidence at murder trials showed significant associations with other variables. Before controls were added, an association was found between the amount of *Law & Order* viewed and perceptions of the amount of forensic evidence needed to convict in a murder trial. After controls were introduced, the *Law & Order* significance level increased, showing an even greater association between the variables. Also, the variables associated with the amount of television individuals watched, specifically *CSI*, showed significance with subject responses concerning evidence at murder trials after controls were introduced. This is the first time the variable *CSI* (how much *CSI* respondents viewed) appeared to have an association with another variable examined. This may be due to the types of crime portrayed by the television show: most offenses appearing on *CSI* are murders or a combination of murder and another offense. This could skew the views of *CSI* watchers in relation to murder trials and forensic evidence.

Conclusion

Overall, data show a correlation between television viewing habits and perceptions of forensic evidence. The amount of television an individual watched was found to have a significant association with how foolproof the individual believed forensic evidence to be. The amount of television watched was significantly associated with perceptions of forensic evidence needed at rape trials. Subjects who watched *CSI* had increased expectations of forensic evidence at murder trials. These findings illustrate that television viewing is associated with perceptions of individuals. There also existed a correlation between the amount of education individuals possessed and perceptions of the infallibility of forensic science. This is an important finding of the study. It seems that as education level rises, individual perceptions related to the infallibility of forensic evidence and its presence at trial changes. Those more highly educated do not necessarily require forensic evidence to be present in court to convict, and they do not believe forensic evidence to be infallible.

Although this research showed an association between television viewing habits and perceptions of forensic evidence, its extent is unknown. What is known is that the correlations revealed in this study, though statistically significant, were fairly small. Along these lines, *CSI* did not produce a large correlation with perceptions of forensic evidence in relation to different case types other than murder.

If a *CSI effect* does exist, it would be expected that it would be represented in more than one area. If television viewing plays a role in the formation of perceptions of the criminal justice system, how do we combat this effect? One way is to address this issue before individuals serve on juries. Perhaps statements could be placed before television programs are aired, stating that the program they are about to watch is not an accurate portrayal of the criminal justice system, its practices, and forensic science. More important, if the *CSI effect* exists, prosecutors must then change the way they address juries and prepare for cases. It may not be plausible to entirely halt the effect of television, but the criminal justice system can learn to evolve with the changing perceptions and address these issues in court. The *CSI effect* needs to be investigated further to determine whether it truly does exist, with a much larger demographic and in different regions across the United States. With this knowledge, the court system could combat some of the effects of television, making the justice system a more balanced and controlled environment.

References

Anderson, P. (1999). American Bar Association report on perceptions of the U.S. Justice System. *Albany Law Review,* 1307, 1319-1327.

Arkes, H. R., & Mellers, B. A. (2002). Do juries meet our expectations? *Law and Human Behavior,* 26(6), 625-639.

Boatswain v. State of Delaware, 872 A.2d 959 (2005).

Bounds, J. D. (2008). Perry Mason. *The Museum of Broadcast Communications.* Retrieved from http://www.museum.tv/archives/etv/P/html P/perrymason/perrymason.htm

Brickell, W. (2008). Is it the *CSI effect* or do we just distrust juries? *Criminal Justice,* 23(8), 10-17. Retrieved from ProQuest Database.

Briody, M. (2004). The effects of DNA evidence on homicide cases in court. *Australian and New Zealand Journal of Criminology,* 27(2), 231-253.

Bruckheimer, J. (Producer). (2000-2009). *CSI: Crime Scene Investigation* [Television series]. Hollywood, CA: CBS Broadcasting Inc.

Cf. Coffin v. United States, 156 U.S. 432 (1895).

Devine, D. J., Clayton, L. D., Dunford, B. B., Seying, R., & Price, J. (2001). Jury decision making : 54 years of empirical research on deliberating groups. *Psychology, Public Policy, and Law,* 7(3), 622-727.

Douthit, R. & Regler, T. (Producer). (1996-2009). *Judge Judy* [Television series]. Hollywood, CA: CBS Broadcasting Inc.

Gamson, W. A., Croteau, D., Hoynes, W., & Sasson, T. (1992). Media images and the social construction of reality. *Annual Review of Sociology,* 18, 373-393.

Gerbner, G., Gross, L., Morgan, M., & Signorielli, N. (1980). Some additional comments on cultivation analysis. *The Public Opinion Quarterly,* 44 (3), 408-410.

Hallgrimsdotter, H. K., Phillips, R., & Benoit, C. (2006). Fallen women and rescued girls: Social stigma and media narratives of the sex industry in Victoria, B. C., from 1980 to 2005. *Canadian Review of Sociology and Anthropology,* 43(3), 265-280.

In Re Winship, 397 U.S. 358, 364 (1970).

Koehler, J. J. (2001). When are people persuaded by DNA match statistics? *Law and Human Behavior,* 25(5), 493-513.

Lillquist, E. (2002). Recasting reasonable doubt: Decision theory and the virtues of variability, 36 U.C. Davis L. Rev. 85, 112 (2002).

Miles v. United States, 103 U.S. 304, 312 (1881).

Mopas, M. (2007). Examining the *'CSI Effect'* through an ANT Lens. *Crime Media Culture,* 3(1), 110-117.

Nielson Media Group. (2006). *CSI remains top-scripted television series.* Retrieved November 10, 2008 from http://www.nielsonmedia.com.

Peelo, M., Francis, B., Soothill, K., Pearson, J., & Ackerly, E. (2004). Newspaper reporting and the public construction of homicide. *British Journal of Criminology,* 44 (2), 256-275.

People v. Bennett, 9 N.Y. 137, 144 (1872).

People v. Bennett, 49 N.Y. 520, 144 (1872).

People v. Smith, 162 N.Y. 520, 528-529 (App. Ct. 1900).

Podlas, K. (2006). *"The CSI Effect"*: Exposing the media myth. *Fordham Intellectual Property,* Media, and Entertainment Law Journal, 16, 429-465.

Roane, K. R. (2005). *"The CSI Effect:* How TV is driving jury verdicts all across America." *US News & World,* p. 48.

Robbers, M. L. (2008). Blinded by science: The social construction of reality in forensic television shows and its effect on criminal jury trials. *Criminal Justice Policy Review,* 19(1). 84-102. Retrieved from http://cjp.sagepub.com/cgi/reprint/19/1/84.

Shelton, D. E. (2007). The *'CSI Effect'* : Does it really exist? *National Institute of Justice Journal,* 259. Retrieved November 12, 2008 from http://www.ojp.usdoj.gov/nij/journals/259/csi-effect.htm.

Shelton, D. E., Kim, Y. S., & Barak, G. (2006). A study of juror expectations and demands concerning scientific evidence: Does the *'CSI Effect'* exist? *Vanderbilt Journal of Entertainment and Technology Law,* 9(2), 331-368.

Thompson, W. C. (1997). Accepting lower standards: The National Research Council's second report on forensic DNA evidence. *Jurimetrics,* 37, 405, 412.

U.S. v. Addison, 498 F.2d 741, 744 (D.C. Cir. 1974).

Vergeer, M., Lubbers, M., & Scheepers, P. (2000). Exposure to newspapers and attitudes toward ethnic minorities: A longitudinal analysis. *Howard Journal of Communications,* 11(2), 127-143.

Discussion Questions

1. Describe how *CSI: Crime Scene Investigation* provides inaccurate information on crime scene processing.

2. Describe the phenomenon known as the *CSI effect.* How do definitions provided differ?

3. What is the benefit of studying jury behavior and decisions?

4. Mauck distributed survey questionnaires to prospective jurors. Describe the process of locating these subjects. What ethical issues were involved in selecting the participants?

5. If a *CSI effect* truly does exist, what policy/procedure changes, if any, would you propose?

Chapter 12
AFTER TEENS CLICK AND PRESS SEND: SEXTING AND THE LAW

Jennifer M. Balboni, Ph.D. Curry College

Introduction

"If you don't send your boyfriend naked pictures, then I feel bad for him."

— Pop megastar Rihanna,
on whether she regretted sexting her
former beau after the pictures later hit the
World Wide Web (BBC, 2009)

The phenomenon of sexting, the transmission of nude or semi-nude photos via digital communication, has exploded in frequency among young people in the United States over the last several years. In one large-scale study, 33% of teen boys and 25% of teen girls claim to have been exposed, in some way, to such photos that were initially intended to be private (National Campaign to Prevent Teen and Unplanned Pregnancy, 2009). This type of behavior may be shocking to some, but for many teens, evidence suggests that the practice is often viewed as a form of cyber-flirting and bravado (MTV, 2010). Rihanna's response, when questioned about the widely publicized nude photos of her, emphasizes the idea that sexting is neither inappropriate nor consequential for young people; other celebrity sexting incidents have reinforced this idea. Similar to Rihanna, rocker Pete Wentz and *High School Musical* star, Vanessa Hudgens also had risqué pictures (originally intended to be private) of themselves posted online (Hewitt, 2009). Interestingly, the incidents appear to have no serious long-term implications for the young stars. The lack of scandal may normalize the already prevalent behavior in many teens' eyes.

In stark contrast to celebrity nonchalance on the issue, the legal system has begun to deal with what this behavior means and whether it is, in fact, a crime. Although teens may not believe their behavior is inappropriate, sexting images of minors may fall under federal and state child pornography statutes. Taking the actual photo could constitute creating child pornography, sending the photo could constitute distributing child pornography, and keeping the photo could constitute possession of child pornography. The legal ramifications for such charges are steep: besides all the usual implications of a felony conviction (such as serving time in prison, probation, etc.), convictions under such laws can include registry on sex offender lists. Such registries, initially intended to protect the public by informing them about sexual predators in the community, can carry lifelong consequences that restrict people's ability to live in specific areas (for instance, near school zones), to attend college, or to work in certain occupations (such as teachers, nurses, or sports coaches).

In an effort to deal with the phenomenon of sexting, many state legislatures created focus groups to study the issue or introduced anti-sexting legislation; and at least eight states effectively passed such legislation (NCSL, 2010; NCSL, 2009). The goals of such legislation have differed: some laws have explicitly closed loopholes in child pornography statutes, identifying sexting as a crime and applying serious penalties; other legislation has tried to adjust penalties for juveniles involved in sexting, through decriminalization or referrals to juvenile court. Many states have initiated legislation designed to educate youth before the behavior becomes a problem.

This chapter will present a content analysis of this legislation, exploring both the intended and the unintended consequences. The chapter will also present a review of the legal concerns associated with minor-to-minor sexting, including issues of voluntariness and coercion, using a review of articles in major newspapers in 2009 and 2010. Finally, alternative strategies, using education and awareness programs will be discussed.

Methodology

To better understand sexting as a legal entity, I began by searching Lexis/Nexis, reviewing federal and state statutes, court rulings, public records, and other news sources. Using Lexis/Nexis and multiple other search engines, I found recent legislation to review for content analysis. Through these analyses, I also reviewed media coverage to understand trends in prosecuting sexting cases. I developed typologies to help categorize the trends in prosecution and new sexting legislation.

Voluntariness and Distribution

Before delving into case law or recent legislation, it is important to consider voluntariness and distribution, which deeply complicate the legal issue of sexting. One youth sending a picture to his or her significant other may seem fairly innocuous, and some might think this behavior is perhaps best left for parents to deal with. Unfortunately for the youth, the shelf life in cyberspace for such photos can be forever; photos that may have started as impetuous flirtation can be distributed "downstream," ending up viewed by people it was never intended for (Richards & Calvert, 2009). In effect, disseminating such photos may be the new millennium's "locker room" talk—a way for teens to brag about their sexual accomplishments. However, downstreaming is, at best, exploitive; at worst, it is harassing and damaging. The idea that such pictures are permanently "out there" in cyberspace could be devastating to a young person, ruining one's reputation and jeopardizing social standing in myriad ways. Recently, there have been two documented cases where teenagers committed suicide after pictures of them were distributed beyond the primary party (Singal, 2010). Unlike the starlets who seem to have weathered sexting blips relatively unscathed, "real-world" sexting carries both short and potentially long-term legal, social, and personal consequences for those involved.

Sexting and Prosecutorial Discretion

Police and prosecutors have struggled with how to approach sexting, with varying responses. Until 2009, no laws explicitly dealt with sexting. Lacking specific legislation, some prosecutors invoked existing child pornography statutes to such cases. Although it is well recognized that these statutes were originally intended to address adults sexually exploiting youth, many state statutes do not specify that the perpetrator must be over the age of majority (the age of when one is considered an "adult"), leaving an opening for prosecutors to charge youth involved under these statutes. A Berkshire, Massachusetts, District Attorney commented:

> To be clear, we do not want to use the criminal justice system to punish young people for making poor choices using communication technology. This behavior, however, can have devastating and long-term consequences for all involved. As a result, many jurisdictions have felt compelled to use the criminal justice system, and we will as well if appropriate and necessary (2010, p 2).

Further, because of the way some states wrote child pornography laws, both sender and receiver can be prosecuted—even if the receiver may not have known what was in the cellular message (Diaz, 2009).

Some legal professionals criticize the viewing of sexting cases through the same lens that child pornography cases are. Critics charge that most sexting images to date would not meet the standard legal definition of pornography. As one defense attorney put:

> We're largely dealing with erotic-type photos, topless photos, sometimes girls covering their breasts. That's a lot of what you see coming out with celebrities today as well…. The anecdotal evidence suggests that the majority of photos wouldn't even meet

the federal [child pornography] standard (Richards and Calvert, 2009, p 13).

Despite this, these photos of minors are shocking to adults, and many in law enforcement assume (correctly or otherwise) that such photos constitute child pornography. Prosecutors, however, may use other charging options for some of these cases: broadly phrased harassment or transmission of lewd material statutes could potentially be used in these cases. More commonly, though, the media picks up on reports of prosecutors employing child pornography statutes to handle this behavior. In 2009, the government prosecuted several sexting cases as felonies, with varying sentences. For example, Wisconsin officials charged a 17-year-old boy with possession of child pornography after he posted nude pictures of his girlfriend online (Stone, 2009). A 16-year-old New York boy who forwarded nude images of his girlfriend faced up to seven years in prison (Stone, 2009). In Ohio, a 15-year-old girl sent classmates risqué photos of herself and was initially charged with child pornography. She accepted a plea agreement in the case, the terms of which included no cell phone usage, limited Internet use, and a curfew (eschoolnews, 2009).

Depending upon the state codes, offenders faced the possibility of having to register as a sex offender for some period of time or indefinitely. The sexting conviction of 18-year-old Floridian Philip Alpert, who sent nude pictures of his 16-year-old girlfriend to her family and friends following a fight (NCSL, 2009), landed his profile on a sex offender registry until age 43 and resulted in his being banned from the community college he was set to attend (Richards & Calvert, 2009). Because of his new legal status, he can no longer live with his father, whose house is located in a school zone (Richards & Calvert, 2009).

With few exceptions, most cases involved dissemination of sexting images, rather than sexting between mutually consenting parties (Stone, 2009). Although felony prosecutions do not appear to be commonplace, those cases that are prosecuted as felonies are often media-looped, giving the illusion that large numbers of children are being hauled off to prison. Still, these cases are important in that they demonstrate the wide latitude that prosecutors have in charging sexting cases and may represent a glimpse of what might come in the disposition of these cases.

Case Law

There is very little case law addressing youth sexting from state or federal appellate courts, with *Miller v. Skumanick* (2009) being the one notable exception. In this case, the District Attorney in Wyoming County, Pennsylvania confiscated several cell phones containing nude or risqué pictures of nearly 20 minors. The involved girls and their parents were then required to attend a meeting with District Attorney Skumanick, where he warned them that he had enough evidence to prosecute each of them for felony possessing or distributing child pornography, which would require each to register as sex offenders for a minimum of eight years (Bazelon, 2010; Searcey, 2009). Skumanick then told them that if the youth would participate in an awareness program and probation, then he would not further prosecute; however, they would need to sign statements quickly to settle the matter if they wanted to avoid prosecution. (Interestingly, the District Attorney did not similarly threaten the boys who both viewed and distributed the images [Bazelon, 2010]). Part of Skumanick's suggested programming required the girls were to write essays about what they did wrong and "what it means to be a girl in today's society" (Bazelon, 2010).

The prosecutor's conduct both angered the parents and attracted interest from the ACLU, who jointly filed a lawsuit in federal court requesting a Temporary Restraining Order (TRO) against the DA, alleging that the prosecutor violated the youth's "freedom of expression" (Searcey, 2009). The parents claimed that signing such a statement effectively amounted to a guilty plea. Moreover, the parents argued that having their children write such an essay amounted to "compelled speech," a violation under the First Amendment. They further argued that several of the pictures were risqué but not pornographic per Pennsylvania law and therefore not illegal: two were of girls in their bras, one was of girl in her bathing suit, and one showed a young girl's exposed breasts. Finally, they argued that having the State compel their children in such a way interfered with their parenting preferences, (albeit loosely) violating the Fourteenth Amendment.

Notably, the District Court allowed the TRO, and the District Attorney was "enjoined" (commanded) from pressing charges against the children (*Miller v. Skumanick*, 2009). Such a decision, although limited in scope to this jurisdiction, is significant in that the District Court was perhaps inclined to see the behavior as more inappropriate than criminal. Appellate review in future cases will begin to define how courts see such behavior.

Legislative Movement on Sexting

To date, at least 22 states have deliberated, in some way, on sexting. Some drafted or passed legislation. Legislative study groups in other states indicated either a need for further consideration or that the topic should not be pursued.

The new legislation generally takes one of three forms. Much of it carves out a minor-to-minor exception, effectively charging down or decriminalizing the conduct. Conversely, other states effectively have charged up, making child pornography laws more explicit about including the transmission of sexual photos via the Internet or cell phone. Finally, other states are discussing the role of education on the topic.

Carving out an Exception for Youth—Vermont has been the pioneer in successfully enacting comprehensive sexting legislation that includes an exception in cases of voluntary sexting among minors, establishing "age gap provisions" (NCLS, 2009). Youth sexting would be handled by family court and those involved would not subject to sex offender registry requirements. The law also provides for expungement of records from family court at the age of 18 (No. 58, a125) and addresses the issue of when a minor receives a sext message:

> It shall not be a violation of this subdivision if the person took reasonable steps, whether successful or not, to destroy or eliminate the visual depiction (Sect 2802b).

This provision allows the juvenile the opportunity to simply destroy the picture, thus not being guilty of possession for simply opening his/her message. The legislation also discusses differing consequences if the sexting is a first or subsequent event. In all, it provides a fairly thorough response to a complicated issue.

Nebraska attempts to achieve dual purposes with its new sexting legislation. Legislative Bill 97 specifically identifies when a "person knowingly possess[es] any visual depiction of sexually explicit conduct ... which has a child [involved]" as a felony, thus eliminating any loophole for adult child pornographers. However, the law also addresses issues of youth involvement, coercion, and voluntariness. The following circumstances may provide grounds for an affirmative defense:

a. The visual depiction portrays no person other than the defendant

b. (i) the defendant was less than nineteen year of age; (ii) the visual depiction of sexually explicit conduct portrays a child who is fifteen years of age or older; (iii) the visual depiction was knowingly and voluntarily generated by the child depicted therein; (iv) the visual depiction was knowingly and voluntarily provided by the child depicted in the visual depiction; (v) the visual depiction contains only one child; (vi) the defendant has not provided or made available the visual depiction to another person except the child depicted who originally sent the visual depiction to the defendant; and (vii) the defendant did not coerce the child in the visual depiction to either create or send the visual depiction (Nebraska, Bill 97).

Such legislation addresses adult exploitation of youth sexting, as well as protects youth who might have become foolishly entangled in or who have engaged in consensual sexting. Indiana has drafted legislation with similar defenses for minor-to-minor sexting (NCSL, 2010). Similarly, several states, including Arizona, created statutes that classify certain sexting as misdemeanors (NCSL, 2010). For example, Utah amended their child pornography statute (HB 97) to include "the act of viewing child pornography." However, they made some allowance for youthful poor choices, making such behavior a misdemeanor rather than a felony if the person is under 17 (Love, 2009). Still, a misdemeanor is a very different response from the Vermont's law, which abdicates jurisdiction to the family court (in most circumstances), as well as from Nebraska, which provides for an affirmative defense.

At the time of this writing, the Iowa and Oklahoma legislatures were exploring carving out some type of youthful exception for sexting (Gad-City Times, 2010; Talley, 2009), and Indiana (SR 90) has sent the topic to study group for further exploration. Interestingly, a bill in the Illinois Senate seeks to define sexting between minors as a crime, but creatively it would be punishable by community service, and by writing term papers and apology letters (Beacon News, 2009). Finally, Ohio lawmakers introduced a bill in April 2009 that would make sexting a first-degree misdemeanor for minors under 18. The same behavior for adults would carry a felony charge (Richter, 2010).

Leaving it up to the Prosecutors—Other states have not placed such legislative restrictions on prosecutorial discretion. Both New Hampshire and Virginia explored the issue of sexting through study groups, eventually concluding that they needed no new laws to cover such behavior. The New Hampshire legislature reviewed carving out a youth-to-youth exception for sexting cases where no coercion and further distribution was involved (Brattleboro Reformer, 2009). After a few weeks in study group, the legislators backed off from the idea, saying, "We weren't convinced it was enough of a trend to introduce a new law" (Fahey, 2009, p. 8). Similarly, the Virginia Commission members refused to pursue legislation, calling it a "minefield." Instead, they felt that charging decisions should be left to individual prosecutors (Associated Press, Dec 15, 2009).

Charging Up—Other states have gone a different route entirely, focusing on the potential threat that such new technology presents to children. Many statutes do not specifically note that digital communication involving sexual acts with underage youth is prohibited, which has created a loophole in some states for true sexual predators. Consider the case of Commonwealth v. Zubiel (2010). Law enforcement involved in a sting operation caught Zubiel trying to solicit sex online from what he believed to be a 13-year-old girl. He was charged with four counts of attempting to distribute harmful material to minors. The law banned "handwritten or printed material," but it did not prohibit instant messaging or texting. Taking a very literal interpretation of the statute, the Supreme Judicial Court overturned Zubiel's conviction, noting that if the legislature wanted to make that behavior illegal, it needed to expressly do so (Salzman & Ellement, 2010). The governor and legislature responded by stating they would promptly introduce legislation to close the loophole, but at the time of this writing no such legislation has been passed.

Other states are also trying to address the dangers posed by gaps in current laws. Rather than trying to create exceptions for minors, some states have introduced, and sometimes passed, laws that explicitly target sexting as a crime. Colorado House Bill 09-1132 (HB) changed the current child pornography statutes, which prohibit "dissemination of offensive material to children, harassment, stalking, Internet luring and sexual exploitation of children," to include telephone and data networks. Oregon passed legislation (HB 2641) delineating online communication as part of the child pornography statute. While Colorado and Oregon's statutes indeed address a particular danger, it does not appear that they have planned around the more common minor-to-minor sexting complications. Both of these statutes could potentially make criminal prosecution of youth easier in sexting cases.

Education—Several states have drafted or passed legislation that targets education programs about sexting for young people (NCSL, 2010). New Jersey has several bills under consideration (AB 3754, 4068, 4069, 4070), which would create a diversion program for youth charged with sexting and provide funding for education programs designed to prevent sexting. Additionally, the legislation would require cellular companies to provide information on sexting to their customers.

Conclusion

Despite all the media exposure, large numbers of prosecutors are not marching, pitchforks in hand, to charge youth involved in largely consensual sexting cases under child pornography statutes. However, this does not mean that sexting does not merit legislative action. The issue is not one of mass prosecution of unwitting youth; it is rather one of potentially unchecked prosecutorial discretion. Without the appropriate tools, prosecutors might feel like the lesser of two evils would be prosecution under existing statutes rather than no prosecution at all.

Rather than relying on prosecutors' creativity or discretion, lawmakers do need to respond. As was jarringly evident in the Zubiel case, real sexual predators exist. Any loopholes in the law that would prevent prosecution of such adults who exploit children—such as those existing statutes that do not cover cellular transmission of legitimate child pornography—need to be closed. These laws need to be crafted carefully. Making the law clear about sexting is imperative, but it is equally important to create specific youth exceptions so misguided youth do not face lifelong consequences. Further, thoughtfully crafted legislation should delineate consensual sexting from that which involves further distribution, and thus, coercion and harassment, such as the Vermont statute does. Decriminalization, by family or juvenile court involvement in cases involving minors, is perhaps a better response than reducing the behavior to a misdemeanor status, since family court at least offers the opportunity to avoid a permanent record that would follow the youth forever.

What is painfully clear is that not only are teens unaware of the potential legal consequences, but they are also strikingly uninformed about potentially serious personal and social consequences of sexting. What begins as mutual sexting can quickly turn into harassment, ruining reputations, and causing incredible stress. In light of possible negative outcomes and given that sexting has become commonplace for many young people, communities need to look beyond the criminal justice system for a more comprehensive response. Simply, prevention and education efforts should multiply. Recently, MTV aired a documentary on the topic, and the popular television station sponsors a website, athinline.org—both designed to educate youth on the consequences of sexting. These efforts are critical. The government can support such tactics, as well. For example, New Jersey Senator Melendez was able to procure nearly $500,000 for youth-based Internet safety programs (State News Service, 2009; Young, 2009). This is an incredibly important piece: if legislation designed to build awareness for youth around the dangers of sexting is going to work, there needs to be funding. Further, the New Jersey legislature recently proposed legislation that would require cellular carriers to inform customers about sexting. Such information should include how to disable text or picture features from teens' phones. Emerging technology, including a soon-to-be-released application that blocks nudity in pictures, may be another option for parents.

Although we should applaud efforts like that of a Berkshire, Massachusetts District Attorney, who held dozens of sessions on sexting for parents and schools, we should not claim the district attorney's office as our first line of defense against this behavior. Toward this end, schools and nonprofits can take the lead, preferably with funding backed by legislative mandates. After all, an ounce of prevention is worth much more than a pound of any criminal justice cure.

References

Bazelon, Emily. (2010, March 18). How not to prosecute a sexting case. *Slate.* Retrieved June 29, 2010, from http://www.slate.com/id/2248281/.

BBC. (2009, November 26). Rihanna says naked photos were "humiliating." Retrieved 12/1/2010 from http://news.bbc.co.uk/2/hi/8380602.stm

Beacon News. (2009, July 7). Bill in state house seeks to make sexting illegal. *Chicago Sun Times*, p. 13.

Berkshire County District Attorney. (2009). District Attorney Holds Press Conference on Problem of "Sexting" in Berkshire County. *The Official Website of the Berkshire District Attorney's Office.* Retrieved

12/1/2010 from http://www.mass.gov/?pageID=bermodulechunk&L= 1&L0=Home&sid=Dber&b=terminalcontent&f=nu_2009_0303_se xting_press_conference&csid=Dber.

Diaz, M. (2009, July 27). 'Sexting:' Both sender and receiver can face charges. *South Florida Sun Sentinel,* p.3. Retrieved from LexisNexis database.

Eschoolnews.com (2009, April 17). States consider new 'sexting' laws. Retrieved 9/8/2009, from http://www.eschoolnews.com/2009/04/17/ states-consider-new-sexting-laws/

Fahey, T. (2009, September 10). Ad hoc panel: 'Sexting' does not warrant legislation. *The Union Leader,* p. 8.

General Assembly of the State of Vermont. §125 2009.

Hewitt, B. (2009, March 30). The dangers of 'sexting'. *People.* Retrieved on 12/1/2010 from http://www.people.com/people/archive/article/0,20 271181,00.html.

Love, N. (2009, August 25). N.H. lawmakers discuss "sexting". Brattleboro Reformer, News. Retrieved from LexisNexis database.

Menendez announces $463,399 in funding for children internet education. (2009, August 19). *State News Service.* Retrieved from LexisNexis database.

MTV Networks. 2010. *Sexting in America: When privates go public* [documentary].

National Campaign to Prevent Teen and Unplanned Pregnancy and CosmoGirl.com. (2009, September). The national campaign to prevent teen and unplanned pregnancy and cosmogirl.com reveal results of sex and tech survey. *NCPTUP.org* Retrieved on 9/16/2009 from http://www.thenationalcampaign.org/sextech/PDF/SexTech_ PressReleaseFIN.pdf

National Conference of State Legislatures. (2009). *2009 legislation related to "sexting."* Retrieved 6/29/2010 from http://www.ncsl.org/ ?tabid=17756

National Conference of State Legislatures. (2009, July/August). *Trends and transitions; the vexing issue of 'sexting'.* Retrieved 1/8/2010 from http://www.ncsl.org/?tabid=18006.

New laws go into effect July 1. (2009, June 29) *State News Service.* Retrieved from LexisNexis database. Oregon Legislative Assembly. House Bill § 2641 2009.

Richards, R & Calvert, C. (2009). When sex and cell phones collide: Inside the prosecution of a teen sexting case. *Hastings Communications and Entertainment Law Journal,* 32, 1-37.

Richter, E. (2010, January 10). Sexting bill getting big push. *Dayton Daily News.* Retrieved January 10, 2010 from http://www.ohio.com/ news/ohio/81086387.html

Saltzman, J. & Ellement, J. (2010, February 6). SJC says lewd IMs to minors not illegal. *The Boston Globe,* p. A1.

Searcey, Dionne. (2009, April 29). A lawyer, some teens and a fight over 'sexting." *The Wall Street Journal.* Retrieved on 9/8/2009 from http://www.boston.com/bostonglobe/editorial_opinion/oped/articles /2010/01/08/panic_over_teen_sexting_eclipses_bigger_threat/

'Sexting' legislation refused. (2009, December 15). Associated Press.

Shipkowski, B. (2009, July 19). NJ Assemblywoman moves to combat teen "sexting." *Associated Press State and Local Wire.*

Singal, J. (2010, January 8). Panic over teen 'sexting' eclipses bigger threat. *The Boston Globe.* Op-ed section. Retrieved on 12/12010 from http://www.boston.com/bostonglobe/editorial_opinion/oped/articles /2010/01/08/panic_over_teen_sexting_eclipses_bigger_threat/

State of Colorado. House Bill §09-1132. (2009).

State of Nebraska. LB § 97. (2009)

State of Utah. Sexual Exploitation of a Minor. H.B. §97. (2009).

Stone, G. (2009, March 13). 'Sexting' teens can go too far. *ABC News.*

Talley, T. (2009, June 16). Oklahoma House members request interim studies. *The Journal Record.* p. 2. Retrieved from LexisNexis database.

Young, E. (2009, July 21). 3 Bills target 'sexting' by kids; put emphasis on education. *The Record,* p. A04.

Discussion Questions

1. Define crime. Is sexting a crime? Why or why not?

2. Is sexting a "victimless" crime? Why or why not? Compare it with other "victimless" crimes.

3. What are some of the personal, social, and legal implications of sexting?

4. Differentiate among the three general forms of anti-sexting legislation.

5. Stories highlighting felony sexting convictions often media looped. What problems can arise from this?

6. How would you create an anti-sexting awareness program for teenagers today?

7. If you wanted to know more about youth awareness of the consequences of sexting, who would you study and how would you get your information?

Chapter 13
DOMESTIC VIOLENCE SHELTERS: SERVICES PROVIDED, REQUESTED, AND RECEIVED

Jaclyn Smith, M.A. University of Maryland
Angela Moore, Ph.D. National Institute of Justice[1]

Introduction

Domestic violence, also known as intimate partner violence or interpersonal violence,[2] is a global crime problem that permeates and crosses socioeconomic status, gender, age, sexual orientation, race, and ethnicity (Broude & Greene, 1983; National Coalition of Anti-Violence Programs, 2009; Straus, 1977; WHO, 2005). In the United States, about 25% of women and 8% of men will experience violence at the hand of an intimate partner at some point during their lives (Tjaden & Thoennes, 2000). The consequences of this violence are well documented. Victims suffer physical injuries or death (Catalano, 2007; Tjaden & Thoennes, 2000), mental health problems, or other psychological trauma (Carlson, McNutt, Choi, & Rose, 2002). Many victims lack social support or employment networks (Brown, Trangsrud, & Linnemeyer, 2009; Plichta, 2004). Children raised in homes with domestic violence are at risk for physical injuries and developmental and mental health problems (Sternberg et al., 1993). Domestic violence is also costly. Annual economic impact estimates range from $8.3 to $67 billion (Max, Rice, Finkelstein, Bardwell, & Ledbetter, 2004; Miller, Cohen & Wiersema, 1996).

Research on the magnitude and outcomes associated with domestic violence prompted a number of public policy responses to assist victims and to prevent continued abuse. Many of these policies concentrate on law enforcement and judicial system interventions, including mandatory arrest, no-drop prosecution, and specialized training for criminal justice personnel (Chanley, Chanley, & Campbell, 2001; Hollenshead, Dai, Ragsdale, Massey & Scott, 2006). Other interventions focus on community-based programs, including non-residential and residential domestic violence programs that offer a variety of preventative, educational, and crisis services.

---

[1]   Opinions, findings, conclusions, and points of view expressed in this work are those of the author and do not reflect the official position or policies of the U.S. Department of Justice.

[2]   Although domestic violence, intimate partner violence, and interpersonal violence are often used interchangeably in the literature, for clarity we use the term domestic violence throughout this chapter.

This chapter begins with a discussion on the historical growth and expansion of services for victims of domestic violence, particularly focusing on domestic violence shelters in the United States. We then explore the components of community-based services using a sample of residential domestic violence shelters. We provide a description of domestic violence shelter services, staff, and other program-level characteristics. Finally, we examine victim needs and services provided using a sample of clients who stayed in shelter and discuss what this analysis means for the field.

Literature Review

Shelters were among the first specialized support services available to domestic violence victims. Initially, shelters were limited to helping women escape abusive relationships by providing social support and a temporary place to live. Over time, shelter networks have grown substantially and are now a critical element of any coordinated community response to domestic violence. The approximately 2,000 domestic violence shelters in the United States provide a variety of services, including emergency shelter, 24-hour crisis hotlines, support groups, counseling services, advocacy, community outreach and training, and programs for children (National Network to End Domestic Violence, 2010). The increased diversity of residential and non-residential victim services is a major advancement in the response to domestic violence.

Services
Domestic violence programs should offer clients five core services: crisis services, advocacy, support groups, counseling, and shelter (Macy, Giattina, Sangster, Crosby, & Montijo, 2009). Crisis services help ensure clients' immediate safety and enhance their ability to cope with crises (Macy et al., 2009). Advocacy services address clients' needs in several areas, including employment, education, housing, finance, legal, and child-related issues (McDermott & Garofalo, 2004). Advocates are particularly important because they facilitate participation in the criminal justice process and help clients understand their legal options (Thelen, 2000). Support groups and counseling services educate women and family members about domestic violence, decrease social isolation, increase empowerment, and help clients with safety planning (Macy et al., 2009; Tutty & Rothery, 2002). Shelter services promote physical and psychological safety, help clients regain control over their lives, and serve as a gateway for other services (Bennett, Schewe, Howard, & Wasco, 2004).

Results from the 2009 National Census of Domestic Violence Services (NCDVS) illustrate the range of services provided by domestic violence programs (NNEDV, 2010). In the 24-hour period examined, programs averaged more than 960 hotline calls per hour. Ninety percent of these programs offered emergency shelter. A significant majority of programs offered a variety of advocacy services. More than 90% of participating shelter programs offered individual, group, and court accompaniment advocacy. More than 80% offered advocacy services related to public benefits, housing, child welfare, mental health, and substance abuse. Seventy-seven percent of programs offered advocacy related to disability and immigration issues, and 62% offered advocacy related to pet placement. Counseling was the least offered core service, at just over 50%.

Service Outcomes

Despite the expansion of shelter-based services for domestic violence victims and the proliferation of research on domestic violence, there are few empirical evaluations of the short- and long-term effects of these services (Berk, Newton, & Berk, 1986; Abel, 2000; Stover, Meadows, & Kaufaman, 2009). Many of the evaluations assessed the impact of shelter stay on future violence; however, some evaluations have considered other outcomes related to quality of life.

Berk et al. (1986) studied the impact of domestic violence shelter services on later spousal abuse. That study found that shelter stay reduced the likelihood of future violence, but the effects depended on the actions of the client. Shelter stay dramatically reduced the likelihood of new violence when clients engaged in additional help-seeking behaviors (i.e., called the police, obtained a restraining order, prosecuted their batterer, sought counseling, or obtained help from an attorney). Otherwise, shelter stay had no impact (Berk et al., 1986).

Evaluations conducted since the Berk et al. (1986) study support the study's findings. Dutton-Douglas and Dionne (1991) studied the effectiveness of shelter support groups and counseling services. They found that although women viewed support groups more favorably than counseling agencies, women's support groups were not more effective in preventing future violence. A more recent study from Krishnan, Hilbert, and McNeill (2001) found that almost half the clients reported a decrease in domestic violence incidents and an increase in their safety because of the services they received while in shelter.

In 1992, Sullivan, Tan, Basta, Rumptz, and Davidson examined the short- and long-term impact of advocacy services on women leaving domestic violence shelters. Their study demonstrated the importance of advocacy in reducing domestic violence. More than twice as many women receiving advocacy services experienced no violence after two years, compared to women who did not receive such services (Bybee & Sullivan, 2002; Sullivan & Bybee, 1999). This suggests that advocacy services are associated with positive changes on other quality of life outcomes. Women who received advocacy services had fewer symptoms of depression, had more social support, and had less difficulty obtaining community resources.

Findings from a statewide evaluation of domestic violence services supports the research discussed above and deepens the field's understanding of the effectiveness of hotline, shelter, and counseling services. All services examined during the evaluation were associated with positive quality of life outcomes (Bennett, Riger, Schewe, Howard, & Wasco, 2004). In particular, clients reported an improvement in their decision making ability during their participation in counseling and advocacy programs. Hotlines helped clients obtain information about violence and provided a source of support. Clients also reported feeling safer while in shelter (Bennett et al., 2004).

In contrast to the positive results reported by Bybee and Sullivan (2002) and Bennett et al. (2004), other research finds only partial support or no support for domestic violence shelter services and quality of life outcomes. Cox and Stoltenberg (1991) assessed how shelter-based group counseling services helped clients with social adjustment, personal development skills, and vocational guidance; overall, results were mixed.[3] Of the two groups that received counseling, one group had significantly less depression, anxiety, and hostility whereas the other group had significant improvement in self-esteem. Brown, Trangsrug, and Linnemeyer (2009) found that women in their study still experienced significant barriers to life two years post-shelter stay. All clients but one were dissatisfied with housing, 50% of the women had concerns about their romantic relationships, and 50% reported health problems. Brown et al. (2009) also found that although the majority of women reported an expectation to return to work after shelter, some women changed their mind at the two-year follow-up.

Services Needed and Provided

Although domestic violence cuts across all demographic groups, it is important to understand how different personal characteristics influence the help-seeking behaviors and needs of victims. Research on the help-seeking behaviors of victims from minority populations is limited, but it suggests different cultural backgrounds and practices are influential and warrant attention (Hollenshead, Dai, Ragsdale, Massey, & Scott, 2006; Krishnan, Hilbert, VanLeeuween, & Kolia, 1997).

Even among minorities who seek help, some research suggests contextual differences impact shelter use and requested services. One study exploring environmental factors influencing African-American women indicated they faced many obstacles, including severe abuse, poverty, unemployment, and the need for numerous resources (Sullivan & Rumptz, 1994). Another study that compared the characteristics of

---

[3]   The results are mixed because both groups received the same treatment, and since the groups were randomly assigned, the outcome should have been the same.

Caucasian and Hispanic women residing in shelter in New Mexico found important differences. Hispanics were more likely to be married (as opposed to divorced or separated), had more children, and had lower levels of education (Krishnan et al., 2001). Most importantly, Hispanics reported substantially less help-seeking behavior from informal and formal support providers (i.e., family and friends, medical, counseling).

Hollenshead et al. (2006) examined the relationship between ethnicity and age and the impact that relationships might have on preference for a particular type of social service. Overall, they found that African Americans underuse social services and were more likely to use law enforcement services over family violence center services. Even among African Americans who requested family violence center services, most sought legal services rather than social support. In contrast, Caucasians more frequently selected family violence center services and were more likely to select services related to counseling.

Krishnan, Hilbert, McNeil, and Newman (2004) compared the needs of those domestic violence clients in shelter who indicated that they would return to their abusive partner upon exit versus those that would not. Those who indicated they would return reported higher frequency of alcohol use and had higher rates of depression, and they were less likely to seek services during their shelter stay. Although Krishnan et al. (2004) did not find specific racial differences, they found that clients who were older, who had more children, and who were married were significantly more likely to indicate a desire to return to their partner after their shelter stay.

Grossman, Kawalski, and Margrave (2005) assessed how race and location (urban versus rural) interact to influence clients' help-seeking behaviors and needs. Across measures of race and location, the services most requested by clients were emotional support and legal help. Here, racial differences did exist; compared to Caucasians, African Americans in both settings needed more services, including housing, emergency shelter, transportation, and education and training.

The literature suggests that domestic violence victim services, particularly those offered in shelters, are beneficial. In most studies, women reported feeling safer and better able to effectively cope and plan for their future. However, additional research is needed before substantive conclusions are made regarding the effectiveness of shelter-based services, especially in light of research that suggests not all clients experience these benefits equally. Not all victims think shelter-based services are for them. Moreover, research in this field is often limited because of small sample sizes and a lack of demographic diversity. Sample attrition has been a problem, and reliance on convenience or opportunity rather than random or probability-based samples limit the ability to generalize these findings.

Methods

Using data originally collected by Lyon, Lane, and Menard (2008), we conducted a secondary analysis with the goal of exploring domestic violence service delivery, client needs, and services received. We analyzed data from the eight states included in the Lyon et al. (2008) research, using information from their previous reporting year, over a six-month study period.

Sampling

The Lyon et al. (2008) study purposively selected eight states for inclusion to better reflect various geographic regions and population demographics. Each state's domestic violence coalition invited all domestic violence programs that offered emergency shelter to participate in the study. Representatives from each participating program completed a survey that solicited information on staffing, services, and clients served throughout the previous reporting year. Table 13-1 provides the number of participating programs by state.

The Lyon et al. (2008) study included surveys of shelter clients, as well. They asked all those served during the six-month study period to anonymously complete two surveys: one at entrance to and one at exit from the shelter. These surveys collected information on the types of help clients requested upon entrance to the shelter, the degree to which they received each type of help during their shelter stay, and demographic information. Table 13-2 breaks down client participation by state and number of surveys completed. An additional 566 clients completed both surveys, but they are excluded from all analyses in this chapter. Only clients who completed either the entrance survey or the exit survey are included in the analyses presented below. As such, clients who completed the entrance survey are not the same individuals who completed the exit survey.

Analyses

Our initial goal with this secondary analysis was to better understand the volume, accessibility, and diversity of domestic violence shelters; our second goal was to examine client needs and services provided. To address the first goal, we used basic frequencies, counts of the variables of interest, and cross-tabular analyses to show correlations among variables. To address the second goal, we used basic frequencies, cross-tabular analyses, and logistic regression, which allowed us to predict services requested and the extent to which receipt of services was based on client demographic characteristics.[4]

Table 13-1. Program Participation by State

State	Number of Participating Programs
Tennessee	35
Florida	34
Michigan	33
Illinois	32
Washington	30
Oklahoma	26
Connecticut	17
New Mexico	11
TOTAL	218

Table 13-2. Client Participation by State

State	Entrance Survey	Exit Survey	Total
Tennessee	216	133	349
Florida	503	216	719
Michigan	266	88	354
Illinois	356	226	582
Washington	193	103	296
Oklahoma	149	83	232
Connecticut	77	24	101
New Mexico	72	58	130
Missing	48	33	81
Total	1880	964	2844

---

[4] Predictions are explained in terms of odd ratios, or comparing the likelihood that a certain event is the same for two groups. In this chapter, the odd ratios express the probability of clients requesting or obtaining services given different demographic characteristics. An odds ratio of 1.0 indicates no relationship between the variables of interest. An odds ratio of less than 1.0 indicates an inverse or negative relationship whereas an odds ratio of greater than 1.0 indicates a positive relationship. In the tables that follow, all relationships that are significant at the .05 level or less are indicated with an asterisk.

Results

Program-Level Information

The median number of full-time, paid staff at a domestic violence program was 12, with a range of 1-99 paid employees. Fewer than 10% of programs employed 30 or more staff members. Volunteers supported most programs (only 4% of programs did not have any volunteers), with a range of 0-250, but on average, a program had just eight volunteers per month to assist paid staff in providing services. Staff members and volunteers provided services in several languages besides English; the largest number of programs offered services in Spanish (72%), followed by American Sign Language (20%), and German (8%). Figure 13-1 illustrates the lack of staff diversity.

Figure 13-1

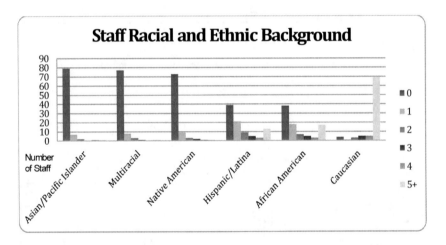

Figure 13-2 summarizes services offered by the domestic violence shelters; programs offered an average of seven services, with a range of 2-12. Childcare services were offered least often by programs (47%) whereas advocacy services were offered most often (91%). Of the programs that offered advocacy services, more than 90% of those services focused on housing advocacy, and more than 70% offered advocacy related to health, civil court, criminal court, government benefits, child protection, job placement, and immigration. Approximately 50% of the programs offered other services, for example, sexual assault services, transportation, and language classes.

Figure 13-2

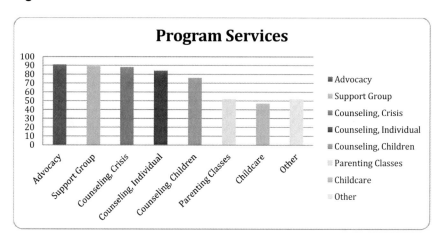

Separate from the aforementioned services, approximately 30% of programs offered one or more specialized services. The most common service was substance abuse treatment or counseling (17%). Seven percent of programs offered culturally—or ethnically—specific services, such as Latina support groups, Hispanic outreach, traditional Native American medicine, and women of color empowerment programs. Only 3% of specialized programs offered services for the elderly, and just 2% offered services for the lesbian, gay, bisexual, transgender (LGBT) community.[5] Figure 13-3 illustrates the percentage of programs that accommodated different types of disabilities. Overall, 2% did not offer any accommodations for the disabled, whereas 36% provided accommodations for all five types of disabilities.

Figure 13-3

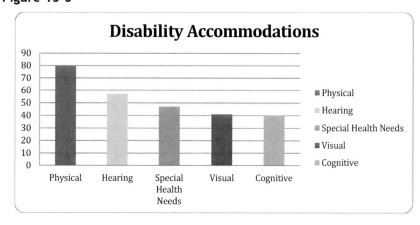

---

[5]   Information not portrayed graphically.

More than three-quarters of the programs had 40 or fewer beds with which to serve the median 189 clients. Programs averaged 101 clients served, with a range of 2-865. One shelter served as many as 2,107 clients. The number of children served ranged from one to more than one thousand, with a median of 82. Less than a quarter of programs reported adult male clients.[6] Of those programs that served men, the median was two, with a range of 1-60.

Client-Level Information

Respondents who completed the survey at entrance and those who completed the survey upon exit from the shelter were similar across most demographic characteristics. Approximately 90% were female. A little more than half were minorities, age 34 or younger, with a high school or GED education. Although there was no significant difference in the number of minor children, clients who completed the exit survey were more likely to have fewer children with them in shelter compared to clients who only completed the survey upon entrance. Table 13-3 summarizes the demographic characteristics of the two samples. Clients requested an average of 16 services, with a range of 0-38. We collapsed these services into 11 major categories, presented in Figure 13-4.

Table 13-3. Client Demographic Information

	Entrance Survey	Exit Survey		Entrance Survey	Exit Survey
Race/Ethnicity			Education		
Caucasian	48%	47%	Grade 8 or less	5%	5%
African American*	24	20	Grade 9-11	21	19
Hispanic/Latina	12	11	High School/GED	29	26
Multiracial	7	8	Some College	31	32
Native American	4	5	College	7	8
Asian/Pacific Islander	1	1	Graduate	2	3
Other	1	1			

---

[6] To our knowledge, none of the programs explicitly excluded men from services. The small number of men served may be due to men's reluctance to seek help as victims of domestic violence.

	Entrance Survey	Exit Survey		Entrance Survey	Exit Survey
Age			**Sexual Orientation**		
17 or younger	0.3%	0.2%	Heterosexual	82%	87%
18-24	18	20	Bisexual	3	2
25-34	32	32	Lesbian/Gay	1	1
35-49	35	31	Other	1	2
50-64	9	8			
64 +	1	1			
Number of Minor Children			**Number of Children in Shelter***		
Zero	16%	18%	Zero	19%	25%
One	20	18	One	20	17
Two	21	17	Two	15	13
Three	10	11	Three	6	6
Four +	10	5	Four +	5	3

Figure 13-4

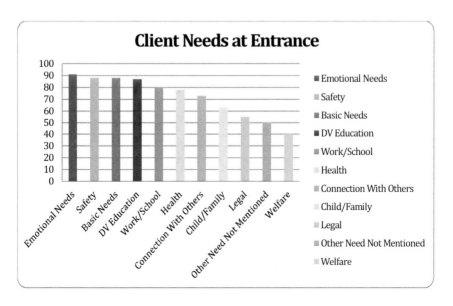

Results from the logistic regression analysis presented in Table 13-4 show significant demographic differences in types of services requested. The number of children in shelter increased the odds that clients requested children/family and legal services, but decreased the odds of requesting services related to their emotional needs and health. Each additional child with the client while in shelter increased the odds of that client requesting child/family services by a factor of 6.5, increased the odds of requesting legal help by a factor of 1.2, decreased the odds of requesting health services by a factor of .82, and decreased the odds of requesting services related to emotional needs by a factor of .76. Race was only minimally associated with different need requests upon entrance to the shelter. Hispanic clients were 1.5 times as likely to request legal help compared to Caucasian clients whereas African American clients were 1.5 times as likely to request child/family services compared to Caucasian clients.

Table 13-4. Logistic Regression Results—Requested Services at Entrance

Need Category	Predictor Variables				
	African American	Hispanic	Age	Education	Children
	Odds Ratio				
Emotional Needs	1.246	1.106	1.163	.836	.764*
Safety	1.051	1.401	1.352*	.883	.909
Basic Needs	.971	.554*	1.045	.877	.982
DV Education	.919	.978	1.257	.785*	.939
Work/School	1.339	.980	.708*	.793*	.983
Health	1.098	1.597	1.213*	.971	.823*
Connection	1.059	1.088	1.151	1.095	.941
Child/Family	1.541*	1.866	.708*	.906	6.589*
Legal	1.029	1.525*	1.063	.990	1.245*
Welfare	.553*	1.178	1.053	.870*	1.051

* = p < .05

Table 13-5 summarizes the relationship between demographic characteristics and specific legal services requested at entrance. Only two demographic characteristics were significantly related to the majority of legal services: being African American and having children in shelter. Being African American increased the odds of clients requesting help related to their batterer's arrest by a factor of 2.5, but decreased the odds that they would request help with other legal services such as child protection, child welfare, divorce, and custody. In contrast, the number of children with clients in shelter increased their odds of requesting legal help related to children protection, child welfare, custody, and divorce.

Table 13-5. Logistic Regression Results—Requested Legal Services at Entrance

Predictor Variables					
Legal Service	African American	Hispanic	Age	Education	Children
	Odds Ratio				
Child Protection	.610*	1.586*	.934	.941	1.245*
Child Welfare	.533*	1.306	.792*	.912	1.186*
Restraining/ Protection Order	.935	1.297	1.095	1.017	1.067
Abuser Arrest	2.454*	1.448	.977	.967	.944
Client Arrest	1.438	1.066	1.087	1.199	.763
Custody	.213*	.975	.929	.916	1.330*
Divorce	.512*	1.222	1.514*	1.047	1.337*
Immigration	1.105	3.411*	.901	.886	.984

* = p < .05

In addition to exploring the needs requested by clients upon entrance to shelter, we also explored the relationship between demographic characteristics and services received while in shelter. The next two tables present the findings from the exit survey. Table 13-6 shows that level of education and number of children with a client in shelter was inversely related to receiving more than half of all services needed. Only two demographic characteristics, client age and being African American, increased the odds that clients received all the help they requested while in shelter. In particular, African American clients were nearly twice as likely to receive services for their children and other family members, and each additional increase in age increased the odds of receiving help with work and school services by a factor of 1.2.

Table 13-6. Logistic Regression Results—Services Received While in Shelter

Predictor Variables						
Need Category	African American	Hispanic	Age	Education	Children	Length of Stay
	Odds Ratio					
Emotional Needs	1.427	.841	1.029	.777*	.821*	.997
Safety	1.367	1.302	1.039	.796*	.916	.996
Basic Needs	1.100	1.391	1.159	.852	.944	.997
DV Education	1.117	1.285	.962	.841	.859	.999
Work/School	1.570	1.237	1.221*	.839	.775*	.996
Health	1.522	1.476	1.147	.816*	.937	.999
Connection	1.256	1.340	.901	.938	.825*	.994*
Child/Family	1.904*	.644	1.134	.789*	.451*	.998
Legal	1.134	.632	1.016	.704*	.790*	.998
Welfare	1.332	.879	.870	.900	.763*	.996

* = p < .05

As demonstrated in Table 13-7, the level of education was the only demographic variable consistently related to specific legal services received while in shelter. Each unit increase in education level decreased the odds that clients received all the help they sought with legal services. African American clients had decreased odds of receiving help they sought relating to restraining and protection orders. Length of stay was the only variable that significantly increased the odds that a client received all requested legal help related to restraining and protection orders.

Table 13-7. Logistic Regression Results—Legal Services Received
          While in Shelter

Legal Service	Predictor Variables					
	African American	Hispanic	Age	Education	Children	Length of Stay
	Odds Ratio					
Child Protection	.787	.939	.817	.562*	1.059	1.002
Child Welfare	.711	.656	.851	.620*	.925	1.004
Restraining/ Protection Order	.435*	.762	.863	.613*	1.031	1.017*
Abuser Arrest	1.354	1.193	1.032	.428*	.860	.999
Client Arrest	2.841	.373	1.264	.174*	.647	.990
Custody	.725	.574	1.188	.489*	.683*	1.001
Divorce	.599	.574	1.345	.507*	.744	1.004
Immigration	.233	.224	.733	.343*	.643	1.017

* = p < .05

Discussion

We analyzed data from the Lyon et al. (2008) survey on domestic violence shelters to investigate those shelters' volume, accessibility, and diversity of services provided. On average, residential domestic violence shelter programs had 12 paid employees that serviced nearly 200 clients during the previous reporting year. This supports other research findings that domestic violence shelters are understaffed (NNEDV, 2010). Consistent with the literature, we found that programs offered a variety of services to meet the complex needs of their clients, including specialized services and culturally sensitive services. Services were offered in a variety of languages besides English, but most commonly in Spanish.

Although prior research found that less than 50% of domestic violence shelters offered counseling, we found more than 80% offered individual counseling, and more than 90% offered crisis counseling. More than 90% of all programs offered clients at least one type of advocacy service, and many programs offered multiple types of advocacy. Despite the fact that more than three-quarters of all clients had children with them while in shelter, programs had very few child-related services. This gap is alarming as nearly half of all clients sought child-related services during their stay. Stephens, McDonald, and Jouriles (2000) speculate that there are several challenges that limit the ability of shelter programs to implement child services, including the limited number of staff, space, funding, and length of time spent at the shelter (see also Poole, Beran, & Thurston, 2008).

Clients in our analysis of the Lyon et al. (2008) study averaged 16 need requests when they entered the shelter; demographic differences resulted in differences in the types of needs requested. In particular, clients who had a greater number of children with them in shelter were less likely to request help related to their emotional needs and health and more likely to request child, family, and legal services. Client age was also an important factor: older clients were more likely to request safety and health services, but less likely to request help with work, school, and family services. The likelihood of requesting specific legal services differed based on race or ethnicity. In particular, Hispanic clients were more likely to request immigration and child protection legal services. African American clients were twice as likely to request legal services leading to their abuser's arrest, but less likely to request other legal services such as child protection, child welfare, custody, and divorce.

Most demographic variables were not significantly related to whether clients actually received the services sought while in shelter, which is encouraging. Yet, clients with a higher level of education and clients with a greater number of children in shelter were less likely to get help related to safety or to maintaining connections with others, with children and family issues, with legal concerns, and with emotional needs. There were only two instances in which demographic character-istics increased the likelihood of obtaining all the help clients requested. Being African American increased the chances of obtaining all the help wanted regarding child and family needs, and being older increased the likelihood of getting all the help they requested as related to school and work. Specific to legal services, clients with a higher level of education were less likely to receive all the help they sought with child protection, child welfare, restraining and protection orders, abuser and client arrest, custody, divorce, and immigration.

Our analyses reaffirm existing literature in the field and further demonstrate the substantial diversity that exists among clients in domestic violence shelters. Given these differences, programs must tailor their services to meet the needs of clients represented.

Clearly, one size does not fit all.

Strengths and Limitations

The preliminary findings from this secondary analysis are an impor-tant contribution to the literature. To our knowledge, this is the first cross-state study of residential domestic violence shelters with a large enough sample to document the range of services provided; to describe the requested needs of clients in shelter; to explore the extent to which these services were provided; and to assess how these findings differ across different demographic characteristics. The ability of Lyon et al. (2008) to facilitate the cooperation of the eight state domestic violence coalitions, who in turn worked with the shelters to provide the data, is unprecedented.

Despite these strengths, the findings may not be generalizable. Since the states were nonrandomly selected and not all programs participated, it is unclear how well the larger population is represented. Client results were based on those victims who went to the shelter for services. Victims who seek services likely differ from those victims who do not. All this makes our results vulnerable to selection bias, when samples comprise individuals who self-select themselves into the study as opposed to being randomly selected to participate. Furthermore, despite the relatively large sample size of the Lyon et al. data, there were some key demographic groups not adequately represented, including men, the elderly, the LGBT community, and some racial and ethnic groups.

Future Research

Although knowledge regarding the dynamics of domestic violence has advanced, little is known about the structure, components, content of services, and evaluations of community-based domestic violence programs. These knowledge gaps are troubling for several reasons. First, shelter programs and related services are expensive. Chanely, Chanely, and Campbell (2001) estimate the annual operating cost of a shelter between $654,655 and $960,100. Service providers, policymakers, and funding agencies need to be confident that the limited resources available for these programs are used appropriately and efficiently. Second, policymakers and funding agencies increasingly favor evidence-based practices. Research in this field does not yet lend to identification, replication, and dissemination of the crucial components of effective service provisions. Finally, shelter programs are expected to meet the increasingly complex and diverse needs of domestic violence victims, which includes providing culturally competent services. It is unfair to hold shelter programs to these expectations unless we can identify the needs of the populations to be served (including desired outcomes) and develop and evaluate strategies to meet such needs.

Conclusion

Domestic violence is recognized as a serious and widespread public health issue. Over the past several decades, law enforcement, courts, and community-based service providers have implemented interventions to assist victims and prevent future violence. Domestic violence shelters provide a wide range of services to an increasingly diverse population and have become the cornerstone to a coordinated community approach to addressing domestic violence. Unfortunately, despite the greater attention in research, the effectiveness of these services—and who they benefit most—remains a largely unanswered question.

References

Abel, E. M. (2000). Psychosocial treatments for battered women: A review of empirical research. *Research on Social Work Practice* 10(1): 55-77.

Bennett, L., Riger, S., Schewe, P., Howard, A. & Wasco, S. (2004). Effectiveness of hotline, advocacy, counseling, and shelter services for victims of domestic violence: A statewide evaluation. *Journal of Interpersonal Violence* 19(7): 815-829.

Berk, R., Newton, P. & Berk, S. (1986). What a difference a day makes: An empirical study of the impact of shelters for battered women. *Journal of Marriage and the Family* 48(3): 481-490.

Broude, G. & Greene, S. (1983). Cross-cultural codes on husband wife relationships. *Ethnology* 22(3): 263-280.

Brown, C., Trangsrud, H. B., & Linnemeyer, R. M. (2009). Battered women's process of leaving: A 2-year followup. *Journal of Career Assessment* 17(4): 439-456.

Bybee, D. L. & Sullivan, C. M. (2002). The process through which an advocacy intervention resulted in positive change for battered women over time. *American Journal of Community Psychology* 30(1): 103-132.

Carlson, B. E., McNutt, L., Choi, D. Y. & Rose, I. M. (2002). Intimate partner abuse and mental health: The role of social support and other protective factors. *Violence Against Women* 8(6): 720-745.

Catalano, S. (2007). *Intimate Partner Violence in the United States.* Washington, DC: U.S. Department of Justice, Bureau of Justice Statistics, NCJ 210675.

Chanely, S., Chanley, J. & Campbell, H. (2001). Providing refuge: The value of domestic violence shelter services. *The American Review of Public Administration* 31(4): 393-412.

Cox, J. W. & Stoltenberg, C. (1991). Evaluation of treatment programs: Battered wives. *Journal of Family Violence* 6(4): 395-413.

Dutton-Douglas, M. A. & Dionne, D. (1991). *Counseling and shelter services for battered women.* Cincinnati, OH: Anderson.

Grossman, S. S., Kawalski, A. & Margrave, C. (2005). Rural versus urban victims of violence: The interplay of race and region. *Journal of Family Violence* 20(2): 71-81.

Hollenshead, J. H., Dai, Y., Ragsdale, M. K., Massey, E. & Scott, R. (2006). Relationship between two types of help seeking behavior in domestic violence victims. *Journal of Family Violence* 21(4): 271-279.

Krishnan, S. P., Hilbert, J., VanLeeuwen, D. & Kolia, R. (1997). Documenting domestic violence among ethnically diverse populations: Results from a preliminary study. *Family and Community Health* 20(3): 32-48.

Krishnan, S. P., Hilbert, J. C. & McNeil, K. (2001). *Understanding domestic violence in multi-ethnic rural communities: A focus on collaborations among the courts, the law enforcement agencies, and shelters.* Washington, DC: U.S. Department of Justice, National Institute of Justice, NCJ 191863.

Krishnan, S. P., Hilbert, J. C., McNeil, K. & Newman, I. (2004). From respite to transition: Women's use of domestic violence shelters in rural New Mexico. *Journal of Family Violence* 19(3): 165-173.

Lyon, E., Lane, S. & Menard, A. (2008). Meeting survivors' needs: A multi-state study of domestic violence shelter experiences. Washington, DC: U.S. Department of Justice, National Institute of Justice, NCJ 225025.

Macy, R., Giattina, M. Sangster, T., Crosby, C. & Montijo, N.J. (2009). Domestic violence and sexual assault services: Inside the black box. *Aggression and Violence Behavior* 14(5): 359 - 373.

Max, W., Rice, D. P., Finkelstein, E., Bardwell, R. A. & Leadbetter, S. (2004). The economic toll of intimate partner violence against women in the United States. *Violence and Victims* 19(3): 259-72.

McDermott, M. J. & Garofalo, J. (2004). When advocacy for domestic violence victims backfires: Types and sources of victim disempowerment. *Violence Against Women* 10(11): 1245-1266.

Miller, T, Cohen, M., & Wiersema, B. (1996). Victim costs and consequences: A new look. Washington, DC: U.S. Department of Justice, National Institute of Justice, NCJ 155282.

National Coalition of Anti-Violence Programs (2009). Lesbian, gay, bisexual, transgender, and queer domestic violence in the United States in 2008. Retrieved December 22, 2010 from *http://www.ncavp.org/publications/NationalPubs.aspx*

National Network to End Domestic Violence (2010). Domestic violence census counts 2009. Retrieved December 22, 2010 from *http://www.nnedv.org/resources/census/2009-census-report.html*

Plichta, S. B. (2004). Intimate partner violence and physical health consequences: Policy and practice implications. *Journal of Interpersonal Violence* 19(11): 1296-1323.

Stephens, N., McDonald, R. & Jouriles, E. N. (2000). Helping children who reside at shelters for battered women: Lessons learned. *Journal of Aggression, Maltreatment, and Trauma* 3(2): 147-160.

Straus, M. A. (1977). "Wifebeating: How common and why" *Victimology: An International Journal* 2 (3/4): 443-458.

Sternberg, K., Lamb, M., Greenbaum, C. Cicchetti, D., Dawud, S., Manela, R., Krispin, O. & Lorey. F. (1993). Effects of domestic violence on children's behavior problems and depression. *Developmental Psychology* 29(1): 44-52.

Sullivan, C. M. & Rumptz, M. H. (1994). Adjustment and needs of African-American women who utilized a domestic violence shelter. *Violence and Victimization* 9(3): 275-286.

Sullivan, C. M., Tan, C., Basta, J., Rumptz, M. & Davidson, W. W. (1992). An advocacy intervention program for women with abusive partners: Initial evaluation. *American Journal of Community Psychology* 20(3): 309-332.

Sullivan, C. M. & Bybee, D. (1999). Reducing violence using community-based advocacy for women with abusive partners. *Journal of Consulting and Clinical Psychology* 67(1): 43-53.

Stover, C. S., Meadows, A. L. & Kaufman, J. (2009). Interventions for intimate partner violence: Review and implications for evidence-based practices. *Professional Psychology: Research and Practice* 40(3): 223-233.

Thelen, R. (2000). Advocacy in a coordinated community response: Overview and highlights of three programs. Retrieved December 22, 2010 from *http://www.mincava.umn.edu*

Tjaden, P. & Thoennes, N. (2000). *Full report of the prevalence, incidence, and consequences of violence against women.* Washington, DC: U.S. Department of Justice, National Institute of Justice, NCJ 183781.

Tutty, L. M. & Rothery, M. A. (2002). Beyond shelters: Support groups and community-based advocacy for abused women. In A.R. Roberts (Ed.) *Handbook of domestic violence intervention strategies* (pp. 396-418). New York: Oxford.

World Health Organization (2005). WHO Multi-Country study on women's health and domestic violence against women. Retrieved December 22, 2010 from *http://www.who.int/gender/violence/who_multicountry_study/en/*

Discussion Questions

1. Describe the core services offered by domestic violence programs.

2. The economic impact of domestic violence is billions of dollars each year. What do you think contributes to this number?

3. In what specific areas did results show a disjunction between the services sought by domestic violence clients and service available and received? What factors limit a shelter's ability to provide such services?

4. When it comes to shelter clients and shelter services, does one size fit all?

5. Why is it so important to increase the body of literature on the structure, components, and services of community-based domestic violence programming?

Chapter 14
EXAMINING THE QUALITY AND EFFECTIVENESS OF A COUNTY JUVENILE TREATMENT (DRUG) COURT

Martin S. Floss, Ph.D. Hilbert College
Linda Bernstein, MBA, Hilbert College

Introduction

Youth in an Upstate New York community were facing many problems: high drop-out rates, a very high level of teenage pregnancy, and increased use of heroin, crack cocaine, Ecstasy, Ketamine, and Oxycontin. This region was also facing fiscal crises in its towns and the county's urban center. In response to these serious concerns, area leaders combined efforts to respond more effectively to the needs and behaviors of many of its youth. They hoped that a Juvenile Treatment Court (JTC) would be the most effective and efficient approach to dealing with troubled, high-risk youth living in the county.

Area leaders began by establishing a planning team—comprised of county judges, prosecutors, youth advocates (who provide legal representation for youth taken into custody), treatment providers, county probation, and a criminal justice professor—who would help design and evaluate the court. The team applied for and received a federal planning grant, which allowed them to attend weeklong conferences specifically designed to facilitate the establishment of juvenile treatment courts. Ultimately, they obtained a large federal grant, and soon the county's Juvenile Treatment Court (JTC) was up and running. This chapter describes the planning group's efforts to evaluate the quality and effectiveness of the court. Essentially, the group assessed whether the JTC was implemented as planned and whether it achieved its goals.

To improve your understanding of current efforts at reform, we begin with a brief review of the history of the legal treatment of juveniles and of the drug court/juvenile treatment court movement. This is followed by a description of the screening and selection criteria used by the drug court team and of the groups studied and the dataset compiled. Finally, this chapter concludes with a summary of the JTC evaluation highlights, interpretation of findings, and some concluding thoughts.

History of Juvenile Justice in America

Thoughts and practices regarding youth have changed dramatically over the centuries. This county's Juvenile Treatment Court simply represents a recent approach at improving the lives of children who have violated community rules and find themselves in trouble. Early societies made no distinction between juveniles and adults concerning criminal behavior—if rules were broken, punishments followed. In many societies, children faced the same system of justice as adults, and punishments included whippings, mutilation, banishment, torture, and even death (Bartollas & Miller, 1998). Children often had no rights whatsoever.

The settlers' overwhelming need for labor influenced Early American treatment of children. They did not view children as fragile or under-developed adults, and subsequently, government officials indentured misbehaving youth into the service of adults. By the early 1800s, however, states became increasingly concerned about the welfare of children. As industrialization and urbanization increased, so too did the corresponding number of wayward and incorrigible youth.

Groups of educated middle- and upper-class women emerged as "Child Savers," believing that the salvation of these youth could be achieved through the development of the "ideal child" (Bartollas & Miller, 1998). They could "save" these wayward youth by instilling the following ideals: supervision, discipline, modesty, diligence, and obedience. Child Savers emphasized *supervision* and believed that adults should never leave children alone; they believed that *discipline* could help children develop self-control and should be used when appropriate—"to spare the rod is to spoil the child." *Modesty, diligence,* and, most important, *obedience* acted as the pillars needed to create productive citizens (Empey, 1992).

Child Savers developed large "Houses of Refuge" as progressive places of reform. The Houses addressed the many abuses that reformers helped identify and, for the first time, separated the neglected, abused, and delinquent youth from institutionalized adult criminals. By 1899, the first juvenile court was ushered into existence (Bartollas & Miller, 1998), especially by those involved in the Child Savers Movement (Frontline, 2008).

Juvenile courts were comparatively informal; they did not include traditional courtrooms or other legal trappings associated with adult courts, such as prosecuting and defense attorneys or jury trials. Children did not have to commit a crime to land in juvenile court; they could come to the court based on a complaint from a citizen, parent, police officer, or school official (Bartollas & Miller, 1998). Three related interests guided these courts: (1) the role of the parent, (2) the protection of the child, and (3) the responsibility of the state (Siegel & Senna, 1997). For many years, the public paid little attention to the rights of or official "treatment" of these youth. A series of landmark cases, beginning in 1966 with the Supreme Court case of *Kent v. the United States,* marked the beginning of the "juvenile rights" era. In response to *Kent,* Supreme Court Judge Abe Fortas stated:

> *There is evidence, in fact, that there may be grounds for*
> *concern that the child receives the worse of both worlds;*
> *that he gets neither the protection accorded to adults nor*
> *the solicitous care and regenerative treatment postulated*
> *for children (Kent v. United States, 383 U.S. 541, 86 S.*
> Ct. 1045, 16 Led 2d 84, [1966]).

The philosophical foundation of the juvenile court is built on the fundamental concepts of *parens patraie* (i.e., the State as benevolent parent) and *in loco parentis* (in place of parents) (Rogers & Mays, 1987). Although landmark cases provided American youth many basic due process rights, juvenile courts remain informal, non-adversarial, and more civil than criminal in nature (Rogers & Mays, 1987). The best interests of the child, the treatment of individual needs and problems, and the prevention of future misbehavior are central to the juvenile court. Unfortunately, many juvenile courts have become overloaded; dealing with many long-term problems associated with high-risk youth is extremely difficult.

The Drug Court Movement

By the 1980s, several converging forces resulted in the development of drug courts. First, an increased focus on the relationship between drugs and crime resulted in the need to crackdown on drugs. The "war on drugs" had the unintended consequence of over-burdening the criminal justice system. Specifically, the "war" resulted in increased drug-related arrests, prosecutions, and case filing (Banks & Gottfredson, 2004; Finn & Newlyn, 1997). Faced with a backlog of cases, the criminal justice system began to recognize the need for alternative methods of processing drug offenders. Treatment professionals persuaded many criminal justice functionaries that well-organized, community-based programs could be effective if they were flexible enough to address a wide variety of offender needs (Listwan, Sundt, Hosinger, & Latessa, 2003).

In 1989, few could imagine that a small diversionary "pilot program" would revolutionize the way the American justice system handled criminal offenders with substance abuse problems. By 2006, there were 1,665 drug courts operating in the United States and nearly 400 more being planned (whitehousedrugpolicy.gov). The federal government's support and early indicators of success contributed to the rapid growth of adult and, later, juvenile drug courts.

Drug courts are generally behavior-oriented, with clear rules and expectations. One of the primary aspects of drug courts is close judicial supervision—tied to immediate sanctions for behaviors that are harmful or that violate program rules and incentives for productive and healthy behaviors. Another fundamental component is the presence of a collaborative, supportive court team that provides a wide range of treatment options for the non-violent substance-abusing defendant (Burdon, Roll, Prendergast, & Rawson, 2001; Kassebaum & Okamoto, 2001). Additional key components associated with drug courts include early identification and screening of offenders, random drug testing, continuous monitoring of drug court activities, collaboration with local community agencies, and strict judicial monitoring (Kimbrough, 1998; Volkow, 2006).

By the turn of the twenty-first century, researchers and program evaluators had evaluated several notable drug courts, with somewhat consistent findings, and raised new questions for further consideration. Using information from his and other drug court evaluations, a leading researcher from American University, Steven Belenko (2001), concluded that drug use and criminal activity were relatively reduced while offenders participated in drug court programs (2001). He also found that participants were typically poorly educated males lacking successful employment histories and who had been extensively involved with the law. The fact that drug use and criminal behavior could be reduced was good news because researchers had shown that drug court participants who had previously sought help (outside the drug court setting) for substance abuse or addiction problems did not fare well in treatment (Belenko & Peugh, 1999; Belenko, Peugh, Califano, Usdansky & Foster, 1998). Belenko (2001) maintained that drug courts consistently demonstrated the ability to reduce drug use and criminal activity, and they were able to do so at a significant cost savings compared with traditional criminal justice responses.

Once researchers demonstrated that drug court participants improved their behavior while involved in the program, focus shifted whether these courts could reduce future rates of recidivism. While early drug courts enjoyed much anecdotal support, they failed to receive much empirical support. In fact, one early attempt to assess the success of drug courts in reducing recidivism, conducted by Belenko, Fagan, and Dumanovsky (1994), found that offenders processed through a specialty narcotics courtroom were more likely to be rearrested (53%) than those processed through a traditional courtroom (51%). This difference in arrest rates did not result in any significant differences in reconviction or re-incarceration rates, however. Similarly, Deschenes and Greenwood (1994) failed to find any significant differences in rearrest rates in the experimental evaluation of the Maricopa County (AZ) drug court.

More recently, research has demonstrated positive changes affected by drug courts, as well. In Ohio, for instance, felony-level drug court participants were significantly less likely to be rearrested than a comparable group of probationers (32% vs. 44%). This finding was duplicated with misdemeanor drug courts, with 41% of municipal drug court participants being rearrested compared with 49% of comparable probations (Latessa, Shaffer, & Lowenkamp, 2002).

New York's Center for Court Innovation compared recidivism rates among drug court graduates, attendees from six drug courts, and control groups of similar defendants who did not enter a drug court. They found that all six drug courts analyzed—Bronx, Brooklyn, Queens, Suffolk, Syracuse, and Rochester—produced recidivism reductions compared with conventional case processing (Rempel, Fox-Dralstein, Cissner, Cohen, Lariola, Farole, Bader & Magnani, 2003). Because New York State tracked defendants at least three years after their initial arrest and at least one year following drug court program completion, these results indicated that positive drug court outcomes are durable over time.

Juvenile Drug Courts

A *juvenile drug court* is a special docket within a juvenile court to which selected delinquency cases or cases involving disobedient, truant, runaway, or similar "beyond control" juveniles are deferred for handling by a designated judge. These cases involve youth whose behavior is believed to be exacerbated by substance use. The juvenile drug court judge maintains close oversight of each case assigned through frequent (often weekly) status hearings with the parties involved. The judge also works with the drug court "team" of treatment, juvenile justice agency, social service, education, and other service providers, in addition to the prosecutor and defense counsel, to determine how best to address each juvenile's substance use and related problems (Cooper, Nerney, Parnham, & Smith, 1999, p. 1).

Considering the growth of adult drug courts nationwide, it is no great surprise that, in 1995, the "drug court" concept was adapted and used to cope with nonviolent youth engaged in the juvenile justice system (Cooper et al., 1999). It quickly became evident, however, that far greater complexities existed for dealing with adolescent substance abusers. Approaches utilized would need to intensively address youth, their substance abuse, their families, their school, and their peers (McGee, Merrigan, Parnham, & Smith, 2000). According to the Office of Juvenile Justice and Delinquency Prevention (OJJDP) (1998), juvenile drug courts have shown that they can provide greater access to community-based and government-provided social, medical, mental health, and substance abuse services than traditional approaches for dealing with youth substance abuse, delinquency, and troubled behavior (Kimbrough, 1998).

Cooper et al. (1999) set forth a framework for successful juvenile drug courts. They argued that to be successful, juvenile drug courts needed to be educationally appropriate and able to address the many needs of youth (including medical) in a credible and culturally relevant way. They needed to incorporate restorative justice/community-based forms of accountability. The courts needed to help build a strong support structure for participants, and ultimately provide the foundation for short- and long-term strategies for becoming drug free.

Because juvenile drug courts have not been around as long as the adult versions, they have not undergone as many or as extensive evaluations. Hence, we know more about adult drug courts than juvenile drug courts in terms of their ability to achieve goals, such as reducing substance abuse or recidivism, changing destructive behaviors, or increasing public safety. So far, research on recidivism rates associated with juvenile drug courts has been mixed. For example, American University, in conjunction with the Bureau of Justice Administration, compiled the findings of 13 different juvenile drug court evaluations from across the nation. Two juvenile drug courts in North Dakota reported that as few as 16% of participants recidivated within one year, versus 57% of the comparison group. On the other hand, evaluations of Oregon's Clark and Multnomah counties revealed that 66% of the youth were rearrested for a new offense within 12-months of enrolling in the drug court program. In Bibb County, Georgia, 26% of juvenile drug court graduates were rearrested (resulting in 1 conviction), compared with 56% of those youth terminated from the juvenile drug court (with 5 convictions). The statewide evaluation in Ohio during 2002 reported that 56% of juvenile drug court participants were rearrested, compared with 75% of those in the comparison group. Finally, in Kalamazoo, Michigan, 2004 recidivism rates among juvenile drug court participants tracked for one year were similar to those of the probation control group (Bureau of Justice Administration, 2006).

In sum, initial evidence supports the efficacy of juvenile drug courts to positively impact several key elements central to their mission. It appears that drug courts in many jurisdictions have either reduced or had comparable recidivism rates among youth, compared with traditional responses to similar behavior. Of the few evaluations with sufficient data to examine the impact of the juvenile drug court on the education of clients, all seemed to have a positive impact on important issues related to school (e.g., improved grades and improved attendance) (Bureau of Justice Administration, 2006). Finally, while juvenile drug courts are not cheap to implement and administer effectively, they appear less expensive than traditional approaches—especially in terms of confinement or long-term placements (Belenko, 2001).

Screening, Selection, and Description of the County Juvenile Treatment Court (JTC)

The county juvenile treatment court (JTC) at the heart of this review was designed to help non-violent juveniles ages 13 to 16 who have chemical or alcohol abuse problems (and their families). The county probation department directly referred many of these juveniles to the JTC based on probation violations. Potential JTC candidates progressed through both legal and clinical screening processes to quickly determine whether they were suitable for entering the JTC. A member of the drug court team from the county attorney's office reviewed all candidates to confirm that they did not have previous violent or drug distribution charges, and a licensed treatment professional ensured that each candidate was clinically appropriate to enter the JTC.

The screening process for youth referred to JTC was quick, typically producing decisions regarding inclusion into the court before the next scheduled drug court session. For those youth included in the program, the first step was for the caring team of professionals to develop a comprehensive treatment plan. This included assessing educational needs, so the JTC could help youth receive proper support to address any shortcomings. JTC participants needing inpatient treatment had priority placement in several area facilities; treatment could begin within days of admission into the JTC.

The JTC served post-adjudicated youth who have pled guilty to the original charge(s) initially, but who would achieve an Adjournment Contemplating Dismissal (ACD) upon graduation from the JTC program. Youth must complete, among other things, one full year of sobriety before they could graduate. A cornerstone of the JTC has been that all participants had immediate and complete access to law-guardians, who informed them of their rights, of the details of the court, and of any alternatives. The JTC resolved cases by two means only: successful graduation or termination from the court (meaning no ACD).

All who entered the JTC progressed through a set of "phases" that ultimately led to graduation. For example, Phase I required participants to be drug and alcohol free for 30 days and involved *weekly* court appearances, random drug screens at least twice a week, and successful involvement in an education program. Meanwhile, the probation department conducted home visits and in-office interviews to determine the level of monitoring. Phase II required completion of 4 months, 90 consecutive days of clean drug tests, and work toward the completion of treatment activities. Phase III required 4 months of consecutive clean drug screens for drugs and alcohol, *monthly* court appearances, completion of treatment plans, tasks, and goals, and approval by the treatment team. Participants could be dismissed from the JTC for any of several reasons: conviction of selling a controlled substance, conviction of a violent felony, knowingly tampering with or submitting a false or adulterated sample, or any other failure to follow the rules, or request of the counseling or drug court team.

Evaluation Methodology and Highlights of the JTC

Evaluation research is typically made of two parts: process (quality) and impact (outcome) evaluations. In this case, the process evaluation examined whether the JTC was implemented and operated as planned, and the impact evaluation studied whether the court's stated goals and objectives were achieved. We collected a combination of *quantitative* (analysis based on the statistical summary of data) and *qualitative* (analysis presented in the researchers own words, such as focus groups, interviews, and courtroom observations) information (Stier Adler, & Clark, 2011). We began our evaluation efforts before any youth entered the JTC, and members of the drug court team continued collecting data on at least a weekly basis for more than 5 years, allowing for further evaluation.

Overall, there were four main goals of the JTC:

1. Implement an effective juvenile treatment court, based on a case-management system, that used a comprehensive range of treatment services under close scrutiny of the justice system;
2. Reduce recidivism/increase public safety while protecting the individual rights of the juvenile drug court participants;
3. Increase prosocial and responsible behaviors of the juvenile drug court participants who would subsequently live healthier lives; and
4. Increase family involvement in the lives of the juvenile drug court participants

Due to space limitations, what follows will be highlights from the process evaluation, tied to goal #1, and the outcomes associated with goal #2. These highlights will reveal some of the things that we learned by evaluating the quality and effectiveness of the JTC.

To begin, by 2008 there had been 211 individuals who had contact with the JTC. Of these, 22 (10%) graduated from the program, 52 (25%) failed, and the remainder (65%) were deemed ineligible to participate in the program. Considering only those who actually entered the court, 24% successfully graduated, 56% failed, and 20% remained open at the time of the evaluation. The process evaluation involved following all participants through the JTC court process, and the impact evaluation compared graduates of the JTC to both JTC participants who failed out of the court and another group of youth taken into custody for similar reasons but were assigned Juvenile Intensive Supervision Probation (JISP) rather than allowed to participate in the JTC. This last group was matched to the graduating group in terms of age and ethnicity.

Most (87%) of the youth who entered the JTC were male. More than half were White (53%); African Americans represented a quarter of the population (24%), and roughly 5% were Hispanic/Latino. The average age of the JTC participants was 15 years old, with the two youngest members being 12 and the four oldest were 17 when they entered the court. Moreover, participants reported first using drugs at a fairly early age, most commonly ages 12-14, with four reporting drug use as early as ages 7 or 8. Participants indicated that alcohol and marijuana were their drugs of choice, followed by cocaine.

Also troubling was that many of the youth entering the JTC reported multiple forms of abuse and victimization. For example, 15% of the youth entering JTC stated that they had been the victim of a violent crime; 10% had been physically abused by someone close to them, and 14% had been emotionally abused by someone they knew. Many also suffered from some form of mental illness, with 30% reporting they had received counseling for mental health problems and another 15% reporting a period of hospitalization for mental health reasons. Tragically, 9 individuals (8%) of this court population reported that their lives became so difficult that they had attempted suicide.

Regarding the charges faced by youth who entered the JTC, most (64%) were arraigned on non-drug misdemeanor charges, followed by 30% arraigned on non-drug felony charges, with 6 (3%) facing misdemeanor drug charges and 2 (1%) being arraigned on felony charges.

The Process and Timing of JTC Participants

By examining the identification, screening, and timing of participants throughout their JTC experience, we concluded that those entering the court were truly high-risk (non-violent) youth facing substantial time in residential placement. On average, JTC participants had 340 days elapse from the time that they were taken into custody to the time they entered court by signing a contract; Figure 14-1 displays this and related timing data. We believe that these youth had attempted other ways to deal with their legal problems and, running out of options, signed the JTC contract and entered the court.

Figure 14-1. Process and Timing of the County Juvenile Treatment Court

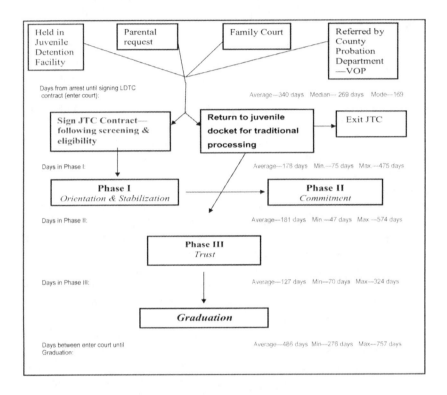

Goal 1 Findings

Through direct observation of pre-court and court proceedings, detailed record analysis, focus groups, and interviews, we found it abundantly clear that the JTC was well planned, effectively implemented, and professionally administered. Virtually all JTC participants received intensive services coupled with close judicial supervision. All who entered the court immediately received individualized treatment plans created by treatment professionals in close cooperation with the JTC. Because this JTC was located within a larger jurisdiction, court participants and their families could benefit from many treatment and wraparound support services, including age-appropriate treatments for substance abuse, health care, anger management, education, and vocation programs. The court had particularly strong mental health screening and treatment services. Combined with the leveraging abilities of the court and the care of the JTC team, youth and their families were enrolled in an individualized case-management approach that used a comprehensive continuum of treatment services—as described and planned in goal 1.

Comparing Participants by Program Success—Table 14-1 provides a summary of the bivariate (the relationship between two variables) results of JTC participants who successfully graduated from the program compared with those who failed by selected demographic, social, educational, mental health, and criminal justice variables. We used a statistical method called the chi-square test to compare JTC participants by individual attributes. This test allowed us to assess how our observed data related to what we expected to find, given the stated purpose of the JTC.

We divided the variables into individual characteristics and program measures as studies indicate that individual demographics are important indicators of program graduation or termination. The individual characteristics included gender, race, and age. We analyzed participant race and gender to study whether minority status or gender were factors in program completion as previous researchers had shown.

Table 14-1. Bivariate Comparison of JTC Graduates and Failed Participants

Characteristic	*Failed*	*Graduated*
Age (Avg. = 15.1 yrs.) n=63; p.<.589		
13 years old	1 (50%)	1 (50%)
14 years old	7 (67%)	4 (33%)
15 years old	23 (67%)	11 (33%)
16 years old	10 (67%)	5 (33%)
17 years old	1 (100%)	0 (0%)
Gender n = 74; p. <.801		
Male	46 (71%)	19 (29%)
Female	6 (67%)	3 (33%)
Race n = 74; p. <.169		
Caucasian	29 (63%)	17 (37%)
African American	18 (85%)	3 (15%)
Latino/Hispanic/Other	5 (71%)	2 (29%)
Education Level n = 74; p<.306		
Enrolled in school full-time	45 (69%)	20 (31%)
Enrolled in school part-time	1 (100%)	0 (0%)
Not in school & employed	0 (0%)	1 (100%)
Not in school & unemployed	6 (86%)	1 (14%)
Physical Abuse by someone close—Ever n = 44; p<.410		
Yes	3 (100%)	0 (0%)
No	28 (68%)	13 (32%)

Characteristic	Failed	Graduated
Emotional Abuse by someone close— Ever n = 45; p<.561		
Yes	3 (60%)	2 (40%)
No	29 (72%)	11 (28%)
Victim of a violent crime **(Ever)** n = 45; p<.329		
Yes	2 (50%)	2 (50%)
No	30 (73%)	11 (27%)
1st Mode of Treatment n = 36; p<1.00		
Inpatient (long-term)	6 (75%)	2 (25%)
Outpatient	21 (75%)	7 (25%)
Mental health counseling **(Ever)** n = 46; p<.380		
Yes	11 (79%)	3 (21%)
No	21 (66%)	11 (34%)
Hospitalized for mental health— Ever n = 44; p<.072		
Yes	6 (100%)	0 (0%)
No	24 (63%)	14 (37%)
Ever Attempted Suicide n = 46; p<.869		
Yes	4 (67%)	2 (33%)
No	28 (70%)	12 (30%)
Type of case n = 68; p.<.781		
Felony Non-Drug	11 (61%)	7 (39%)
Misdemeanor Drug	2 (67%)	1 (33%)
Misdemeanor Non-Drug	33 (70%)	14 (30%)

* = p<.05   ** = p<.01   *** = p<.001

The data show that *none* of the demographic variables were significantly associated with graduating from the program. That is, younger participants were just as likely as older youth to graduate, males and females graduated at similar rates, and any differences in rates of success among White, Black, and Hispanic youth were not different enough to result in a statistically significant finding. Moreover, there was virtually no difference in the expected rates of graduation when comparing 12-17-year-old males with females the same ages (p. < .801).[1] Of these three demographic variables, only the race of the individual showed any difference: White participants graduated at a higher rate (37%) than did Black participants (15%), with Hispanic/Other participants graduating in the middle with a rate of 29%. Yet, the *correct*

---

[1] It is important to note that only 9 young women were considered in this analysis—any findings should be considered tentatively.

interpretation of the data is that there was not a statistically significant difference among any of these variables and, in the long run, we would not expect to find any meaningful differences if we studied additional samples of youth participating in the JTC.

A final variable was based on the type of illegal act committed, namely a drug vs. non-drug offense and whether the act was a felony or misdemeanor. Although the presenting charge was *not* a significant predictor of graduation/failure from the program, those who faced felony charges did better than did those who faced misdemeanor charges. Because those taken into custody and faced felony non-drug related charges had more incentive to successfully graduate from the JTC, is not a complete surprise that they graduated at a higher rate.

Logistic Regression—These findings provide a preliminary glimpse into the relationship between variables and program success. We used a multivariate analysis (allowing the study of multiple measures in cases or groups of cases) technique called case logistic regression to see if the bivariate results presented above hold (still exist) when other variables are *controlled for* or *held constant*. The following model was one that was used to examine the interactions that the age, race, and gender have on graduating from the JTC.

$$\textbf{Probability Graduation/Fail} = \textbf{a} + \textbf{b}_1 \textbf{ (age)} + \textbf{b}_2$$
$$\textbf{(gender)} + \textbf{b}_3 \textbf{ (race)} + \textbf{e}$$

Table 14-2.   Variables in the Equation

	B	S.E.	Sig.	Exp(B)
Age	.042	.035	.226	1.043
Gender(1)	-.751	.872	.389	.427
Race 1			.088	
Race 2	-.826	1.054	.433	.438
Race 3	.737	.908	.417	2.089
Constant	-.913	1.200	.447	.401

Model Summary

-2 Log likelihood	Cox & Snell R Square	Nagelkerke R Square
78.403(a)	.224	.300

We performed this and many other regressions to examine relationships, and, in short, they supported the earlier analysis: none of these factors were significant predictors of graduating from the JTC—even after controlling for the other variables.

Goal 2 Findings

To examine whether the JTC reduced the likelihood of rearrest among participants and graduates, we compared JTC graduates with a group of participants who failed out of the program. We also compared these two groups with similar youth sanctioned to the County Probation Department's Juvenile Intensive Supervision Probation (JISP) program.

Because the JTC court continuously received new cases while graduating successful program participants during each year of operation, we could not use the same length of "time at risk" for recidivism for each person. That is, we were able to track early graduates for more than 4 years, but we could track the progress of the most recent graduates for only a few months.

We established the control/comparison group by picking a similar number of youth from the JISP program and matching them on gender, age, offense, and date entering the program. It was important for us to compare like groups of youths. Each of the three groups compared were among the most difficult cases facing the county system, and group members were running out of alternatives to long-term residential placement.

Following these three groups of youth produced mixed and interesting findings. To begin, just 2 of the 22 (9%) JTC graduates were taken into custody/rearrested within 6 months of graduation. Also positive was that we could identify only one instance in the JTC's then five-year history when a youth was arrested for a crime while actively participating in the program.

Moreover, there was virtually *no difference* between the rearrest rates of those who graduated from the JTC and the JISP control group over the course of the lengthy follow-up period. Again, both groups comprised some of the most difficult cases in the county, and we were able to look at rearrests during four years of post-graduation lapse for early graduates—far longer than other studies. Nine of the 22 (40.9%) JTC graduates were rearrested, as were 35 of 86 (40.6%) from the JISP control group. Although the JTC graduates and the JISP youth recidivated at the same rate, JISP youth were rearrested for far more serious and violent offenses. An unexpected, somewhat ironic finding of our review was that only 6 of the 50 (12%) JTC participants who *failed out* of the program were rearrested during the same follow-up period that was used with the other two groups.

Conclusion

Nearly a decade ago, a group of professionals from different criminal justice and treatment agencies gathered to plan for and find funding to establish a Juvenile Treatment Court. Roughly five years after the JTC opened its doors, we helped the court complete both *process* and *impact* evaluations. Our evaluations were made stronger because they were planned before the program was started and conducted by a team who had been working with the court during the entire time. This allowed us to make a matched control group for use in a quasi-experimental design.

Having a strong evaluation planned from the start played an important role in obtaining large amounts of grant money used to help the county establish this Juvenile Treatment Court. The evaluation was designed to inform decision-makers such as the judge and drug court team about how well the program was being implemented and whether it was having the desired results. We collected a great deal of information using a variety of methods: qualitative approaches—such as focus groups and interviews—and quantitative approaches—such as the analysis of extensive court records that were regularly updated by court personnel and turned into a large dataset. Ultimately, our evaluation will guide future decisions within this community's JTC and among other communities considering this approach to youth crime precipitated by issues of substance abuse.

References

Bartollas, C. & Miller, S. (1998). *Juvenile justice in America* (2nd ed). Upper Saddle River, NJ: Prentice Hall.

Banks, D. & Gottfredson, D. C. (2004). Participation in drug treatment court and time to rearrest. *Justice Quarterly*, 21(3): 637-658.

Belenko, S. (1998). *Research on drug courts: A critical review*. The National Center on Addiction and Substance Abuse at Columbia University: New York.

Belenko, S. (2001). *Research on drug courts: A critical review 2001 Update*. The National Center on Addiction and Substance Abuse at Columbia University: New York.

Belenko, S., Fagan, J.A., & Dumanovsky, T. (1994). The effects of legal sanctions on recidivism in special drug courts. *The Justice System Journal*, 17(1): 53-79.

Belenko, S. J., Peugh, J. A., Califano, Jr., Usdansky, M., & Foster, S. E. (1998). Substance abuse and the prison population: A three-year study by Columbia University reveals widespread substance abuse among offender population. *Corrections Today*, 60:82-89, 154.

Belenko, S. J. & Peugh, J. A. (1999, March). Substance involved women inmates: Challenges to providing effective treatment. *Prison Journal*, 79 (1):23-44.

Brewster, M. P. (2001). An evaluation of the Chester County (PA) drug court program. *Journal of Drug Issues*, 31(1): 177-206.

Burdon, W. M., Roll, J. M., Prendergast, M. L., & Rawson, R. A. (2001). Drug Courts and contingency management. *Journal of Drug Issues*, 37(1) 73-90.

Bureau of Justice Administration. (2006). Recidivism and Other Findings Reported in Selected Evaluations of Juvenile Court Programs: 2000—present. *BJA Drug Court Clearinghouse Project*. School of Public Affairs, American University.

Cooper, C. S., Nerney, M., Parnham, J., & Smth, B. (1999). Juvenile Drug Courts: Where have we been? Where should we be going? *Drug Court Clearinghouse and Technical Assistance Project*. Drug Courts Program Office, Office of Justice Programs. U.S. Department of Justice.

Deschenes, E. P. & Greenwood, P. W. (1994). Maricopa County's drug court: An innovative program for first-time drug offenders on probation. *The Justice System Journal*, 17(1): 99-73.

Empey, L. (1982). *American Delinquency: Its Meanings and Construction*. Dorsey Press: Homewood, IL.

Finn, P., & Newlyn, A. K. (1997). Miami's drug court: A different approach. In L. K. Gaines & P. B. Kraska (eds.), *Drugs, crime, and justice* (pp. 357-374). Prospect Heights, IL: Waveland.

Frontline, Juvenile Justice. *Child or Adult: A Century Long View, Juvenile Justice* (2008). PBS. Retrieved from http://www.pbs.org/wgbh/pages/frontline/shows/juvenile/stats/childadult.html.

Godley, M. D., Dennis, M. L., Funk, R., & Siekmann, M. (1998) *An Evaluation of the Madison County Assessment and Treatment Alternative Court.* Technical Report. Normal, IL: Lighthouse Institute, Chestnut Health Systems.

Gottfredson, D. C., Najaka, S. S. & Kearley, B. (2003). Effectiveness of drug treatment courts: Evidence from a randomized trial. *Criminology & Public Policy*, 2(2): 171-196.

Harrell, A., Mitchell, O., Merrill, J., & Marlowe, D. (2003). *Breaking the Cycle: The research demonstration.* Technical Report. The Urban Institute.

Kassebaum, G., & Okamoto, D. K. (2001). The drug court as a sentencing model. *Journal of Contemporary Criminal Justice*, 17(2): 89-104.

Kimbrough, R. (1998). *Treating juvenile substance abuse: The promise of juvenile drug courts.* Office of Juvenile Justice and Delinquency Prevention.

Kent v. United States, 383 U.S. 541, 86 S. Ct. 1045, 16 Led 2d 84 (1966).

Latessa, E. J., Shaffer, D. K., & Lowenkamp, C. (2002). *Outcome evaluation of Ohio's drug court efforts.* Technical Report. Center for Criminal Justice Research, University of Cincinnati.

Listwan, S. J., Sundt, J. L., Holsinger, A. M., & Latessa, E. J. (2003). The effect of drug court programming on recidivism: The Cincinnati experience. *Crime & Delinquency*, 49(3): 389-411.

McGee, C., Merrigan, T., Parnham, J., & Smith, M. (2000). *Applying drug court concepts in juvenile and family court environments: A primer for judges.* American University, Justice Programs Office, School of Public Affairs.

Rempel, M., Fox-Kralstein, D., & Cissner, A. (2003). *New York State Adult Drug Court Evaluation: Policies, Participants & Impact.* Center for Court Innovation. New York.

Rogers, J. D. & Mays, L. G. (1987). *Juvenile Delinquency and Juvenile Justice.* Wiley: New York.

Siegel, L. & Senna, J. (1997). *Juvenile delinquency: Theory, practice, and law.* (6th ed.). St. Paul, MN: West.

Spohn, C., Piper, R. K., Martin, T., & Frenzel, E. D. (2001). Drug courts and recidivism: The results of an evaluation using two comparison groups and multiple indicators of recidivism. *Journal of Drug Issues*, 31(1): 149-176.

Stier Adler, E. & Clark, R. (2011). *An Invitation to Social Research: How it's done*, 4th edition. Wadsworth Publishing.

Vito, G. F. & Tewksbury, R. A. (1998). The impact of treatment: The Jefferson County (Kentucky) drug court program. *Federal Probation*, 62(2): 46-51.

Volkow, N. D. (2006). *Principles of Drug Abuse Treatment for Criminal Justice Populations: A Research-Based Guide.* U.S. Department of Health and Human Services. (NIH Publication No. 06-5316.) National Institute on Drug Abuse.

Whitehousedrugpolicy.gov. (2006). Office of National Drug Control Policy. Washington D.C.

Discussion Questions

1. How is drug court different in what it hopes to accomplish from regular court?

2. How is the juvenile drug court system different from the adult drug court system? That is, what assumptions are made about how juveniles are treated versus adults?

3. Explain the importance of having matched comparison groups when evaluating a program's success. What measures did the research team take to create comparison groups in this project?

4. Although many students express great concern over privacy issues on Facebook, many disclose personal information on the SNS. Why the disjunction?

5. Explain the concept of nonsocial reinforcement. Provide an example of nonsocial reinforcement, other than those presented in this chapter.

6. If you were a member of the Institutional Review Board, what concerns would need to be addressed prior to approving replication of this study at your college or university?

7. What factors limit the generalizability of these findings?

8. How would you expect results to differ if the subjects of the study were from different demographic groups?

SECTION 5

CORRECTIONS ISSUES AND RESEARCH

Section 5
Corrections Issues and Research

Introduction

Once suspects are apprehended and processed through the legal system, they find themselves in the correctional system. They may be in jail awaiting trial or, if convicted, in jail or prison serving a sentence. They may be serving their sentences outside of institutional walls, through one of many forms of community-based corrections. The papers in this section do not focus on life in prison—there are many excellent works already on this subject (beginning with the Syke's 1958 classic *Society of Captives*), but rather how they got there (West and Smith), what to do with them to improve their chance of successful reintegration, (Brewster), how community members, particularly college students, can become more actively involved in a system of community-based corrections (Greenberg), and how working within corrections can affect families (Paap and McSain).

This section's first chapter deals with incarceration and the intergenerational transmission of crime. West and Smith interviewed children of incarcerated fathers, asking them to organize and recall events that were meaningful to them. Sadly, many of them reported events that produced lives that replicated their fathers' including drug use, instability and crime. West and Smith's work challenges the notion of intergenerational transmission of crime.

Brewster's chapter describes California's Arts in Corrections program, a program designed to give prisoners training in a variety of forms of art and a place to display their work. He interviewed a small group of formerly incarcerated people who participated in this program and found that the program produced many benefits, not only helping the individuals involved. In an era of budget cuts, Brewster's research raises the question of how much society should invest in individuals to benefit the larger group.

Greenberg's chapter discusses probation and getting college students involved in community corrections programs. He describes citizen probation academies and suggests ways students can become involved with these programs including internships. While each institution has a different approach to experiential learning, Greenberg's article should give both students and faculty some inspiration for participating in educational experiences beyond the classroom. Such opportunities can be rewarding for everyone involved, including the agency and the community.

Paap and McSain's chapter presents research that developed from interest generated by classroom discussion about the impact of working corrections on families of the officers. Students conducted interviews with corrections officers, which confirmed much of what they had already learned in the classroom about the impact of being a corrections officer on families. Interestingly, the research revealed another dimension that has rarely been discussed by academics: the impact of working corrections on officer perception of race.

Students may find that these articles portray the corrections field in a new and interesting way. Jails and prisons are here to stay but are becoming excessively expensive options for the criminal justice system and a personally taxing option for offenders, community members, and corrections workers. A non-traditional approach to corrections might solve part of the current overcrowding problem, and in some cases do a better job of rehabilitation.

Involving College Students in Community Corrections

Probation is the most commonly imposed criminal sentence. Yet, many of its parameters are unknown to the public. In recent years, basic probation has been somewhat eclipsed by intermediate sanctions, inmate reentry programs, and a variety of "problem-solving" courts for dealing with cases in particular areas, such as domestic violence, substance abusers, and veterans. College students may become involved in community corrections by applying for existing internship opportunities in probation, parole, courts, and related agencies, serving as volunteer probation officers, and by assisting in the development of citizen probation academies. In this chapter, Greenberg discusses the goals of community corrections and provides a brief overview of the history of citizen involvement in community corrections. He describes the purposes, organization, advantages, and disadvantages of citizen probation academies, and suggests several ways for college students to participate in community corrections.

The Effects of Working Corrections: Role Conflict, Strain Conflict, and Reconceptualizing Race Relations

In this chapter, Paap and McSain explore the effects of working corrections over time using information from ten in-depth qualitative interviews with correctional officers (COs). Respondents discussed levels of stress due to perceived negative stereotyping of correctional officers, job constraints, stresses at home from their behavioral changes over time (which they attributed to work), and a recognition that working in a highly racialized environment has changed their perceptions of race from views considered socially acceptable to views more reflective of the dynamics and demographics within prison walls. They conclude with a discussion of the implications of these changing racial ideologies for the largely white communities where many rural prisons are located.

Sons of Incarcerated Fathers: Following in Dad's Footsteps

The dramatic increase in the incarcerated population in the United States has led to a corresponding increase in the number of children of imprisoned fathers. Although scholars and criminal justice professionals have long recognized existence of intergenerational incarceration, little is known about how individuals, primarily males, follow in their fathers' footsteps. It is widely assumed that the children of incarcerated fathers are at high risk for exposure to parental substance abuse, violence, mental health disorders, and criminality. Exposure to these risk factors predicts poor outcomes for children, but other elements, such as the perception of the father and assignment of blame for the family's hardships, may also contribute to negative outcomes for children of prisoners. In this chapter, West and Smith present information gleaned from interviews with sons of incarcerated fathers who lived with or who had regular contact with their fathers and whose later-life outcomes closely mirrored their fathers' experiences.

Arts-in-Corrections: A Path of Discovery and Redemption

The California Arts-in-Corrections (AIC) program offered high quality, formal art instruction to incarcerated individuals. It was the nation's first prison fine arts program to be administered, in part, by highly skilled and successful civilian artists, who helped meld inmates' impulses to create with the fine arts model of practice, inspiration, and discipline. Whereas many inmates pass the monotonous time in segregated groups in the yard, AIC offered inmates constructive, meaningful ways to momentarily escape the harsh realities of prison. AIC offered hundreds of thousands of hours of art instruction to thousands of inmate-artists during its thirty year run (1980-2010) and produced countless original pieces of extraordinary sensitivity and honesty. More important, the artistic process for many of these convicts provided a path of discovery and redemption. In this chapter, Brewster describes the AIC program and, through interviews with ex-cons who participated in the program and current inmate-artists at San Quentin state prison, discusses its impact on their lives as incarcerated and later free men and women.

Chapter 15
INVOLVING COLLEGE STUDENTS IN COMMUNITY CORRECTIONS

Martin Alan Greenberg, J.D., Ph.D., Associate Professor of CJ; Miles College, Birmingham, AL, Director of Research and Education, New York State Association of Auxiliary Police, Inc.; State University of New York at Ulster (Ret.)

Introduction

In recent years, there have been significant advances in community supervision of offenders. New, sophisticated risk assessment tools determine which offenders require the most supervision and what sort of services they need. In addition, global positioning systems, rapid-result drug tests, and other technology can track offenders' whereabouts or behavior. Supervision, treatment, and reentry programs are incorporating research on how to reduce recidivism. At the same time, there has been huge growth in the number of people on probation or parole (Moore, 2009). According to a 2009 report by the Pew Center on the States, the population of the American corrections system stood at more than 7.3 million, one in every 31 U.S. adults. Although nearly 90 percent of state corrections dollars were being spent on prisons, most of these offenders were being supervised in communities (Pew Center, 2009). The Pew study warned against cutting probation and parole programs that have the potential of reducing crime (Moore, 2009).

Starting in the late 1980s, many U.S. police departments established citizens police academies. These are "mini" police academies, where departments instruct citizens in many facets of police work. Their primary goal has been to develop a positive police–community relationship by providing citizens with exposure to police operations and procedures. A similar program for probation departments can help foster the goals of community corrections. The development of citizen probation academies might create a mechanism for improving probation-community relations and for enhancing public understanding of the problems and goals engendered by the community supervision of offenders.

This chapter explores several ways for involving college students in projects and services concerned with community corrections, beyond internships. Students can also be encouraged to participate in a citizen's probation academy and to serve as volunteer probation officers.

Goals of Community Corrections

Community correctional agencies strive to protect the community by monitoring offenders in the community at the most appropriate level of supervision. Common protection strategies include conditional release supervision, intensive supervision, community service, electronic home monitoring, and drug and alcohol testing. If these methods of offender supervision fail, community correctional agencies may petition the appropriate court or board to send the offender to jail or prison for having violated the terms of release. The agencies charged with preventing recidivism can enhance community protection by focusing more on offender accountability and supervising offenders based on the level of risk they pose to the community.

The process of community corrections begins when the court places an offender under probation supervision or when a paroling authority releases an offender early from prison. In both cases, the offender agrees to abide by "conditions of supervision." The law mandates many general conditions and allows the sentencing/releasing authority to design "special conditions" for the offender if needed. Violation of these conditions may result in revocation of release status and reinstatement of any sentence imposed before placing the offender on community supervision.

Probation or parole officers have arrest powers over their offenders on supervision. In recent years, these officers have worked with other law enforcement agencies to strengthen the supervision of offenders who are members of gangs, sex offenders, or absconders from supervision. Many supervising officers carry a firearm for protection and have responsibilities beyond offender supervision. For example, probation officers prepare presentence reports to aid courts in carrying out their sentencing responsibilities.

The United States experienced a growth in "intermediate sanctions" during the last two decades of the twentieth century. These sanctions include intensive supervision programs, day reporting centers, home confinement programs, and halfway houses. Intermediate sanctions place greater restrictions on probationers or parolees than traditional forms of these sentences. Involving community members actively in the community corrections process facilitates monitoring offenders and connecting offenders with appropriate services. Such involvement may include participation in the planning and implementation of agency programs. Community volunteers and college students can assist in the monitoring of adult and juvenile offenders in an effort to help keep them from engaging in activities that would violate their terms of probation or parole.

A Brief Overview of Citizen Involvement in Corrections

Since 1787, members of the Pennsylvania Prison Society have monitored prison conditions and visited prisoners to assist them with issues ranging from serious medical concerns to reconnecting with family members. A Pennsylvania statute authorizes "Prison Society Official Visitors" access to all Pennsylvania correctional facilities. More than 450 volunteer "Official Visitors" make about 5,000 visits to Pennsylvania jails and prisons each year (Pennsylvania Prison Society, 2009).

The fields of probation and parole, the best-known and most widely practiced alternatives to incarceration, came into fruition during the latter half of the nineteenth century. Perhaps the most important reason for their creation was the inhumane conditions found within the penal institutions of the era (Wodahl & Garland, 2009). Establishing probation and parole in the U.S. relied heavily on the services of volunteers.

The first probation officer was a volunteer named John Augustus. He was a shoemaker, and beginning in 1841, he routinely posted bail at the Boston Police Court for hundreds of petty criminals and helped them find jobs. Augustus believed that the object of the law was to reform criminals and to prevent crime. He had little faith in the ability of prisons to rehabilitate (Wodahl & Garland, 2009).

The first parole officers were volunteers. In 1877, New York's Elmira Reformatory for young men (ages 16 to 30) started a supervised release or parole system that used volunteers. Similarly, the first parole officers from Auburn Correctional Facility were volunteers (Pollock, 2008). According to Wodahl & Garland (2009):

> *After Augustus passed away in 1859, other volunteers carried on his work. The volunteer remained an important figure in the development of probation throughout the nineteenth century. Early probation statutes failed to authorize money for probation officer salaries. It was assumed that supervision duties would be delegated to persons willing to take on this role without compensation. It was not until decades later that probation shifted from a secondary function to be carried out by untrained volunteers to a salient criminal justice function requiring the services of trained professionals* (p. 87S).

During the last half of the twentieth century, two novel types of educational programs involving student participation in criminal justice fields emerged. From 1955 to 1965, the probation department of the Kings County Court in Brooklyn, New York offered college seniors an intensive six-day course in probation. According to Smith and Bassin (1992), students were assigned probation officer mentors and attended lectures offered by probation staff and members of the judiciary.

Since 1972, the Georgetown University Law Center Street Law Program has provided law-related educational services in the District of Columbia and has served as a model for "Street Law" programs both nationally and internationally. The program offers legal education to laypersons while aiding in the professional development of law students. It seeks to provide a greater understanding of the law to those outside the legal profession and to promote the use of interactive educational methods to develop academic, critical thinking, and civic skills. The law students, who serve as law teachers to District of Columbia high school students and community members, are an integral part of these efforts.

More than 60 other law schools have replicated the Georgetown University Law Center program; law students throughout the United States and in more than 25 countries participate in this type of law-related education (LRE). Some participate for academic credit, some participate as part of a *pro bono* or public service requirement, some are paid, and some volunteer. Law schools have provided student-led law-related education programs in local schools, prisons, juvenile justice facilities, and community settings (Street Law, 2009).

In recent decades, some law schools as well as local and state bar associations have begun to offer free law-related education classes to the public. Most often, these programs target adult citizens, and the instructors are local attorneys or judges. A typical name for this type of program is "The People's Law School." For example, the Cleveland Metropolitan Bar Association (CMBA) offered its first "People's Law School" program in the early 1990s (CMBA, 2009).

Most law schools also provide year-long legal clinics that involve their students in other related community affairs. For example, the Frank J. Remington Center at the University of Wisconsin School of Law has at least eight corrections-based clinics, including an "Innocence Project" and a "Restorative Justice Project." The Center's newest clinic is the "Community Supervision Legal Assistance Legal Project." Since 2007, it has helped those under Wisconsin's Department of Corrections' Division of Community Corrections with legal assistance in areas of housing law, employment law, family law, disability law, debt issues, revocation hearings, restitution issues, early release from supervision, and reinstatement of drivers licenses (Remington Center, 2009).

Since 1965, Canadian citizens have been encouraged to contribute in the development and implementation of new correctional policies and programs by serving as volunteer members of citizens' advisory committees (CACs). In 1977, the Canadian government mandated that each unit of the Correctional Service of Canada have a CAC be recognized as a national organization. In 1992, the *Corrections and Conditional Release Act* further solidified the position of the CAC, by stating the importance of public involvement in corrections. By 2006, CACs were operating in almost all Canadian correctional institutions, parole offices, and community correctional centers (Gillis & Trevethan, 2006).

The Traditional Citizen Police Academy Model

In 1977, the Devon and Cornwall Constabulary designed a program to familiarize private citizens with the nature and organization of policing in the United Kingdom. Police personnel volunteered to lead a course, known as the "Police Night School," which met weekly over a ten-week period. The success of this program prompted other police departments to imitate it. Eight years later, in 1985, the Orlando (Florida) Police Department organized the first citizen police academy in the United States (Ferguson, 1985). According to Aryani et al. (2000):

> *Citizen police academies represent a vital part of community-oriented policing. CPAs keep the public involved by making them part of the police family.... [and] provide a productive outlet for the mutual sharing of information and concerns in order to further common goals of communities and law enforcement agencies* (p. 21).

Citizen police academies provide a mechanism for educating the public about various aspects of police work and may include ways to resist crime. Their overall goals are to gain support for police work, to explain the operations of police agencies, and to encourage private citizens to undertake appropriate security measures. Typically, police personnel conduct the classes. Since the mid-1980s, other U.S. communities have followed Orlando's lead. These initiatives have spawned several related programs, including the Citizens' FBI Academy, Junior Police Academies, and Teen Police Academies.

Purposes for Citizen Probation Academies

The purposes for establishing citizen probation academies are similar to those of the citizen police academies; namely, they use education to develop positive relations and partnerships between the probation department and the community at large. They provide an opportunity for citizens to learn about the responsibilities of probation officers.

Citizen attendance at such academies should lead to the creation of a nucleus of responsible, well-informed citizens who understand the tasks and responsibilities of probation officers. Furthermore, it may be possible for an agency to attract volunteers from participants in the academy program. Smith (1993) recognized the value of a volunteer probation officer program decades ago, claiming that such programs would effectively augment probation departments and increase community involvement in the criminal justice system. Table 15-1 lists eight potential roles performed by volunteer probation officers.

Table 15-1. Volunteer Probation Officer Roles

- Casework Assistant: Assist probation and parole officers with caseload-related duties.

- Education: Help youthful offenders get their high school diplomas by providing one-on-one tutoring or by teaching a class.

- Parenting: Teach parenting skills to parents and parents-to-be.

- Community Service: Locate projects and assist in monitoring of service work.

- Interpreters: Provide foreign languages or American Sign Language (ASL) interpretation service.

- Offender Reentry: Assist in developing a well-planned transition for offenders reentering the community.

- Reparative Board Program: Serve on a community team designed to ensure that probationers convicted of low-risk offenses make amends to their victims and to the community.

- Victim Impact Panels: Help instruct a class of offenders about the impacts of DUI on others.

- Victim Liaison: Work with crime victims to ensure their needs are met.

Currently, hundreds of volunteers in four separate programs, including a non-profit support group, help the Orange County (CA) Probation Department in its mission to enhance community safety. Probation volunteers work in a variety of assignments, often directly with youth and adult probationers. The volunteers work with and under the supervision of deputy probation officers. They may aid the department in investigating adult and juvenile cases, monitoring caseloads, performing telephonic compliance checks, verifying address and place of employment, and making home, work, or jail visits. They may contact victims or others for information, provide bilingual services, work with juveniles in drug treatment programs, and more (Volunteer Probation Officer Program, 2009). Table 15-2 summarizes Orange County's citizen volunteer probation programs.

Table 15-2. Orange County Probation Department Volunteer Programs

Volunteers in Probation (VIP) Program — Probation's largest volunteer program with no minimum time commitment for service. A brief program orientation is provided.

Volunteer Probation Officer (VPO) Program — Involves a deeper level of participation, including night training classes and a commitment of at least 20 hours per month of volunteer work for a year.

Volunteer Internship Academy — Santa Ana College in collaboration with the Orange County Probation Department presents this Academy for those interested in seeking employment with the Orange County Probation Department. Students may earn up to a total of 6 units in two consecutive semesters. **First Semester:** Requires 40 hours of classroom lecture provided by experienced staff from the Probation Department who are experts in their field. **Second Semester:** Requires students to complete an internship of a minimum of 120 hours (3 units).

Probation Community Action Association (PCAA) — Probation's non-profit support group. This organization conducts activities aimed at promoting the Probation Department and raising money to underwrite anti-crime programs.

Source: http://egov.ocgov.com/ocgov/Probation/Volunteer%20Programs

---

Students learn about the following topics: the departments mission, values, and ethics; confidentiality; juvenile and adult court; field services; domestic violence; sex offenders; substance abuse; gang violence suppression; and officer safety during the "first semester" of the Orange County Volunteer Internship Academy (see Table 15-2). Additional classes are required to tour juvenile institutions. During the "second semester," students complete several hours of job shadowing (Volunteer Internship Academy, 2009). Table 15-3 indicates the admission qualifications for this internship program.

Table 15-3. Minimum Requirements for Volunteer Internship Academy

- Be at least 18 years of age and provide proof of legal residency in the United States.

- Have successfully completed a Criminal Justice 101 Class or similar training or experience.

- Not be on formal or informal probation or parole for at least one year prior to the start of the VIA Program.

- Not have used illegal drugs for at least one year.

- Obtain a test for tuberculosis with negative results.

- Pass a background check to the satisfaction of the Probation Department.

Source: http://egov.ocgov.com/ocgov/Probation/Volunteer%20Programs/Volunteer %20Internship%20Academy%20(VIA)

Organizing the Citizen Probation Academy

In today's technological society, the Internet should play a central part in any recruiting effort. A department's website can reach large groups as well as provide a way for one-on-one contact. Possible uses of a website include sharing non-confidential department information, presenting crime statistics, announcing and accepting applications for academy classes, providing opportunities for citizen feedback, and using e-mail as a vehicle for communication with the public. Video clips from a department's web site can be an easy way to have community members see and hear what it has to offer.

A citizen probation academy should seek to attract attendees from a variety of backgrounds. Organizers should use the latest Internet channels of communication and local media outlets to recruit participants. They should focus on attracting community members of various ethnicities, professions, cultural backgrounds, age groups, and neighborhoods in the hopes of enriching class discussions and reaching out to as many sections of the community as possible. Table 15-4 indicates suggested qualifications for participation in a citizen probation academy.

Table 15-4. Qualifications for Participation

- 18 years of age
- Completion of an application
- Commitment to attend a 7 week series of classes
- Preference to those who work or reside in community served by department
- Optional criminal background check

It is important to maintain at least some contact with the participants after academy attendance is completed. For example, graduates of some police citizen academies have formed alumni associations that raise funds for crime prevention programs or for specialized units. They can also become involved in the selection of future participants and in the development of the curriculum. Other types of contact include having picnics or similar gatherings, assisting at future academies, and actually becoming an agency volunteer.

Curriculum Design and Instruction

Ideally, the curriculum should be presented over a seven-week period (one 3-hour session per week) and should provide an in-depth understanding of probation services, practices, resources, and the nature of the judicial system in which the agency functions. Although there are various levels of courts in the U.S. (federal, state, and local), state courts handle most cases; individual courts vary in jurisdiction, nomenclature, rules, and method of judicial selection. Hence, the nature of the state judicial system should be an important topic for academies. Additionally, the curriculum should emphasize the unique role of probation officers as both officers of the court and as case managers, and it should review specialized programs in the probation and court systems as well as criminal proceedings from the time of arrest to post conviction actions.

The academy's instructors should be of high quality and involved in the planning for the academy. They should strive to involve the participants as much as possible. Instructors should incorporate classroom demonstrations or hands-on activities at least once per session. They must tailor handouts and other materials to the needs of all participants (Blackwood, 1994).

The curriculum should provide participants with information on the nature of the American correctional system and allow for the discussion of the challenges relating to promoting liberty and public safety in our nation today. Supervised offenders in the community experience a loss of privacy and various degrees of liberty, which can create problems and tensions in offenders. It is important to communicate this to participants. Table 15-5 lists other topics for possible curricular inclusion.

Table 15-5. Additional Academy Topics

Community Anticrime Programs	Domestic Violence
GPS Tracking and Crime Mapping	Inmate Re-Entry
Race, Ethnic and Gender Issues	Cults
Trafficking and Organized Crime	Gangs
Use and Addiction	Victim Services
Community Supervision of People with Mental Illness	White-Collar Crime

Advantages and Disadvantages of CPAs

In the United State, the number of people on probation or parole stands at more than 5 million, up from 1.6 million 25 years ago. One in 45 U.S. adults is under criminal justice supervision in the community (Pew Center, 2009). This tremendous growth requires scrutiny by all concerned citizens. A citizen probation academy can provide an appropriate forum to address this need on a community-wide basis. Through their academy participation, citizens may become more aware of the operations of the criminal justice system. This can better prepare them to support policies based on sound research, rather than relying on abbreviated media portrayals or reports regarding criminal incidents. Additionally, citizens bring a wealth of knowledge of their community and neighborhood problems. In this way, agency personnel can learn firsthand about the concerns of citizens.

Some participants may want to take a more active role to help reduce crime by contributing a service to the department or serving as a volunteer. For example, a bank executive, who participated in a citizen police academy, offered to include crime prevention messages in the monthly statements mailed to depositors (Seelmeyer, 1987). Today, probation departments may be able to improve their websites through the services of a volunteer webmaster and thus be able to extend community outreach efforts. The use of guest instructors from other agencies furthers interagency cooperation, and the internal cooperation necessary for organizing and implementing an academy program can improve departmental morale (Greenberg, 1991). Moreover, through CPA sessions, some college students may come to regard probation or related work as a career goal.

Citizen academies also have their disadvantages. For example, the programs may reach only a small number of residents. The public relations aspects might be overplayed and curtail the delivery of more useful information about the realities of community supervision and the ability of the criminal justice system to contend with crime. At the same time, planning activities for the academy, such as preparing curriculum and screening applicants, might detract from the time and resources of a busy department. Although the expenditures needed to maintain a citizen probation academy are usually minimal, some instructional costs might still be necessary, especially if probation officer instructors or other volunteer agency personnel are unavailable. Moreover, if departments are seeking greater community involvement, they need to develop meaningful after-academy, follow-up opportunities. Nevertheless, the weight of the arguments appears to favor the use of citizen academies (see Cohn, 1996; Blackwood, 1994; Breen & Johnson, 2007; Brewster, Stoloff, & Sanders, 2005; and Stone & Champeny, 2001).

Roles and Responsibilities of Student Interns

Probation officers are engaged in at least three important roles: direct supervision of offenders, counseling of offenders, and documenting and reporting such activities. With high caseloads in many agencies, the services of competent college student interns for help in carrying out crime prevention programs could be invaluable. Student interns can help facilitate the establishment of a citizen probation academy. For example, student interns can help with recruitment and selection of participants, as well as with the actual design and delivery of instruction.

College students can become actively involved in the citizen probation academy. One of the most compelling aspects of utilizing college students in the field of probation, especially for work with juveniles, is that many of these students will be in an age group that is much closer to the age of the juvenile population. Therefore, they may be better able to relate to these individuals and understand their problems. On the other hand, they will need to be carefully trained and supervised to ensure that they stay within the proper bounds of their assignments. In this regard, it seems highly important for instructors contemplating the establishment of such a program to enlist the services of those colleagues who specialize in human relationship education (e.g., psychologists, social workers, etc.). Their assistance would be of great value in setting up an appropriate internship training and orientation program. Table 15-6 presents a brief list of potential roles for college students working with younger clients of the justice system.

> **Table 15-6. Internship Roles for Working with Youth**
>
> Help with the school assignments
> Assist with Youth Court
> Assist in data collection and compilation
> Assist Agency with new project development
> Provide support for students with special needs
> Serve on a weekend crisis intervention team
> Assist in school field trips
> Research, develop, and offer a Youth Citizen Police Academy

Why Students Should Seek Internships

Internships provide many benefits to students. They offer them a chance to learn about a career field from the inside and to gain self-confidence. Students can learn new things, meet new people, and practice communication, networking, and teamwork skills—all valuable additions to the resume and the graduate school application. Internships provide an opportunity for students to apply ideas learned in school and to connect the ideas presented in the classroom to experiences in the professional world. They can demonstrate to potential employers and references that they have initiative and are responsible. Many interns obtain a mentor from within the organization, who can help them learn more about job specifics and provide guidance on the sequence of steps in a particular career path.

Generally, students gain a richer understanding of the relationship between theory and practical application. The experience may test a career objective because of a real world encounter. Students have the opportunity to develop good professional work habits and to become acquainted with people employed in professional occupations. The relationships may grow into a network of contacts for future career pursuits. An internship should also enhance the students' self-confidence as they learn self-reliance and independence and develop skills necessary to interact with populations that are more diverse. At the very least, they can provide a meaningful experience to discuss during job and graduate school interviews.

Conclusion

Dr. Frank Straub, public safety director of Indianapolis, has called upon police departments to re-think their strategies for combating crime by embracing a "smart power" paradigm. According to Straub (2009), "smart power policing skillfully sequences and integrates traditional and non-traditional strategies with broader social programs to prevent crime, build police legitimacy, and engage the community in the 'war on crime'" (para. 5). His agency has partnered with his city's youth bureau, community, faith-based and other organizations to provide an array of services for at-risk youth (Straub, 2009).

"Smart power policing" has a corollary in the field of probation known as "community justice." According to Cole and Smith (2010), community justice is "a philosophy that emphasizes restorative justice, reparation to the victim and the community, problem-solving strategies instead of adversarial procedures, and increased citizen involvement in crime prevention" (p. 512). Student and faculty participation in the field of probation services and in the establishment of citizen probation academies can help forge new probation and community alliances to reduce violence and to build effective crime prevention strategies.

In future years, especially as the American economy struggles for recovery, the need and demand for citizen participation will no doubt increase. Exposing students to a variety of criminal justice positions through volunteer service facilitates their eventual participation in the system as professionals and potentially assists and recruiting, training, and supervising others down the road. These students can become leaders of criminal justice agencies. Furthermore, unless there is greater public knowledge regarding funding disparities for the community supervision of offenders, advances may be lost and community safety jeopardized.

As the number of clients in community corrections continues to grow, so does the demand for agency workers and volunteers. However, constant government cutbacks remain a dominant feature of the American economy. Therefore, it is critical for informed citizens to become actively involved in the field of criminal justice. Citizens are ultimately responsible for their own safety, security, and survival. Opportunities abound for greater citizen participation in the field of community corrections and the need for support is urgent.

References

Aryani, G. A., Garrett, T. D. & Alsabrook, C. L. (2000). The citizen police academy. *The FBI Law Enforcement Bulletin*, 69 (5):16-21.

Blackwood, B. (1994). Citizen police academies. *TELEMASP Monthly Bulletin*, 1 (2):1-8. Retrieved May 4, 2009 from http://www.lemit online.org/telemasp/Pdf/volume%201/vol1no2.pdf

Breen, M. E. & Johnson, B. R. (2007). Citizen police academies: An analysis of enhanced police–community relations among citizen attendees. *The Police Journal*, 80 (3): 246-266.

Brewster, J., Stoloff, M. & Sanders, N. (2005). Effectiveness of citizen police academies in changing the attitudes, beliefs, and behavior of citizen participants. *The American Journal of Criminal Justice*, 30 (1): 21-34.

CMBA (2009). Cleveland Metropolitan Bar Association. Retrieved May 22, 2009 from http://www.clemetrobar.org/about_history.asp?id=23

Cohn, E. G. (1996). The citizen police academy: A recipe for improving police-community relations. *Journal of Criminal Justice*, 24 (3): 265-271.

Cole, G. F. & Smith, C. E. (2010). *The American system of criminal justice*. (12th ed). Belmont, CA: Wadsworth, Cengage Learning.

Ferguson, R. E. (1985). The citizen police academy. *FBI Law Enforcement Bulletin*, 54 (9): 5-7.

Gillis, C. & Trevethan, S. (2006). Involving the community in corrections. The citizens' advisory committees in Canada. Retrieved June 18, 2009 from http://www.icclr.law.ubc.ca/Publications/2008/Book

Greenberg, M. A. (1991). Citizen police academies. *FBI Law Enforcement Bulletin*, 60 (8):10-13.

Moore, S. (2009, March 3). Prison spending outpaces all but Medicaid. *New York Times*, p. A13.

Pennsylvania Prison Society (2009). Official visitors. Retrieved June 23, 2009 from   http://www.prisonsociety.org/adv/ov.shtml

Pew Center on the States (2009). One in 31: The long reach of American corrections. Washington, DC: The Pew Charitable Trusts, March 2009. Retrieved May 14, 2009 from http://www.pewcenteronthe states.org/uploadedFiles/PSPP_1in31_report_FINAL_WEB_3-26-09.pdf

Pollock, J. M. (2008). *Crime and justice in America*. Newark, NJ: LexisNexis.

Remington Center (2009). Clinical projects of the Frank J. Remington Center. Retrieved June 18, 2009 from http://www.law.wisc.edu/ fjr/clinicals/index.html

Seelmeyer, J. (1987). A citizen's police academy, *Law and Order*, 35 (12): 26-29.

Smith, A. B. & Bassin, A. (1992). Kings County Court probation: A laboratory for offender rehabilitation. *Journal of Addictions & Offender Counseling*, 13 (1): 11-23.

Smith, B. M. (1993). Probation department in Michigan finds volunteers make fine officers. *Corrections Today*, 55 (5): 80-82.

Stone, W. E. & Champeny, S. (2001). Assessing a citizen police academy. *Police Practice and Research*, 2 (3): 219-241.

Straub, F. (2009, January 29). Smart policing: It can be done. Retrieved May 12, 2009 from http://thecrimereport.org/2009/01/29/smart-policing-it-can-be-done-really/#more-19196

Street Law (2009). Overview of street law programs. Retrieved May 22, 2009 from http://law.hofstra.edu/studentlife/StudentOrganizations/ StreetLaw/strlaw_overvie w.html

Volunteer Internship Academy (2009). Volunteer Internship Academy (VIA). Orange County, CA. Retrieved May 19, 2009 from http://egov.

ocgov.com/ocgov/Probation/Volunteer%20Programs/Volunteer
%20Internship%20Academy%20(VIA)

Volunteer Probation Officer Program (2009). Volunteer Probation Officer
Program (VOP). Orange County, CA. Retrieved May 19, 2009 from
http://egov.ocgov.com/ocgov/Probation/Volunteer%20Programs/
Volunteer%20Probation%20Officer%20Program%20(VPO)

Wodahl, E.J. & Garland, B. (2009). The evolution of community correc
tions: The enduring influence of the prison. *The Prison Journal*, 89
(1): 81S-104S.

http://egov.ocgov.com/ocgov/Info%20OC/Departments%20&%20Agencies/
Volunteer%20&%20Intern

Discussion Questions

1. Discuss the various roles citizens have played in the American correctional system.

2. Contrast and compare the nature of Street Law Programs and Citizen Police Academies.

3. Identify at least five potential roles performed by volunteer probation officers.

4. What is the value of internship programs in college curricula?

5. Review the list of admission qualifications for volunteer probation interns presented in Table 15-3. Discuss whether these qualifications are appropriate. Should any items be eliminated or added?

6. You are tasked with "pitching" the idea of establishing a citizen probation academy to probation department and government officials in your area. What benefits are there to creating such a program? What concerns would you expect them to have and how would you address them?

7. Consider question #6. You were given permission to establish and operate a citizen probation academy on a trial basis for two years. If you are able to establish evidence of success, the program may become permanent. What steps would you need to take prior to establishing the program? (Note: Recall Chin's chapter *The Case for Sound Social Science Research*). What types of data would you want to collect throughout and/or after program completion?

Chapter 16
THE EFFECTS OF WORKING CORRECTIONS: ROLE CONFLICT, STRAIN CONFLICT, AND RECONCEPTUALIZING RACE RELATIONS

Kris E. Paap, Ph.D., State University of NY—Institute of Technology
Janet McSain, B.A., State University of NY—Institute of Technology

Introduction

Although there has been a lot of research on the work attitudes, work stress, and even work-family conflict experienced by correctional officers (COs) over the past three decades, virtually all has been quantitative and based on survey data collected en masse within the confines of the prisons, using sets of questions formed by researchers (for examples, see Antonio, Young, & Wingeard, 2009; Farkas, 1999; Grossi & Berg, 1991; Hemmens & Stohr, 2001; Kifer, Hemmens, & Stohr, 2003; Klofas & Toch, 1982; Poole & Regoli, 1981; Summerlin, Oehme, Stern, & Valentine, 2010; Tewksbury & Mustaine, 2008). Although surveys can ask very important questions about the COs' sources of stress, relations with coworkers, or work-related burnout, it is important to note that survey topics are *fixed*, meaning that they only cover the topics that the researchers have determined in advance (for examples, see Dial, Downey, & Goodlin, 2010; Lambert & Hogan, 2010; Lambert, Hogan, & Tucker, 2007). Hence, fixed surveys are able to capture only data on the topics *preselected* for the study.

Few projects have met the correctional officers on their turf and asked them to describe, in their words, the nature of their work and how it has changed them across time (see Crawley, 2004 [a British example] and Kauffman, 1988 [a view from the 1970s]). In this simple project, we have done just that. What we have found most helpful about this approach is that it has allowed the COs—not the research team—to determine the important topics. As a result, our topics were not limited to pre-determined ideas; they encompassed the concerns and reflections of the COs. Our results, however, dovetail nicely with the quantitative research on correctional officers (including discussions of work-family conflicts) while offering some surprising findings about racial and ethnic relations.

Background

Understanding the effects of work on correctional officers is a topic of growing importance, partly because the correctional industry itself has been expanding notably in recent decades. Incarceration has been a mainstay of U.S. penal policy throughout our history. Although crime rates have been in decline, our "get tough" sentencing practices and increased calls for accountability have resulted in greater use of prison, longer sentences, and fewer opportunities for early release. In response to a burgeoning prison population, many states have doubled their number of prisons, and the U.S. Bureau of Prisons budget has increased by 1,500% (Clear, Cole, & Reisig, 2000; Gaines & Miller, 2006). Several states in America have more prisons than entire other Western countries have (Bohm & Haley, 2009).

These increases in imprisonment have had profound effects on American society, particularly on low-income communities—and largely communities of color—that have been policed and over-policed in the drug war that has dominated the last four decades of U.S. domestic policy (Barak, Leighton, & Flavin, 2010; Díaz-Cotto, 2007). It is not an exaggeration to write that these policies have transformed many communities for the worse. Some estimate that one in three young African American men in many communities are involved with the criminal justice system (Huling, 1999). Todd Clear (2007) has written about the devastating effects on neighborhoods and communities from having so many people (especially adult males) pulled from them and placed into prisons. Marc Mauer and Meda Chesney-Lind edited a volume in 2002 on the "collateral consequences" of the policies of mass imprisonment on individuals and society. These included the effects on families (Braman, 2002), the effects of more women and mothers being incarcerated by the drug war (Richie, 2002), and the shift in voter demographics caused by the disenfranchisement of many felons (Mauer, 2002). These concerns are very meaningful and very real.

Creation of Prison Economies

Mass imprisonment yields some consequences that are not necessarily negative for the communities that house prison inmates. First, jobs are created during the construction of the facilities; then, jobs are created to staff the facilities, both with permanent full-time staff and outside contractors. Because prisons are often built where they will be most economical (i.e., where land and labor is cheaper), they are often constructed away from cities, in rural and rust-belt (that is, de-industrialized) areas (Farrigan & Glasmeier, n.d.; Huling, 2002; Huling, 1999). As a result, the prison boom tends to benefit some communities significantly, perhaps as much as it devastates others.

In these communities, it makes sense to talk about the creation of a prison economy as a subset of the local economy. Each prison is likely to have hundreds of COs employed, plus administrative, health care, and other civilian staff, not to mention the outside contractors that rely on providing some kind of supplies to the prisons. Although some research suggests that much of the prison purchasing is centralized and more beneficial to the state than local economies (Farrigan & Glasmeier, n.d.), regions still consider prisons as significant contributors to local businesses as well as providers of notably higher salaries for the local population. Although having a prison might not singularly lift an area out of deep poverty, it provides long-term and short-term job opportunities, as well as other economic benefits.

What Sorts of Jobs Come With the Prisons?

The majority of jobs in any correctional facility are likely to be correctional officers (COs)—those concerned with the "care, custody, and control" of the inmates. In state-run facilities, correctional officers' jobs are civil service positions, meaning that candidates must meet minimum requirements (such as being 21 and having a high school diploma or GED) and pass a competitive exam to be accepted into the correctional academy. Once accepted, correctional jobs with the state tend to offer good benefits, long-term security, and a higher than average salary for entry-level work. At the time of this writing, COs in New York State began training at $36,420 and made $43,867 as full COs (New York State Department of Correctional Services, 2011); although surely not a great salary for New York City, it is a decent wage in upstate New York, where most facilities are located.

Despite good wages and benefits, it has been well documented that correctional staff, particularly correctional officers, suffer from work-related stress (Dowden & Tellier, 2004; Garland & McCarty, 2009). What sort of stress, it appears, is open to some debate and varies according to the source of the data. In what one might term the "professional literature" or "trade journals"—materials written by correctional staff for correctional staff (or by practitioners for practitioners)—emphasis is placed on the immediate risks of face-to-face contact with inmates and the likelihood of fights, riots, and potential hostage situations. Writers stress increased gang tensions, overcrowded prisons and jails, and the loss of incentive for inmates to behave when they are ineligible for early release on parole and instead "max out" their sentences (see, for example, Arthur, 2009; Campbell, 2009; Gillan, 2001).

By contrast, academic literature finds work stress to stem from the more mundane aspects of work, including relationships with peers, relationships with supervisors, and bureaucratic aspects of the system that provide COs little control over their work or work environment (Griffin, Hogan, Lambert, Tucker-Gail, & Baker, 2010; Lambert & Hogan, 2010). It is not that academic literature has ignored face-to-face contact and danger-related variables as discussed in the professional literature; instead, the academic has generally found them to be statistically insignificant, meaning that the danger-related stressors with inmates provide little to no meaningful stress to COs over time (see for example, Whitehead & Lindquist, 1986, cited in Lambert, Hogan, & Altheimer, 2009).

Why the discrepancy? It is possible that the CO-based organizations continue to emphasize the danger-based forms of stress rather than matters of job structure, in part because the latter are totally out of their control and thus unlikely to change. Identifying for themselves sources of stress over which they have no control might even worsen the problem. Advocating for greater security around gangs, riots, and potential hostage situations, however, is more likely to meet with support and resources from administration and thus is more under their control. Additionally, the excitement and danger seem to offer a sort of social wage to correctional officers, an adrenaline rush and a risk that challenges the stereotype of COs as highly paid babysitters—a stereotype disturbing to many COs.

Turning the Research Focus to Work-Family Conflict

More recently—perhaps due to research saturation and general agreement on the causes of CO stress in the academic literature—academic research has begun to look at work-family conflict. Work-family conflict is generally defined as how the domains of work and family life spill over into each other, causing trouble in either or both domains (e.g., Lambert, Hogan, Camp, & Ventura, 2006; Triplett, Mullings, & Scarborough, 1999). It is this area of research that most interests us, as it links to our anecdotal evidence of how working corrections both changes a person and disrupts their home and family life. Work-family conflict research that draws broadly from literature on family research has recognized three forms of conflict: *time conflict, strain conflict*, and *role conflict* (Greenhaus & Beutell, 1985; Netemeyer, Boles, & McMurrian, 1996).

Time conflict occurs when the time-based demands of work and family overlap, requiring the worker to be at more than one place at a time. For example, a worker might be scheduled to spend the day with her family (or to provide childcare while her husband works), only to find that the CO on the next shift is not coming in and that she has mandatory overtime. Clearly, her time demands of work are in direct conflict with her time demands of home (Greenhaus & Beutell, 1985; Netemeyer, Boles, & McMurrian, 1996).

Strain conflict occurs when the stresses and strains of work become too much for the worker, and he begins to behave differently at home, taking the stress out on his family members. This can involve being extra "grumpy" or argumentative or yelling; it can involve withdrawing from family and friendship relationships, increasing alcohol consumption, and so forth. Strain conflict, clearly, is a risk factor for *job burnout*, which, in turn, is a risk factor for leaving the job, and thus having further potential consequences for family and community (Greenhaus & Beutell, 1985; Netemeyer, Boles, & McMurrian, 1996).

Role conflict occurs when the worker brings behaviors home from work and uses work-appropriate behaviors in the home setting where they are not appropriate. Examples of this include barking orders loudly at others in the family and following up immediately to see if they have completed the tasks, similar to the way that one might treat an inmate, rather than a maturing twelve-year-old son or daughter (Netemeyer, Boles, & McMurrian, 1996; Greenhaus & Beutell, 1985).

Our interest in researching this topic began with these three forms of conflict, as they were well represented in the anecdotal descriptions that students in a variety of classes had provided about their friends and relatives who worked corrections. These types of strain also provided a framework for us to begin thinking about correctional officers, their lives outside of work, and their families. We then used a senior seminar on work-family conflict to explore these issues in greater depth, focusing on how workers in corrections experienced these conflicts and whether such conflicts changed over time. We gathered information through minimally structured interviews with corrections officers, with hopes of providing insight on work-family stress from the perspective of the officers.

Methods

The data for this project were gathered by students as part of a senior seminar on work-family conflict at a small college in semi-rural area upstate New York. Students were trained in qualitative interviewing, observation, and qualitative data analysis, using training interviews both inside and outside of class. Training interviews were evaluated by faculty and other students. Interviews in-class were evaluated as they occurred; interviews and observation outside of class were transcribed and evaluated subsequently. Textual resources included *Learning From Strangers* (1994) and *Writing Ethnographic Fieldnotes* (1995), both of which contain substantial sections on analysis.

Students in the seminar had the option of picking this project or another project on agricultural safety with children. Five students worked on this project: All were white females in their 20s or early 30s majoring in Sociology or Nursing. All students successfully completed the project.

Sampling and Data Collection

For this project, we used purposive sampling, following the definition provided by Rubin and Rubin (1995). This meant selecting interviewees who were knowledgeable about the topic, who were willing to talk honestly and openly with the interviewers, and who were likely to represent a range of viewpoints. Interviewees also needed to have enough time in the workforce that they would have reasonably adapted to (and changed because of) the work. Students interviewed correctional officers (and spouses or family members as they felt comfortable) with whom they either had or could establish the necessary rapport. No student interviewed only family members, but some had side conversations with family members around the time of the interview, and some family members chimed in during the interview if the interview took place at the respondent's home. We included this information as well. It is possible that the presence of family makes our results more conservative than they might be otherwise, meaning that the COs might have understated the changes that they have experienced.

The campus is in a largely White region where there are five prisons within a 30-minute radius. Students generally conducted these interviews with family and friends, and as a result, most of these interviews took place within the area. Some were within a few hours of the campus. The fact that students interviewed friends and acquaintances of their families might also have caused the interviewees to be more conservative in their responses (that is, to report fewer changes that they might have otherwise), in a desire to appear socially appropriate.

Interviews took place in locations agreed upon by the interviewer and the interviewee—in coffee shops and other public locations or interviewees' homes. Interviews generally lasted between 90 minutes and two hours. Students tape recorded—with the interviewees' consent—and fully transcribed their interviews. Each student completed two interviews, resulting in a total of ten interviews, and a sample of seven males and three females, all between the ages of 35 and 55, and all of whom had children (though some were grown at the time of the interview).

Data Analysis

Students initially coded interviews working independently, meaning that each student individually identified the themes she saw present in the ten interviews. Then, each student recoded the interviews for *intra-coder* reliability. Once all students finished individually coding the interviews, the team came together to re-code the interviews, checking the coding for *inter-coder* reliability (Miles & Huberman, 1994). These codes were then used to write up the team's summary and project results. After the course's conclusion, the course's faculty member and one graduating student (whose name is listed as co-author of this chapter) continued the project, recoding the data again and further confirming inter-coder reliability. It is this last round of coding and analysis that we discuss here.

Results and Discussion

Three broad themes emerged as the COs talked about the effects of working corrections. First, the COs talked about the sense of *Sustenance vs. Satisfaction*, the trade-offs they felt they made for the wages and benefits. The second theme was the *Work-Family Spillover*, the ways in which their work and family lives failed to stay separate and/or balanced. The third—and entirely unexpected—theme that emerged was the *Reconceptualization of Racial and Ethnic Relations*, how working corrections caused the COs to see and to understand race and ethnicity differently than they had before working in corrections. Each of these themes appeared in most (but not necessarily all) of the interviews.

Although all three of the types of the work-family conflict from the quantitative literature conflict (role-conflict, strain-conflict, time-conflict) appeared in the COs' responses, they did not all appear as expected. Specifically, time-conflict appeared as both a positive and negative factor, meaning that the effects of the job were both positive and negative when it came to its time demands. Some of this seems to be due to the COs' flexibility in trading shifts with other COs, not the scheduling itself. We discuss this in greater depth below.

Sustenance vs. Satisfaction: Trading Social Wages of Esteem and Control for Wages and Benefits

The first major theme to emerge is what we came to call "Sustenance vs. Satisfaction," a sense of trade-offs that the COs made for the wages and benefits that allowed them to support themselves and their families in a way that many other jobs in the regional economy would not allow. Our subthemes in this category—"lack of respect" and "lack of power and authority"—reveal the costs that the COs believe they have paid for the wages and benefits they have received.

Benefits and Pay—The first major distinction that virtually all COs made was between a job and a career. Whether or not they stated that they liked their jobs, they stated that the pay and benefits were important, and more often than not, this was what kept them on the job. Given that these are jobs available to individuals with a high school degree in a rust-belt (that is, in a de-industrialized) economy, this is important. Examples of this include the following: "It's a good paying job, good time off and good benefits. Not much more you can ask for. It's a secure job 'cause, ya know, inmates aren't going anywhere." Similarly, "It's a good living. An honest living. I'm not … I didn't get a college degree. But I worked hard to support my family." And as another CO phrased it, "I like the paycheck, its great benefits. We get pretty good health insurance, so my wife can work part-time and not have to worry about working full-time."

Lack of Respect Vis-à-vis Other Law Enforcement Professionals—The job is not without its drawbacks, however, and a number of the COs talked about the way that they believed they were seen by those on the outside, by those who don't work in and presumably don't understand corrections. One CO when asked to clarify what he meant by his "temper at work," said

CO: Maybe that's not really the right word.
Int: OK. What's a more accurate word?
CO: Um … [thinks a minute] … I would say 'force'.
Int: Excessive?
CO: [smirks] Depends on who you ask. People who throw that term around have no idea what it's like inside those walls.

This same officer spoke hotly about the television show *Prison Break*, a cable TV show about two inmates who escape prison(s) and spend several seasons on the run.

CO: You watch that show *Prison Break*?
Int: Yes, I do.
CO: Fucking show. I don't let … [his wife] watch it. That's the problem. Propaganda. Makes the COs look like a bunch of dumb morons. Can you believe it? A whole nation is watching this and rooting for a group of criminals. Scum, murderers, rapists. And you're all rooting for them. You want them to get out. Would you feel that way if one showed up in your backyard or in the playground of … [the local elementary school]?
Int: No, probably not.
CO: No, you wouldn't. You'd be on the phone begging for the help of the same people that you were rooting against.

This theme appeared in other interviews—the perception that COs were thugs and brutes—not so much law enforcement officers as heavyweight babysitters. Some of this apparent disrespect led to a sense of competition with other law enforcement groups. Another CO talked both about the public perception of COs and about the perceived rivalry between cops and COs:

Int: How do people usually respond when they find out you're a corrections officer?

CO: Umm. It's been better since 9-11. Not like cops. People think they can walk on frickin' water or something. But they think it's cool. They tell me they do anyway.

Int: Is there a rivalry between corrections officers and cops?

CO: Not a spoken one. But I know some cops and they wouldn't last five minutes in my job. They think they're so brave. They have two cops, two guns, and one perp. Try four COs and hundreds of inmates and no weapons. Not five minutes.

The way his response is phrased, it sounds like something that is uttered frequently, perhaps like an ideological mantra among prison guards, declaring their rank in regard to police officers. But the mantra sounds like one that needs to be stated due to lack of security, not one that dismisses the fact that cops can "walk on frickin' water."

Lack of power and authority at work—A second cost of the job was heard in the way that the COs described having a lack of power and authority at work. Although all COs were able to talk about the way that they maintained authority with and power over inmates (this is obviously a basic safety requirement of their job), they did not feel that their power and authority were acknowledged, granted, or honored by the administration. One CO described,

> *You don't really have much of a sense of accomplishment for your job 'cause people are people and you can't correct them the way they [supervisors] want you to correct them. So you just go in and do your job and go home. You're not really performing any major function other than just care, custody, and control …*

He continues:

> *Well, not the way I [emphasis his] want to correct them, but I mean there's … can't enforce … Can't force people to change if they don't want to change, and criminals are criminals. Some are worse than others. That's just the way they are. You're not gonna make them any different by what I do. I go there to make sure they survive, and I survive [emphasis his].*

This is something echoed by a respondent in *Doing Prison Work*, who talked about his job as "standing at a bus stop waiting for a bus that never comes" (Crawley 2004).

More important, though, the COs talked about the inability to make a difference within the structures of work and the sense that no matter what they do, it doesn't make a difference to the way that work is done or whether they will get a promotion.

> *...when you first get in the Department you want to be the best you can be and make changes .... And then you realize ... you're not going to make a difference no matter how hard you work, no matter how hard you try, you're still just a number.*

Although some of this sense of being a number can certainly be caused by the sheer size of the prison system and the Department of Corrections (DOC), the COs noted that it is also caused by the way that jobs are structured and by the way that the DOC functions. The same CO continued this thought:

> *In some regard, I think the Department makes you feel like you're just a number to them, too. You're just a body and you go in and do your job. No matter how good you do your job or how bad you do your job, a body is a body, they [administration] could care less. That's just my opinion .... The promotions are all worked out by test scores .... So that means no matter how bad of an officer you are, if you pass the test with a high mark you can be a really bad sergeant. Nobody judges you on how you do your job, it's how well you do on the tests that you take.*
>
> *Officers always feel like we're the ones right in the middle of the jail, working among what's going on, and the administration goes ahead and change things because they feel we need changes here and there, but they never ask the officers our opinions on what to do when they themselves have no idea what's going on, they just make changes based on paperwork ... instead of being there to see what's going on ... on paper it looks like a good idea, [they say] "OK, we'll change it."*

So, despite of all of the power and authority that COs must maintain in the correctional environment, they feel treated somewhat like children on the job, creating a sense of a dead end, of being without a purpose. This is, then, in direct contrast to the danger and risk that for many is a sort of social wage and job benefit that cancels out the stereotypical aspects that correspond to being seen as a "highly paid babysitter."

Taking the Job Home: Rules, Germs, and Role Conflict

A second major drawback of work is apparent in the way that the COs saw themselves bringing the work home with them, actions identified in the literature as role-conflict. The two major ways that COs described this as happening were by imposing more rules at home and by a recognized sense of "germophobia" spreading to the home environment.

Too many rules—In our interviews the COs talked about becoming overly rule-focused with their families. As one CO said, "my kids used to tell me ... that they are not inmates." Some of this tendency might come from the comparisons that the COs made between inmates and children (that neither group can "make their own decisions ..." and that for the inmates it was their decisions that got them to prison). Perhaps the comparisons eventually lead to COs seeing the two groups similarly and requiring similar levels of stewardship.

Families, however, see this overlap differently than a simple comparison taken too far. One wife of a CO actually went so far as to diagnose her husband as having Asperger's syndrome, saying "people with Asperger's are very controlling, they have to control their world, everything has to fit into this neat little box, and if it falls outside that box, they flip." COs, although not generally accepting or talking in terms of such mental health diagnoses, did acknowledge that they became overly rigid with their families, with additional rules and additional needs for order.

Too many germs—COs also showed great concern about the possibility of carrying germs home from work and, frequently and disturbingly, developed fear of germs that made them difficult to live with. The most striking example of this came from a CO who described himself as having become overly focused on cleanliness and germs after an inmate smeared feces on his work phone. It does not take much to imagine the perspective of the CO and to begin to see every surface as potentially covered with unfriendly bacteria. The stories that COs tell of having feces, urine, and semen (generally as a well-mixed concoction) thrown on them (which did not come up in our sample but has come up in many conversations since) likely have similar effects. Even more seriously, prisons are institutions in which hepatitis, AIDS, and tuberculosis are not uncommon. All of these aspects of working in a prison are likely to lead an individual to become very germ-focused.

Work/family time issues—It is well documented that correctional work requires a demanding schedule that frequently includes overtime, often mandatory and without warning. As one can imagine, this greatly complicates the extent to which correctional officers can participate in the care of their children, especially if they cannot be counted on to pick children up or watch the children while their spouses are at work. This alone can put stress on both the individual and his family relationships.

As mentioned earlier, however, the time-conflict issues appeared as a negative more in our anecdotal evidence than in our actual project data. Despite having to work for a facility that operates around the clock ("24 x 7 x 365" as it is often described), a number of COs talked about how their schedules actually *enhanced* their ability to participate in family life—more than they believe other occupations would have allowed for. They largely attributed this to their ability to swap shifts with other COs and create more creative and family-friendly schedules. One CO described how, rather than working four days on and two days off, he could work two doubles and have four days off. Though he admitted that the first day off is a bit of a "recovery day" during which he could not do much around the house, he claimed that the other three days were much more useful than the time he would have otherwise, and the flexibility has been tremendously helpful in avoiding the need for additional childcare. As one CO phrased it, "The hours are nice, too. I work long days, but it's great to have the time off it affords."

Reconceptualizing Race Relations: Seeing Ex-Inmates and Pre-Inmates in Despite of One's Self

The most surprising theme, however, was one that we did not ask about initially, but rather was raised by the COs themselves. We have come to see this as the most important finding of our project. Although we expected to hear the more generalized lack of trust that emerged— with generalized suspicions toward others in corrections (inmates, COs) and of people in general—we did not expect the COs to talk about the ways they began to see—and often tried not to see—race and ethnicity across time. As one CO described,

> I guess working with criminals and inmates, I guess I have a tendency to judge a book by its cover. Sometimes now, the way somebody dresses or how they look, I might say, 'look, there's an ex-inmate or a future inmate' or things like that.

Virtually all the COs who discussed racial and ethnic relations (with one clear exception who used racial epithets with a vengeance) worked to make clear to us that they were not racist or did not want to see themselves as racist, but that they had simply come to see an alternate reality through working corrections. Some suggested that those on the "outside" do not really understand how it actually is. Others just tried to explain the logic that has them straddling the realities of two distinct worlds with two distinct populations and realities. In any case, the COs made it clear that working corrections had changed the way they viewed race and thus racial and ethnic relations. One CO, when asked if the job changed the way he looked at people of color responded:

> Essentially, I want to say no, but I would be lying because yes, it has changed my opinion now ... over the years I've developed ... just been able to distinguish the difference between criminals and Black people, I mean, people are people whether they're Black or White or Hispanic or whatever, so .... Yeah, when I first got on the Department and saw the majority of inmates

Black, and the way they acted and the way they treated us and the way they talked to us about racism, ya know, everything we did, you're a mother f'er, yeah, at first it gets under your skin and you start to lump all people into that category but after a while you kind learn who's who, ya know. Criminals are criminals, people are people.

Another CO described:

CO: I'd like to tell ya that it doesn't affect how I look at people on the outside, but that's just not at all true .... I mean I know in my head that just because the majority of the minorities that I see are criminals and liars, that the I see on the outside are like that [sic]. It's just hard to .... I don't know. It's hard ...

Int: What's hard?

CO: I don't want to be a racist. And I'm not.

Int: OK.

CO: No, I'm not. It's more ... It's a statistical thing .... I want to tell you that I'm not a racist. If I played the odds, based on the numbers, in, say, the stock market, I'd be shrewd or insightful. But if I play the numbers with race, I'm a racist. Does that make sense to you? I mean, does it?

Int: Does it make sense to you?

CO: [laughs] Are you sure you're not a psych major? You haven't answered any of my questions.

This appeal to understanding from the listener is compelling. *"Does that make sense to you? I mean, does it?"* Here are individuals explaining the world they see and trying to interpret it without falling into the trap of being labeled racist. But what does it mean for an individual to work in a system that is clearly skewed by race? The U.S. criminal justice system has well-documented conditions that create racist processes and racist outcomes. These include racial profiling, racial inequalities in sentencing, differences in the ways neighborhoods are policed, and how different groups of people are moved in and out of the system in patterned and unequal ways (Barak, Leighton, & Flavin, 2010; Bosworth & Flavin, 2007; Provine, 2007).

Given all this, is it at all surprising (however disturbing) that White individuals working in the system would develop racist perceptions? This leads us to develop a framework for understanding, rather than for blaming, those who work and struggle with these perceptions within the system, and it needs to be recognized as a risk and effect of the job. These perceptions aren't something that the COs reported being proud of or even something they seemed comfortable with. Instead, they seemed to need to talk about them. Giving COs a way to think and to talk about their experience might be an important part of an in-service training. But can an effective training be provided from within a system already burdened by the processes of racism? Can the system even afford to acknowledge these affects, an acknowledgement that might call the racism of the entire system into question? This suggests, unfortunately, that the training that might allow COs to best deal with their changes in racial ideology may need to come from beyond the institution itself.

Conclusion

Working corrections is an unusual job. As Haney, Banks, and Zimbardo demonstrated so powerfully in the early 1970s, working corrections can change a person dramatically and quickly. Just how correctional officers see themselves being changed, however, has not been sufficiently qualitatively explored. Clearly, it is perceived as a good job in a bad economy, and as one CO explained, "the inmates ain't going anywhere." But working corrections can be stressful, with drawbacks and lasting costs.

Allowing correctional officers to talk freely about the effects of their work from the comfort of their homes reveals some compelling patterns about the nature of working corrections. Some of these—such as the stressors of feeling unsupported at work or bringing one's work roles home, echo the quantitative findings published in the academic literature. Other aspects, particularly the COs' perceptions of race and their mixed emotions about how their views have changed, do not appear elsewhere in the literature. Perhaps these questions about race are simply questions that have never been asked, or perhaps these interviews provided an opening for COs to talk safely about race that they have not had before. Most strikingly, it was a topic raised initially by a CO in one of the first interviews, then incorporated into subsequent interviews by the students. It is something, it appears, that COs are attempting to deal with and want to talk about.

For those of us living in a "prison community," a community in which five prisons dominate the local working-class job market, these changing perceptions about race and ethnicity are both notable and troubling. What do these shifts in racial ideology, occurring over time, mean for the individuals working corrections, for their families, and ultimately for their communities? The prison community where these interviews took place is predominately white (as many rural areas that receive prisons are); there exists little racial or ethnic diversity to counteract the negatively shifting beliefs. Do officers—through language, words, or symbolic interactions—bring these views home to their families, as often is the case with germophobia and authoritarianism? Do they spread to the family and friends? Is a changing racial ideology then a community cost of a regional prison economy? These are questions that future research must address.

References

Antonio, M. E., Young, J. L., & Wingeard, L. M. (2009). When actions and attitude count most: Assessing perceived level of responsibility and support for inmate treatment and rehabilitation programs among correctional employees. *The Prison Journal*, 89(4), 363-382.

Arthur, B. (2009). Managing gangs and STGs: Proactive approaches for safety and success. *Corrections Today Magazine*, 71(1), 8.

Barak, G., Leighton, P., & Flavin, J. (2010). *Class, Race, Gender, and Crime* (3rd ed.). Lanham, MD: Rowman & Littlefield Publishers.

Bohm, R. M. & Haley, K. N. (2009). *Introduction to Criminal Justice* (6th ed.). New York: McGraw-Hill.

Bosworth, M. & Flavin, J. (eds.). (2007). *Race, Gender, & Punishment: From Colonialism to the War on Terror*. New Brunswick, NJ: Rutgers University Press.

Braman, D. (2002). Families and incarceration. In M. Mauer and M. Chesney-Lind (eds.), *Invisible Punishment: The Collateral Consequences of Mass Imprisonment* (pp. 117-135). New York: Free Press.

Campbell, S. (2009). One clique: Why rivals on the street become rivals behind bars. *Corrections Today Magazine*, 71(1), 36-38.

Clear, T. R., Cole, G. F., & Reisig, M. D. (2008). *American Corrections* (8th ed.). Belmont, CA: Wadsworth/Cengage.

Dial, K. C., Downey, R. A., & Goodlin, W. E. (2010). The job in the joint: The impact of generation and gender on work stress in prison. *Journal of Criminal Justice*, 38, 609-615.

Díaz-Cotto, J. (2007). Latina imprisonment and the war on drugs. In M. Bosworth and J. Flavin (eds.), *Race, Gender, & Punishment: From Colonialism to the War on Terror* (pp.184-199). New Brunswick, NJ: Rutgers University Press.

Dowden, C., & Tellier, C. (2003). Predicting work-related stress in correctional officers: A meta-analysis. *Journal of Criminal Justice*, 32, 31-47.

Emerson, R. M., Fretz, R. I., & Shaw, L. L. (1995). *Writing Ethnographic Fieldnotes*. Chicago, IL: University of Chicago Press.

Farkas, M. A. (1999). Correctional officer attitudes toward inmates and working with inmates in a "get tough" era. *Journal of Criminal Justice*, 27(6), 495-506.

Farrigan, T. L., & Glasmeier, A. K. (n.d.) *The Economic Impacts of the Prison Development Boom on Persistently Poor Rural Places*. Retrieved April 29, 2011 from povertyinamerica.mit.edu/products/publications/prison_development/prison_development.pdf

Gaines, L. K., & Miller, R. L. (2006). *Criminal Justice in Action* (4th ed.). Belmont, CA: Wadsworth/Cengage.

Garland, B. E., & McCarty, W. P. (2009). Job satisfaction behind walls and fences: a study of prison health care staff. *Criminal Justice Policy Review*, 20(2), 188-208.

Gillan, T. (2001). The correctional officer: One of the toughest. *Corrections Today*, October 2001, 112-115.

Greenhaus, J. H. & Beutell, N. J. (1985). Sources of conflict between work and family roles. *Academy of Management Review*, 10(1), 76-88.

Griffin, M. L., Hogan, N. L., Lambert, E. G., Tucker-Gail, K. A., & Baker, D. N. (2010). Job involvement, job stress, job satisfaction, and organizational commitment, and the burnout of correctional staff. *Criminal Justice and Behavior*, 37(2), 239-255.

Grossi, E. L., & Berg, B. L. (1991). Stress and job dissatisfaction among correctional officers: An unexpected finding. *International Journal of Offender Therapy and Comparative Criminology*, 35(1), 73-81.

Haney, C., Banks, C., & Zimbardo, P. (1973). Interpersonal dynamics in a simulated prison. *International Journal of Criminology and Penology*, 1(1), 69-97.

Hemmens, C., & Stohr, M. K. (2001). Correctional staff attitudes regarding the use of force in corrections. *Corrections Management Quarterly*, 5(2), 27-40.

Huling, T. L. (1999, April 15-16). *Prisons as a Growth Industry in Rural America: An Exploratory Discussion of the Effects on Young African American Men in the Inner Cities*. Paper presented at the Crisis of the Young African American Male in the Inner Cities conference: A Consultation of the United States Commission on Civil Rights. Retrieved April 22, 2011 from www.prisonpolicy.org/scans/prisons_as_rural_growth.shtml#_ftn6

Huling, T. L. (2002). Building a prison economy in rural America. In M. Mauer and M. Chesney-Lind (eds.), *Invisible Punishment: The Collateral Consequences of Mass Imprisonment* (pp. 197-213). New York: Free Press.

Kauffman, K. (1988). *Prison Officers and Their World*. Cambridge, MA: Harvard University Press.

Kifer, M., Hemmens, C., & Stohr, M. K. (2003). The goals of corrections: Perspectives from the line. *Criminal Justice Review*, 28(1), 47-69.

Klofas, J. & Toch, H. (1982). The guard subculture myth. *The Journal of Research in Crime and Delinquency*, 19(2), 238-254.

Lambert, E. G., & Hogan, N. L. (2010). Wanting change: The relationship of perceptions of organizational innovation with correctional staff job stress, job satisfaction, and organizational commitment. *Criminal Justice Policy Review*, 21(2), 160-184.

Lambert, E. G., Hogan, N. L., & Altheimer, I. (2010). The association between work-family conflict and job burnout among correctional staff: A preliminary study. *American Journal of Criminal Justice,* 35, 37-55.

Lambert, E. G., Hogan, N. L., Altheimer, I., Jiang, S., & Stevenson, M. T. (2010). The relationship between burnout and support for punishment and treatment: A preliminary examination. *International Journal of Offender Therapy and Comparative Criminology,* 54(6), 1004-1022.

Lambert, E. G., Hogan, N. L., Camp, S. D., & Ventura, L. A. (2006). The impact of work-family conflict on correctional staff: A preliminary study. *Criminology and Criminal Justice* 6(4), 371-387.

Lambert, E. G., Hogan, N. L., & Griffin, M. L. (2007). The impact of distributive and procedural justice on correctional staff job stress, job satisfaction, and organizational commitment. *Journal of Criminal Justice,* 35, 644-656.

Lambert, E. G., Hogan, N. L., Paoline, E. A. III, & Baker, D. N. (2005). The good life: The impact of job satisfaction and occupational stressors on correctional staff life satisfaction—An exploratory study. *Journal of Crime and Justice,* 28(2), 1-26.

Lambert, E. G., Hogan, N. L., & Tucker, K. A. (2009). Problems at work: Exploring the role stress among correctional staff. *The Prison Journal,* 89(4), 460-481.

Mauer, M. (2002). Mass imprisonment and the disappearing voters. In M. Mauer and M. Chesney-Lind (eds.), *Invisible Punishment: The Collateral Consequences of Mass Imprisonment* (pp. 50-58). New York: Free Press.

Mauer, M. & Chesney-Lind, M. (eds.). (2002). Invisible Punishment: *The Collateral Consequences of Mass Imprisonment.* New York: Free Press.

Miles, M. B. & Huberman, H. M. (1994). *Qualitative Data Analysis: An Expanded Sourcebook* (2nd ed.). Thousand Oaks, CA: Sage Publications.

Netemeyer, R. G., Boles, J. S., & McMurrian, R. (1996). Development and validation of work-family conflict and family-work conflict scales. *Journal of Applied Psychology,* 81(4), 400-410.

New York State Department of Correctional Services. (2011). *Correction Officer Exam.* http://www.docs.state.nys.us/Jobs/CO_Exam.html

Poole, E. D., & Regoli, R. M. (1981). Alienation in prison: An examination of the work relations of prison guards. *Criminology,* 19(2), 251-270.

Provine, D. M. (2007). *Unequal Under the Law: Race in the War on Drugs.* Chicago, IL: University of Chicago Press.

Richie, B. E. (2002). The social impact of mass incarceration on women. In M. Mauer and M. Chesney-Lind (eds.), *Invisible Punishment: The Collateral Consequences of Mass Imprisonment* (pp. 136-149). New York: Free Press.

Rubin, H. J., & Rubin, I. S. (1995). Qualitative Interviewing: *The Art of Hearing Data*. Thousand Oaks, CA: Sage Publications.

Summerlin, Z., Oehme, K., Stern, N., & Valentine, C. (2010). Disparate levels of stress in police and correctional officers: Preliminary evidence from a pilot study on domestic violence. *Journal of Human Behavior in the Social Environment*, 20(6), 762-777.

Tewksbury, R., & Mustaine, E. E. (2008). Correctional orientations of prison staff. *The Prison Journal*, 88, 207-233.

Toch, H. & Klofas, J. (1982). Alienation and desire for job enrichment among correction officers. *Federal Probation*, 46(1), 35-44.

Triplett, R., Mullings, J. L., & Scarborough, K. E. (1999). Examining the effect of work-home conflict on work-related stress among correctional officers. *Journal of Criminal Justice*, 27(4), 371-385.

Weiss, R. S. (1994). *Learning From Strangers: The Art and Method of Qualitative Interview Studies*. New York: The Free Press.

Whitehead, J. & Lindquist, C. (1986). Correctional officer burnout: A path model. *Journal of Research in Crime and Delinquency*, 23(1): 23-42.

Discussion Questions

1. Several of the corrections officers indicated that "outsiders" don't understand what it's like in a prison. Many of the realities of prison life affect officers outside of the job. To what extent are inmate behaviors a function of individuality or social structure?

2. Describe the three forms of work-family conflict experienced by corrections officers. Relate these types of conflict to their career that you are hoping to someday have.

3. What impact does a correctional facility have on the community where it is situated?

4. What are some of the "collateral consequences" of mass imprisonment listed in the background section of this chapter? Can you think of any others?

5. Given that the interviewers had some sort of a pre-existing relationship with the subjects prior to the interviews, the authors suggest that the answers to the questions might have been more conservative than they perhaps would have disclosed to someone else. Why would this be? Do you agree?

6. What did the interviewers do to ensure reliability? Were these steps really necessary?

Chapter 17
SONS OF INCARCERATED FATHERS: FOLLOWING IN DAD'S FOOTSTEPS

Mary West-Smith, Ph.D. University of Northern Colorado

Introduction

Sons often follow their fathers' footsteps, even when they lead to prison. Many criminological theories have attempted to explain the relationship between a child's behavior and parental incarceration, including biological and biosocial theories, social disorganization theories, and learning theories. However, none of these explanations addresses the effects of paternal incarceration on children. Despite abundant speculation, there is little empirical evidence to differentiate the effects of paternal incarceration from the effects of other risk factors typically found in these children's lives.

Literature Review

Much of what we know about inmate fathers and their children comes from Bureau of Justice Statistics (BJS) surveys of inmates. BJS data estimated that in 2007, about 1,553,000 minor children had fathers in either state or federal prisons (Glaze & Maruschak, 2009). Although inmate fathers are similar to childless inmates in many ways, data reveal some differences. Poverty, substance abuse, mental illness, and minority status are common in both populations; however, inmate fathers are somewhat older and are slightly more likely to be of a racial or ethnic minority, to be married or separated, and to be drug recidivists with criminal histories. Close to one-half of state and federal inmates reported living with at least one minor child in the month before arrest or incarceration, most of whom identified themselves as the primary financial supporter of their children. The majority of inmate fathers also reported regular contact with their minor children, indicating ongoing relationships between them and their children (Glaze & Maruschak, 2009).

A few studies, many from decades ago, focused on inmate fathers, spouses of incarcerated men, or programs for incarcerated fathers. These studies examined paternal incarceration in relation to financial or emotional problems, increased caregiver stress, possible decreased child supervision, and familial alienation (see Carlson & Cervera, 1992; Fishman, 1990; Fritsch and Burkhead, 1981; Gabel, 1992; Gabel & Schindledecker, 1992; Girshick, 1996; Hairston, 1987; Hairston, 1989;

Hairston, 1995; Hairston, 1998; Johnson, 1992; Johnson, 1995a; Morris, 1965; Sack, 1977; Sack, Seidler, & Thomas, 1976; Swan, 1981). Researchers linked paternal incarceration to abnormal childhood behaviors including internalizing problems such as anxiety, hypervigilance, depression, and withdrawal; externalizing problems such as anger, agitation, oppositional behavior, and aggression; changes in appetite or sleep patterns; school problems; and symptoms of grieving (Boswell & Wedge, 2002; Carlson & Cervera, 1992; Fishman, 1990; Fritsch & Burkhead, 1981; Girshick, 1996; Johnson, 1995a; Johnson, 1995b). Many of these behaviors, however, are similar to those demonstrated by children exposed to marital violence (Holden, 1998; Osofsky, 1998), by children of substance-abusing parents (Feig, 1998; McMahon & Luthar, 1998), and by children exposed to abuse or neglect (Feig, 1998).

According to Boswell (2002), there is no systematic method for identifying children of incarcerated fathers; however, they likely resemble characteristics of their fathers, who are predominately of a racial or ethnic minority and poor and frequently from families with high levels of disruption (Simmons, 2000). They also likely share many of the characteristics of children exposed to childhood trauma long before their parents were incarcerated and may have experienced previous physical or emotional experiences such as abuse or neglect, domestic or community violence, parental substance abuse, or separation from family members (Fishman, 1990; Johnson, 1995a; Johnson, 1995b; Johnson & Waldfogel, 2002).

Although few scholars suggest that a male influence is essential, most recognize that the father figures' behavior can significantly affect their children (Day & Lamb, 2004). Fathers play multiple roles important to the development and prosperity of their children, such as breadwinner, playmate, and educator (Bronstein, 1988; Day, Gavazzi, & Adcock, 2001; Lamb, 2004; Marsiglio & Cohen, 2000; Tamis-LaMonda, Shannon, Cabrera, & Lamb, 2004; Yogman, Cooley, & Kindlon, 1988). Research has also identified links between father absence and antisocial behavior in children (Pfiffner, McBurnett, & Rathouz, 2001), early onset of offending among male juveniles (Gibson & Tibbetts, 2000), economic and psychological difficulties (Amato & Gilbreth, 1999; Florsheim, 2000), and educational attainment and employment (McLanahan & Teitler, 1998). In a study of the short-term effects of parental separation on adolescent delinquency and depression, Videon (2002) found that the effects of separation depended on the nature of the relationship prior to separation: close father-son relationships prior to separation were linked to greater levels of delinquency after the separation.

Although father absence might have negative effects on children, the beneficial effects of father presence might depend on his lack of antisocial behaviors. Jaffee, Moffitt, Caspi, and Taylor (2003) identified a relationship between the time fathers spent with their children and their children's conduct problems: the more time spent with fathers who engaged in antisocial behavior, the more conduct problems the children exhibited. Children of incarcerated fathers, men who may frequently exhibit antisocial behaviors, may differ substantially from children whose fathers are absent because of divorce, occupation, or death.

Methods

My analysis focused on a subset of twenty male subjects from a larger study of children of incarcerated fathers that included male and female respondents. The Institutional Review Board approving this research required that subjects be over age eighteen, thus necessitating the use of retrospective data. Children of incarcerated fathers who experience negative outcomes such as incarceration or other forms of institutionalization or homelessness are much easier to identify and recruit than those who are not involved with organizations that control or provide services for high-risk populations. A primary challenge in studying children of incarcerated fathers is the difficulty in identifying and recruiting potential study participants not affiliated with these types of organizations. Children who are doing well despite their fathers' incarceration are a hidden population and typically do not advertise the fact that their fathers are in prison, making them difficult to identify and recruit for study purposes. Thus, my analysis recruited subjects from jails, treatment facilities, homeless shelters, or parole offices.

Many respondents were in institutions or were leading highly transient lives, which limited their availability and access. As such, traditional participatory ethnographic field research was not an option for investigating their lives. However, as Becker (1996) argued, a one-time intensive interview that helps the researcher understand the subjective reality of study participants is an appropriate ethnographic method. The use of a subjective oral history is a suitable method for providing a voice for largely ignored individuals or groups and can allow researchers complete understanding of how subjects interpret the effects of important events in their lives (Fontena & Frey, 1994)

Because little is known about the lives of children of incarcerated fathers, it was important to focus not only on the incarceration of the father but to allow subjects during their interviews to elaborate on their lives both before and after the fathers' imprisonment. I used a form of the Life History Calendar (Caspi et al., 1996; Freedman et al., 1988; Lin, Ensel, & Lai, 1997) during the interviews to help subjects organize and recall events from their often chaotic pasts in a time-ordered manner and to elaborate on topics that were meaningful to them. Narratives should not be viewed as historical truths, since study subjects typically selectively recall events that hold importance to them and will construct stories of their past that help them to make sense of their lives (Burr & Butt, 2000; Reissman, 2002). Since the focus of the research was on the meaning subjects ascribed to events in their lives, I did not assume that the life histories they recounted necessarily reflected factual reality.

I interviewed the subjects in private interview rooms. Reissman (2002) recommends that because analysis is inherent in the process of transcription, qualitative researchers should be involved in the transcription of oral accounts of their subjects. I was also concerned that participants' manner of speech might not be understood by a professional transcriber and that the long pauses, tears, laughter, or other indicators of emotion, potentially critical elements in understanding the context of what was being said, would be lost if others transcribed the recorded interviews. Therefore, I transcribed each recording. I created a database that allowed me to initially code the presence or absence of specific childhood risk factors. Through ongoing data collection and analysis, an additional unanticipated theme emerged: the perception of the father as either a bad father or as a man who made attempts to be a good father.

Findings

My analysis focuses on twenty male subjects who were facing many challenges in their lives and who were not self-supporting or in college. All had lived with or had regular contact with their fathers as children. The average age at the time of the interview was 26, with an age range of 18 to 47. Thirteen subjects were White, three were African-American, two were of Hispanic ethnicity, and two were Native American. Fourteen described their fathers in exclusively or primarily positive terms while six described their fathers in exclusively negative terms. All had followed closely in their fathers' footsteps; most were living lives filled with substance abuse, instability, and criminality. The experiences and outcomes for many children of incarcerated fathers differ from the lives of these subjects (who did not fare well). Not all participants in the original study faced the same types of childhood adversity or experienced such negative outcomes. But the subjects for the current analysis had much in common. The primary difference in members of this group was how the sons perceived their fathers: some idealized their fathers, some viewed their fathers as flawed men who tried their best, and some hated their fathers.

Growing Up At Risk

Children of incarcerated fathers are likely to experience exposure to risk factors for negative outcomes, such as parental substance abuse, family violence, child abuse and/or neglect, criminal behaviors, residential instability, and poverty. Participants in my study experienced common risk factors. For example, paternal substance abuse was the norm: nineteen of the twenty subjects described fathers who had alcohol and/or drug addictions. Twelve of these subjects, when discussing their fathers' drug or alcohol problems, stated that their fathers would use any drug available, indicating a poly-substance abuse problem. For the rest, their fathers' primary drugs of choice were heroin, crack cocaine, or methamphetamine. Only two subjects described fathers whose drug of choice was alcohol. In both of these cases, the fathers were incarcerated for near-fatal assaults during bar fights while they were extremely intoxicated.

In additional to paternal substance abuse or addiction, most of the subjects' mothers had serious substance abuse problems. Fifteen of the twenty subjects described mothers who also suffered from extreme levels of drug or alcohol abuse, eight of whom were identified as poly-substance abusers. The mothers not described as poly-substance abusers had particular drugs of choice, and, like the fathers, were addicted to heroin, crack cocaine, or methamphetamine. The mothers' substance abuse problems typically prevented them from being able to adequately care for their children, either before or after the father went to prison, and seven of the subjects ended up in foster care as a result. However, none of these men described their new lives in foster care as an improvement over their old lives of chaos and neglect.

Almost all study participants grew up in an environment where excessive drug or alcohol use was the norm. Substance abuse did not seem unusual to them when they were children; almost everyone in their environment used drugs or alcohol extensively. Several subjects described being introduced to drug or alcohol use at a very early age by family members, often the mother or father.

Family violence was also a frequent theme: twelve of the twenty subjects described witnessing violence between their parents, and sixteen described violence directed at the children by either the mother or father or examples of extreme neglect. Although the father was the common perpetrator of physical violence, a few subjects identified their mothers as extremely violent toward their fathers or the children. Besides the father's violence, new father figures, typically after the biological father was sent to prison, continued the patterns of family violence.

Several subjects experienced residential instability. Nine of the twenty subjects described frequent family movement that involved staying with relatives or friends at times, homelessness and shelter stays, and placement in foster care prior to the father's imprisonment. These frequent moves often required changing schools. Eleven of the twenty subjects led lives of relative residential stability prior to their fathers' incarceration. After the fathers went to prison, the situation changed for most of these respondents. For those who were financially dependent on fathers, the loss of the father typically led to high levels of residential instability. If the father's income directly contributed to maintaining a residence, the mothers often could not keep the family home. For those who experienced high levels of residential instability prior to the imprisonment of the father, little changed after the father went to prison and frequent movements continued. After the fathers went to prison, eighteen of the twenty subjects described frequent changes of residence. Only two subjects lived in families that maintained a family home throughout the subjects' childhoods. Both had mothers who had access to financial resources that allowed them to keep the family home after the loss of the fathers' financial contributions.

Because many subjects lived with their fathers prior to imprisonment, thirteen were present at the arrest of their fathers. Witnessing the arrest of a family member may be a traumatic event in a child's life if the child has a close relationship with the arrested person. The effects of seeing a parent handcuffed, often forced to lie on the ground, and taken away by the police may be similar to witnessing an assault on a parent (Mazza, 2002). The memory of their father's arrest was vivid in each of those subjects who were present when it occurred. All described the arrest as the start of their lifelong hatred of police: police represented the point at which their lives dramatically changed for the worse. Given their environment, these subjects were likely to develop distrust and disdain for the police anyway, but witnessing the arrest of the father might have reinforced such attitudes through particularly dramatic and deeply imbedded memories.

Perception of the Father

In our society, the concept of "father" has a unique and specific meaning. The good father provides for, protects, and loves his children. The bad father is the opposite: a man who may cause harm to the child or who fails to provide for, to protect, or to demonstrate that he cares for, much less loves, his children. Although outsiders may be able to assess the "goodness" or "badness" of a particular father, the way a child views his or her father may not necessarily match the symbolic image of fatherhood that resides in our collective imagination. How people define their reality depends on the interpretation they assign to a given situation (Mead, 1934). For children, how the father is perceived may depend less on an objective reality and more on the lens through which their world is viewed. A father who does not conform to our ideal father may yet be viewed as a good father and an appropriate role model by his child.

Although none of the subjects described fathers who most outside observers would classify as good fathers, fourteen of the twenty subjects identified their fathers as good fathers. They portrayed their fathers as men who did their best to provide for, protect, and love their children. Several acknowledged that their fathers, when under the influence of drugs or alcohol, behaved in ways that did not conform with their ideas of a good father, yet they insisted that at other times, their fathers were good fathers. The remaining six subjects had nothing good to say about their fathers.

The Bad Father—All six subjects who spoke of their fathers in exclusively negative terms stressed antisocial characteristics of their fathers. One of the subjects was sexually abused by his father. Another described how his father had been sent to prison for a felonious assault on him when he was a small child. This subject was in jail at the time of the interview for an assault on his father:

> *I ended up having to live with my father again after I was hurt bad in a car wreck. I had nowhere else to go. But I would have been better off being homeless because it wouldn't have beaten me down as much. My dad lets all these other people, tramps and stuff, stay with him, but he kicked me out, his own son. I'm here in jail now for assault on my dad. For doing what he usually does to me.*

The remaining four subjects described distant fathers who rejected their children or who did little to provide for them. These fathers were described as placing their own needs, often for drugs, before the needs of their children. One subject described how difficult it was to grow up without a reliable father figure:

> *I can't really tell you what that was like to not really have a dad. The dad is supposed to be the leader in the house. I mean, he's supposed to teach you things that your mom can't teach you. My dad never hit me, but he never taught me anything. I was pretty much left to do what I wanted. All he ever taught me was how to cook crack.*

This subject was forced to live with his father after his mother, unable to care for him, sent him there. After his father's imprisonment, he was left to live with his paternal grandmother, an alcoholic who also was unable to care for or supervise him. He took the knowledge he learned from his father—how to cook crack—and used it to financially support himself.

Playing with a child, teaching a child a sport, and encouraging that child may help define a caring father. Subjects who viewed their fathers positively recalled interacting with their fathers in a playful manner, but this type of interaction was missing from almost all accounts of those who viewed their fathers negatively. One subject justified his rejection of school and sports:

> *It was like he never really did anything with me. You know how most fathers ... they take their kids to go play catch or*

something like that? They just mess around and be boys. But me and him, we never did that. And then when I was playing basketball, he'd never be there for any games. And I was like "What the hell, there's no point in trying harder." My uncles ... they were always there for their kids' football games and stuff like that. But my dad was never there.

Those with negative views of their fathers never identified a time during which they had good relationships with each other, although several described attempts to reach out to their fathers when they became adults, only to again be disappointed. One respondent described such an effort:

I think the last time I talked to him was like a month ago and that was for three minutes on the phone. That was like three minutes for six years—the length of time I was in foster care because of him. That's not an even trade-off. We've always been on really bad terms. We're still on bad terms. One time I talked to him on the phone and it was clear he'd completely forgotten who I was. It took him a while to realize it was me.

These subjects did not discuss themes of financial support, nurturing, and playing together, unless they were citing the lack of these characteristics as proof that their fathers were not good fathers. Almost all subjects described fathers who abused substances, engaged in criminal activity, or who were violent. Their portrayals of their fathers uniformly provide images of men who were distant and who placed their own desires above the needs and interests of their children. Almost all spoke of their disappointment that their fathers were not men who met the traditional image of the good father.

The Good Father—All subjects who spoke of their fathers in primarily or exclusively positive terms described men who were also drug or alcohol-dependent and criminally active. Yet the image of the good father—the man who provides for, protects, and loves his children—was present in all of these accounts. An additional consistent theme was that of the father as playmate: all of these men described fathers who took the time to interact with their children in traditional father-son activities. One subject, whose father supported his family by dealing drugs, described his relationship with his father:

I was a daddy's boy. We didn't have a mother figure in our lives then, so me and my dad were really tight. He didn't work, so he stayed home and took care of us ... my brother and sister and me. We spent a lot of time together. When I was little, I remember things like taking naps on the couch with him.

After his father was arrested for drug distribution and sent to prison, the lives of this respondent and his two siblings descended into chaos. They were initially placed in foster care, then later shuffled among various family members, all of whom were described as having extreme alcohol or drug addictions and unable to adequately care for the children. Several years later, after the father's release from prison, the subject and his brother returned to live with their father:

> *It was great. My dad had this three bedroom house ... just me and my dad and my brother. My dad was working, but he was growing a lot of pot, too. He gave us everything we wanted—dirt bikes, guitars, drum sets. I loved it. I had a great life.*

Of course, this subject's idyllic life did not last long. The father's drug and alcohol use accelerated, and he was again arrested and sent to prison for drug possession and distribution. This time, the family's assets were seized in as part of a drug forfeiture and this subject's life again descended into chaos.

Another subject described how his father tried to be a good father, but his drug addiction got in the way:

> *We used to go horseback riding, we went fishing, a lot of the dad stuff. I mean, he's a good dad, but he just had the partying stuff. He always wanted to know what I was interested in. I really love my dad, and I always try to back him up. My dad is real intelligent; he went to college and everything. He could have been a doctor, but he was just into drugs and alcohol and just jacked all that up.*

This same respondent went on to detail a later event that still haunts him. He witnessed his father's near-fatal shooting during a struggle over a gun with a police informant:

> *After my dad got out of the hospital, he was in trouble for having the gun. He'd already had a habitual offender charge before that, so he was looking at some time. He took off on the run. He called me up and asked me to get my stuff together, so he could have someone pick me up. I was on the run with my dad for about a year. Me and my dad had always had a good relationship, but we got real close that year. But we were drinking a lot, using a lot of drugs ... coke, smoking coke, stuff like that. We went through a lot that year, but we had a lot of fun, too.*

The time spent with his father did not last. Subjects who lived with their fathers typically had the relationship interrupted by their father's incarceration in jail and prison. All stressed the point that when the father was available, he made time for and attempted to care for his children.

Having enough to eat was also common theme for many of these respondents. The absence of the father often meant that the children went hungry. One subject, whose heroin-addicted father was in and out of his life and whose heroin-addicted mother could not provide for the children in the absence of his father, described life when his father was not in jail or prison:

> My dad always seemed to be able to take care of his habit and his kids. He was always able to have money; no matter what we needed, he'd always find a way to get it for us. I really admired my dad. When he was around, we always had food and stuff like that.

For many subjects like this young man, personal interactions with their fathers were infrequent, yet they held onto memories of fathers who demonstrated their love by occasionally playing sports with their sons, by taking them on a camping or fishing trip or two, or by making sure that the children had enough to eat.

Seven of the fourteen subjects who viewed their fathers positively described highly unstable housing prior to their father's imprisonment. The remaining seven described fathers who, while often engaged in drug use and criminal activities in front of the children, could provide a level of financial security that did not require frequent changes in residence. The loss of the father had profound effects on those subjects who did not have financially stable mothers or help from extended family members to maintain the family home. One subject described his anger at the loss of his father, his home, and almost all of his possessions:

> We had a really nice house. I had my own room; we had a big-screen TV, and all kinds of stuff. We lost everything. My mom sold the house, but all the money she made from selling it went to pay the attorneys. We stayed in the house for a little while and then we had to move. And my mom was freaking out. My mom didn't have a job; most of the money was gone. We moved into this really crappy apartment because it was all we could afford.

With no job skills, little work experience, and no childcare, this mother took a job that often left her children home alone in this new, poverty-stricken neighborhood. Like other subjects whose mothers struggled financially to support their children in the absence of the father, these children changed schools and made new friends with groups of adolescents who used drugs, skipped school, and committed increasingly serious acts of delinquency. The mothers in these cases were generally described as struggling to provide for their children, but, because they were forced to work and leave the children to their own devices, they were unable to adequately supervise their children. One subject ascribed his descent into committing more frequent and severe acts of delinquency to the lack of parental supervision after his father went to prison on an attempted murder conviction, a crime committed while the father was extremely intoxicated:

> What would have helped my family was if he just didn't go to prison. If he'd just gotten help for his alcoholism. After he went to prison, my mom had to work all the time, and we were alone a lot. If there had just been somebody else around to take the time to keep us from getting into trouble. We were just raising ourselves.

Assigning the Blame

A family's ability to cope with a stressful event can depend on how the family interprets the event. An incarcerated father's status within the family can be preserved if family members can blame others, such as the police, the courts, or criminal associates, for the crime and imprisonment, thereby externalizing the blame for the stressor event (Carlson & Cervera, 1992). Maintaining an inmate's identity as a father identity may depend upon his family's willingness to view his incarceration as the responsibility of others.

Study participants who viewed their fathers positively placed blame on others, especially the criminal justice system, for their fathers' incarceration and the challenges their families faced, while subjects who viewed their fathers negatively assigned much of the blame to their fathers. One subject who viewed his father positively discussed how different his life might have been if his heroin-addicted parents had been able to get clean and lead normal lives:

> It's made me a hard-headed kid. If my dad would have been there, maybe things would have been different. Maybe my mom and dad might have still been drug addicts. But we'll never know how things could have been. Because they [the criminal justice system] took his life. They never really gave him a chance. At the time [I was in foster care and residential treatment facilities], I was just so mad and angry. And that wouldn't have happened if my dad was around. Cause I would have been at home with my dad. All these "maybes, what-ifs, should haves." Maybe that shit wouldn't have happened to me and I could have been a totally different person, if my dad would have been around to help me. My life could have been a whole lot better if I was with my Pops or somebody that's family. Just to know that I'm not all alone.

Like many other subjects, this interviewee viewed the criminal justice system as responsible for what happened to his family. His expressed desire to have a more traditional family and a good father-son relationship was common, as were the perceived challenges that the criminal justice system created for these families.

Subjects who were involved with child protective services after their fathers went to prison typically also blamed the governmental systems that were supposed to protect children as creating many of the hardships they endured. One subject expressed his contempt for a system that is supposed to help families in trouble:

> *After my dad went to prison, DSS really fucked up my family. My mom couldn't take care of us, and my dad's brother wanted to adopt me, but they wouldn't let him. They just let me rot in foster care. My grandma died, and no one even told me. They ruined my whole family. They always talk about what is in the best interest of the child. But taking kids away from their families and never letting them see them again is not in the best interest of the child. It really fucks you up. Right now, Social Services is going to help pay for me to go to college. Big deal. They took my life away from me. They took away my family.*

Subjects who viewed their fathers positively generally recognized their parents' inability to provide an adequate level of care, but they all seemed to feel their lives were much worse away from their families than while living with them. The fathers' actions may have started the chain of events that led to negative outcomes for their children, but subjects were harshly critical of and placed much of the blame for their current life situations on the governmental systems that were supposed to protect and correct.

Conclusion

If, as McHugh (1968) argued, the personal definition of a situation implies the reality of the situation, it matters little what others may think. A father who does not meet our socially-constructed definition of a good father may be defined otherwise by the child. If a child perceives his father as a man who attempts to care for his children, even if those attempts appear feeble to others, can the father, from the child's perspective, be worthy of the child's love and admiration? Perhaps more importantly, can that father be an appropriate role model for that child?

It is tempting to assume that children who reject their fathers will not emulate their behaviors. But in the current analysis, the outcomes for those sons who admired their fathers, despite their antisocial tendencies, and those who loathed their fathers, not because of their antisocial tendencies but because of the harm inflicted on them by their fathers, were similar. All subjects in the current analysis were very much like their fathers. All had serious substance abuse problems, including histories of extensive use of alcohol, marijuana, methamphetamine, crack cocaine, or heroin. Except for one subject who struggled with serious mental health challenges and crack cocaine and heroin addictions, all were criminally active and had spent time in juvenile or adult correctional facilities. Their self-described criminality included violent, property, drug, and weapons offenses and frequently mirrored the crimes for which their fathers were sent to prison.

There are surely many elements that contribute to intergenerational incarceration. Exposure to multiple risk factors, such as familial substance abuse, criminality, and instability all increase the risk that sons will follow in their fathers' footsteps. But the role the father plays in the life of the child may also be important. Those subjects who rejected their fathers were angry men, but their anger was directed primarily at their fathers. They did not place all the blame on "the system" for their current circumstances. Those who accepted their fathers were also angry men, but their anger was directed toward a conventional society that supports a system they perceived as actively colluding to destroy their families. It will be difficult for any of these men to turn their lives around and avoid future involvement with the criminal justice system, given their current circumstances. But it may be especially difficult for those who view conventional society as responsible for the destruction of their families and as the reason for living lives filled with many challenges.

References

Amato, P., & Gilbreth, J. (1999). Nonresident fathers and the children's well-being: A meta-analysis. *Journal of Marriage & the Family,* 61, 557-573.

Becker, H. S. (1996). The epistemology of qualitative research. In R. Jessor, A. Colby, & R. Schwender (eds.) Essays on ethnography and human development (pp. 53-71). Chicago: University of Chicago Press.

Boswell, G. (2002). Imprisoned fathers: The children's view. *The Howard Journal*, 41, 14-26.

Boswell, G., & Wedge, P. (2002). *Imprisoned fathers and their children.* London: Jessica Kingsley.

Bronstein, P. (1988). Father-child interaction: Implications for gender role socialization. In P. Bronstein and C. Cowan (eds.), *Fatherhood Today: Men's Changing Role in the Family* (pp. 107-124). New York: Wiley.

Burr, V., & Butt, T. (2000). Psychological distress and postmodern thought. In D. Fee (ed.), *Pathology and the postmodern: Mental illness as discourse and experience* (pp. 116-140). London: Sage.

Carlson B. E., & Cervera, N. (1992). *Inmates and Their Wives: Incarceration and Family Life.* Westport, CT: Greenwood Press.

Caspi, A., Moffitt, T. E., Thornton, A., Freedman, D., Amell, J. W., Harrington, H., Smeijers, J., & Silva, P. A. (1996). The life history calendar: A research and clinical assessment method for collecting retrospective event-history data. *International Journal of Methods in Psychiatric Research,* 6, 101-114.

Day, R. D., Gavazzi, S., & Adcock, A. (2001). Compelling family processes. In A. Thronton (ed.), *The well-being of children and families: Research and data needs* (pp. 103-126). Ann Arbor, MI: University of Michigan Press.

Day, R. D., & Lamb, M. E. (2004). Conceptualizing and measuring father involvement: Pathways, problems, and progress. In R. D. Day & M. E. Lamb, (Eds.), *Conceptualizing and Measuring Father Involvement* (pp. 1-15). Mahwah, New Jersey: Erlbaum.

Feig, L. (1998). Understanding the problem: The gap between substance abuse programs and child welfare services. In R. L. Hampton, V. Senatore, & T. P. Gullotta (eds.), *Substance Abuse, Family Violence, and Child Welfare: Bridging Perspectives* (pp. 62-95). Thousand Oaks, CA: Sage.

Fishman, L. T. (1990). *Women at the wall: a study of prisoners' wives doing time on the outside.* Albany, NY: State University of New York Press.

Florsheim, P. (2000). The economic and psychological dynamics of nonresident paternal involvement. In R. Taylor & M. C. Wang (eds.) *Resilience across contexts: Family, work, culture, and community* (pp. 55-87). Mahwah, NJ: Erlbaum.

Fontana, A., & Frey, J. H. (1994). Interviewing: The art of science. In N. K. Denzin & Y. S. Lincoln (eds.) *Handbook of qualitative research* (pp. 361-376). Thousand Oaks, CA: Sage Publications.

Freedman, D., Thornton, A., Camburn, D, Alwin, D, & Young-DeMarco, L. (1988). The life history calendar: A technique for colleting retrospective data. *Sociological Methodology,* 18, 37-68.

Fritsch, T. A., & Burkhead, J. D. (1981). Behavioral reactions of children to parental absence due to imprisonment. *Family Relations,* 30, 83-88.

Gabel, S. (1992). Behavioral problems in sons of incarcerated or otherwise absent fathers: The issues of separation. *Family Process,* 31, 303-314.

Gabel S., & Schindledecker, R. (1992). Incarceration in parents of day hospital youth: relationship to parental substance abuse and suspected child abuse/maltreatment. *International Journal of Partial Hospitalization,* 8 (1), 77-87.

Gibson, C., & Tibbetts, S. (2000). A biosocial interaction in predicting early onset of offending. *Psychological Reports,* 86, 509-518.

Girshick, L. B. (1996). *Soledad women: Wives of prisoners speak out.* Westport, CN: Praeger.

Glaze, L. E., & Maruschak, L. M. (2009). *Parents in prison and their minor children.* Bureau of Justice Special Report, NCJ 222984. Washington, DC: U.S. Department of Justice.

Hairston, C. F. (1987). Family ties during imprisonment: Do they influence future criminal activity? *Federal Probation,* 52, 48-52.

Hairston, C. F. (1989). Men in prison: Family characteristics and parenting views. *Journal of Offender Counseling, Services and Rehabilitation,* 14, 23-30.

Hairston, C. F. (1995). Fathers in prison. In K. Gabel & D. Johnson (eds.), *Children of Incarcerated Parents* (pp.31-40). New York: Lexington.

Hairston, C. F. (1998). The forgotten parent: understanding the forces that influence incarcerated fathers' relationships with their children. *Child Welfare,* 77, 617-639.

Holden, G. W., & Barker, T. (2004). Fathers in violent homes. In M. E. Lamb (ed.), *The Role of the Father in Child Development* (pp. 417-445). New York: John Wiley & Sons.

Jaffee, S. R., Moffitt, T. E., Caspi, A., & Taylor, A. (2003). Life with (or without) father: The benefits of living with two biological parents depend on the father's antisocial behavior. *Child Development,* 74, 109-126.

Johnson, D. (1995a). The care and placement of prisoners' children. In K. Gabel & D. Johnson (eds.), *Children of Incarcerated Parents* (pp.103-123). New York: Lexington Books.

Johnson, D. (1995). Effects of parental incarceration. In K. Gabel & D. Johnson (eds.), *Children of Incarcerated Parents* (pp. 59-88). New York: Lexington Books.

Johnson, E. I., & Waldfogel, J. (2002). Parental incarceration: Recent trends and implications for child welfare. *Social Service Review,* 76, 460-479.

Lamb, M. E. (2004). The role of the father: An introduction. In M. E. Lamb, (ed.), *The Role of the Father in Child Development* (4th Ed.), (pp. 1-31). New York: Wiley.

Lin, N., Ensel, W. M., & Lai, W. G. (1997). Construction and use of the life history calendar: reliability and validity of recall data. In I. H. Gotlib & B. Wheaton (eds.), *Stress and Adversity Over the Life Course: Trajectories and Turning Points* (pp. 50-72). Cambridge: Cambridge University Press.

Marsiglio, W., & Cohen, M. (2000). Contextualizing father involvement and paternal influence: Sociological and qualitative themes. *Marriage and the Family Review,* 29, 75-95.

Mazza, C. (2002). And then the world fell apart: The children of incarcerated fathers. Families in Society: *The Journal of Contemporary Human Services,* 83, 521-529.

McHugh, P. (1968). *Defining the situation: The organization of meaning in social interaction.* Indianapolis, IN: Bobbs-Merrill.

McLanahan, S., & Teitler, J. (1998). The consequences of father absence. In M. Lamb (Ed.) *Parenting and Child Development in "Nontraditional" Families* (pp. 83-102). Mahwah, NJ: Erlbaum.

McMahon, T. J., & Luthar, S. S. (1998). Bridging the gap for children as their parents enter substance abuse treatment. In R. L, Hampton, V. Senatore, & T. P. Gullotta (eds.), *Substance Abuse, Family Violence, and Child Welfare: Bridging Perspectives* (pp. 143-187). Thousand Oaks, CA: Sage.

Mead, G. H (1934). *Mind, self and society.* Chicago: University of Chicago Press.

Morris, P. (1965). Prisoners and their families. New York: Hart.

Osofsky, J. D. (1995). The effects of exposure to violence on young children. *American Psychologist,* 50, 782-788.

Pfiffner, L., McBurnett, K., & Rathouz, P. (2001). Father absence and familial antisocial characteristics. *Journal of Abnormal Child Psychology,* 29 (5), 357-367.

Reissman, C. K. (2002). Narrative analysis. In A. M. Huberman & M. B. Miles (eds.), *The Qualitative Researchers'Companion,* (pp. 217-270). Thousand Oaks, CA: Sage.

Sack, W. H. (1977). Children of imprisoned fathers. *Psychiatry,* 40, 163-174.

Sack, W. H., Seidler, T., & Harris, S. (1976). Children of imprisoned parents: A psychosocial exploration. *American Journal of Orthopsychiatry,* 46, 618-628.

Simmons, C. W. (2000). *Children of incarcerated parents.* California Research Bureau Note, 7(2).

Swan, A. (1981) *Families of black prisoners: Survival and progress.* Boston: G. K. Hall.

Tamis-LeMonda, C. S., Shannon, J. D., Cabrera, N. J., & Lamb, M. E. (2004). Fathers and mothers at play with their 2- and 3-year-olds: Contributions to language and cognitive development. *Child Development,* 75, 1806-1820.

Videon, T. (2002). The effects of parent adolescent relationships and parental separation on adolescent well-being. *Journal of Marriage and Family,* 64, 489-503.

Yogman, M., Cooley, J., & Kindlon, D. (1988). Fathers, infants and toddlers: A developing relationship. In P. Bronstein & C. Cowan (eds.), *Fatherhood Today: Men's Changing Role in the Family* (pp. 53-65). New York: Wiley.

Discussion Questions

1. To what extend do you think that the inter-generational transmission of crime is inevitable? Support your answer by outlining the theories on which this research is based.

2. Why was it difficult to conduct this research? What were the methodological hurdles the author had to work around?

3. What is an IRB, and why is it important to have research like this approved by an IRB?

4. Would you expect the impact of maternal incarceration on children to differ from what this study revealed as the impact of paternal incarceration? Explain.

5. What limitations might have been created by relying on information from only subjects recruited from jails, treatment facilities, homeless shelters, and parole officers?

6. Why was it important for West-Smith to interview the subjects herself?

Chapter 18
ARTS-IN-CORRECTIONS: A PATH OF DISCOVERY AND REDEMPTION

Lawrence Brewster, Ph.D. University of San Francisco

Introduction

Housed in North Block at San Quentin in his early years of incarceration, "Jake," an African-American raised on the mean streets of East Los Angeles, sought diversion "doing anything other than staring out the cell window hoping to catch a glimpse of passing seagulls." He started working on soap and wood carvings and soon realized he had a talent for sculpting anything from tiny angels to miniature guitars and, eventually, people. The real challenge was capturing the face and giving life to the figure. He worked hours at a time, determined to master his craft. Frustrated with the limitations of soap carvings, he experimented with turning soap into paste to mimic clay and made even more intricate and lifelike sculptures.

One day he was putting the finishing touches on a bass guitar when a guard looked into his cell and complimented him on his work. The guard encouraged Jake to become involved in the Arts-in-Corrections (AIC) program, a relatively new program at that time. It was 1982, and Jake was doing a bid of fifteen-to-life for multiple armed robberies. Prior to this, the nineteen-year-old had never been incarcerated. He was scared and wanted to find a way to survive prison physically and psychologically. The AIC program might just have been the answer. Jake had artistic talent, but no formal fine arts instruction, until his involvement in Arts-in-Corrections.

Jake ended up serving sixteen years, divided among four California institutions: Pelican Bay, San Quentin, Deuel Vocational Institution at Tracy, and the Sierra Conservation Center at Jamestown. I first met Jake at San Quentin State Prison while conducting a cost-benefit study of the Arts-in-Corrections program in 1983. Our second meeting was twenty-five years later, when I had the opportunity to interview ex-cons who had been students in the program. At that point, Jake had been out of prison eleven years and was making his living as a sculptor. He described how the AIC program provided him an opportunity to grow his artistic talents and to build self-confidence, especially when his work gained recognition outside of prison.

Although the 1983 study found Arts-in-Corrections cost-effective, it was still too soon to determine its impact on inmates after their release. A 1987 recidivism study found a significantly reduced rate of recidivism for AIC participants, compared with the general population of parolees. Even more encouraging, AIC participants faired significantly better the longer they were out of prison *(California Department of Corrections, 1987)*. Thirty years after the program was launched in 1980, I evaluated the impact of the program through these interviews with former program participants, AIC classroom observations, and interviews with current inmate-artists at San Quentin State Prison.

Arts-in-Corrections

The California legislation established the Arts-in-Corrections (AIC) program in 1980, based on the successful pilot Prison Arts Project started in 1977 at California Medical Facility at Vacaville. Individual and group instruction was offered in the arts and fine craft disciplines. Arts in Corrections emphasized engaging inmates in the creative process, rather than focusing merely on arts production. According to Brewster (1983), program objectives were:

- To provide instruction and guidance to inmates in the visual, literary, performing and media, and fine craft disciplines.
- To provide, through professional success models in the arts, an opportunity for inmates to learn, to experience, and to be rewarded for individual responsibility, self-discipline, and hard work.
- To provide a constructive leisure time activity as a means of releasing energy not dissipated in work, relieving tensions created by confinement, spurring the passage of time, and promoting the physical and mental health of inmates.
- To reduce institutional tension among inmates and between inmates and staff.
- To provide public service to local communities through art projects and concerts.
- To increase participants' constructive self-sufficiency and heighten self-esteem.

Eloise Smith, the person most responsible for the design and implementation of AIC, believed that participation in prison fine arts programs like Arts-in-Corrections provided inmates with creative outlets, structure to facilitate concentration and focus, models of self-motivated creative discipline, examples of universal ideals, and aesthetic and low-risk problem solving skills. Three program evalua-tions—a 1983 cost-benefit study, the 1987 recidivism study, and this qualitative study—provided evidence that AIC was highly effective and relatively low cost; however, in February 2010, the program was discontinued, eliminated by California's state government in the midst of a severe budget crisis.

The 2008-2010 Qualitative Study

For this qualitative study, I interviewed twenty-one formerly incarcerated people who participated in the Arts-in-Corrections Program. Fourteen of these were male. They ranged in age from mid-thirties to early sixties, with most in their late forties and early fifties. Their crimes included: possession and sale of drugs, second-degree murder, vehicular manslaughter (drinking and driving), fraud, robbery, prison escape, and sex offenses. Time served ranged from five to twenty-three years; time since release ranged from three to seventeen years. Most participants were incarcerated during their late teens or early twenties and had been raised in poor or working-class neighborhoods. Participants included Hispanics, African-Americans, Caucasians, and an older Japanese woman. At the time of their incarceration, a few did not have a high school diploma at the time of their incarceration, and only four had a college education. Fifty-eight percent pursued other programs besides AIC during their incarceration, including two-year and four-year College degree programs and specialized vocational training. Sixteen were using alcohol or drugs at the time of their arrest and conviction.

These former program participants self-identified as musicians, writers, sculptors, painters, poets, magicians, ceramicists, print makers, and guitar and violin makers. Only three—all musicians—had formal training in the arts before their incarceration and involvement in AIC (Brewster, 2010). Among the writers, two were avid readers during their child and teen years, and one had earned an undergraduate degree in English. In addition to interviewing these formerly incarcerated participants of AIC, I observed writing, painting, and printmaking classes and interviewed artist-instructors at San Quentin State Prison. To maintain anonymity, all names have been changed in this report.[1]

Self-Discovery: Taking a Different Path

The irony for many was that prison provided them with the opportunity for the first time to take stock of their lives; to ask why they had been so self-destructive and to determine what they could do to change their lives for the better. A common refrain was that the art program helped light a spark of self-worth and provided them an identity. They were artists, not just inmates known only by a prison-issued number.

---

[1]   See Brewster's "The California Arts-in-Corrections Music Programme: A Qualitative Study" in *The International Journal of Community Music* for a discussion of the AIC music program.

The early twentieth-century American painter and teacher, Robert Henri, believed that each person has what he called the "art spirit." He taught that any one can "become an inventive, searching, daring, self-expressing creature" if only our art spirit is nurtured and allowed to be freely expressed (Henri, 2007, p. 11). This is reflected in the comments made by study participants. They spoke about discovering their talents and passion for art and the importance of the artistic process as the "final salvation of our minds from prison insanity. Our art, in whatever form, tells us, our families, fellow inmates, and society that we, too, are still valuable."

I repeatedly heard from former and current inmates that the Arts-in-Corrections program taught them how to work at their art with a sense of purpose and focused discipline. The ultimate prize for most was earned self-respect, human dignity, self-esteem, and self-discovery. They attribute much of their success to AIC and other educational and training programs they pursued while in prison. They offer themselves as evidence that rehabilitation is possible. Although it was never intended as a job creation program, five of the twenty-one interviewed are earning part or all their living through their art, as magicians, string instrument makers, musicians, and sculptors.

"Leon" is an excellent example of an inmate who chose to take a different path. At an early age, he expected to end up in prison like his father, two uncles, and so many other Black brothers from his south Los Angeles neighborhood. He looked forward to it, romanticizing prison as a place where real men earned badges of courage and respect. He followed his role models' footsteps and ultimately served more than twenty years. However, during this time, Leon eventually decided he wanted a more for himself and his seven children. He wanted to teach his children that there is a better life than the one he, his father, and his uncles lived. Over time, Leon started reading, taking college courses, and participating in a twelve-step program and a peer counseling group. His changed attitude and determination to better himself led him to spend more time alone, avoiding trouble as much as possible while on the inside. Eventually, Leon found his way into Arts-in-Corrections, and through the program, discovered his talents as a songwriter, playwright, actor, and painter.

While in the program, Leon co-wrote and acted in two plays, composed several rap songs, and discovered his talent for drawing and painting. Since his release nearly four years ago, he completed a novel, co-wrote and acted in a play, and continues to write songs and paint, all while working a full-time job to support his wife and children. He talked about the satisfaction he receives from completing projects and the importance of teaching his children that they too can do anything they set their minds to as long as they are willing to work hard and finish what they start. He stated:

Arts-in-Corrections taught me above all the importance of completing projects. I think one of the problems with young people today is that they don't finish what they start. They may get interested in something but often don't follow through. I was like that for most of my life. But not anymore. I've learned with the help of others, especially the art instructors, how satisfying it is to complete tasks and get better at what you are doing in the process.

For example, I've worked hard to get better at my writing and drawing. I decided a few years ago to set myself a writing schedule. My goal is to write three pages a day. Some days I might be on a roll and complete ten pages, and other days maybe only one page gets written. But at least that is one more page than I had the day before. That's how I managed to write my first novel, and it feels good to have finished that project. I don't know if it's any good, but a few of my friends have read it and liked it. My satisfaction comes in knowing that I wrote a book. My children call me a writer and actor. They saw me in a play I co-wrote and after the show my little girl said, "Daddy, you're an actor." It makes me feel good as a person and father and I'm forever grateful to the Arts-in-Corrections program for helping me to develop my talents and, more important, for teaching me how to work.

Claire Braz-Valentine, a long-time writing instructor with Arts-in-Corrections, shared a letter she received from a former student. The writer thanked her and described his success since leaving prison:

I took a course in writing at Soledad where you were an instructor. I would like to thank you! I have used the things you showed me to go on to a great career in the motorcycle industry. Much of the work I do involves writing ads and scripts for the sales department. I also have been doing some minor writing and have had three of my stories published. I now own my own home and will be starting a motorcycle shop next year. I took your classes in the mid-1990s and wouldn't expect you to remember me but I thought you might like to hear of 'one that got away! (From the system that is …). I truly believe you were partially respon-sible for my success. (Anonymous, personal communication with Claire Braz-Valentine, date. [Claire Braz-Valentine shared this letter on the condition the author would remain anonymous]).

Many of the men interviewed were first-time offenders and fearful of what awaited them in prison. Early on, there is tremendous pressure to affiliate with their own kind, defined by race, either by joining a gang or at least hanging with people of the same color. Some, like "John," decided this wasn't for them and looked for ways to spend their time more constructively. John was twenty-eight when he was sent to Soledad Prison on a nine-year rape conviction. It was his first time in prison. John described what it was like for him:

> *My first impression when I arrived at Soledad was that I'd probably never leave there alive. I didn't really know what I should do to survive. Prison is very segregated along racial and ethnic lines. So my first response was, okay, well, I'll hang out with the white guys and see where that leads me. But it just wasn't going to be my thing and I knew it.*

John explained that he wanted to avoid the path taken by so many gangbangers in prison:

> *It was probably about three months into my time at Soledad that I really started to think about maybe getting out and trying to navigate a path through the system that would keep me from becoming an institutionalized type of individual ... I just didn't want to lose any more of my humanity. And once I started thinking about my life and how I ended up in prison ... the first step was really standing in front of the mirror for an hour and staring myself down and searching for some real hard truths. I asked myself what I was about, calling myself a liar, and really just having a conversation with myself and being very, very honest. And then I decided I was going to try to improve myself.*

John talked about the many opportunities available at the time he was incarcerated:

> *Fortunately, when I was at Soledad there were a lot of ways to remake your life. There was an eighteen month, cutting-edge computer program sponsored by Silicon Valley companies that resulted in 100 percent job placement for ex-cons. There were different industries such as textiles and furniture that provided job skills. There were AA and bachelor programs offered through the local community college and San Jose State University. And there was the Arts-in-Corrections program. I took advantage of every program I could get into. My greatest transformation came through Arts-in-Corrections however. I discovered my talent and passion for writing and making things out of leather.*

Jake, who we met earlier, spoke of a similar transformation when he explained the meaning of sculpting and the artistic process in his life:

When you are doing your art, you don't care if you are locked down for months if you have materials and your imagination. When you work at your art, you are meditating. You are focused, able to shut out the noise and fear of prison life. You turn off the monkey mind, and you no longer think about the streets or fear or girls. You get focused and quiet al.l the chatter, because you have found another way to be free. That's what the Arts-in-Corrections and my art gave to me: another way to be free, to reach your calm state of mind.

Similarly, "Jasmine" attributes her renewed will to live to the Arts-in-Corrections program. As a very young girl, she and her family, of Japanese descent, lived in an internment camp during World War II. She and her husband (now deceased) were well-educated; both were teachers. Jasmine also was a medical illustrator. She was an older woman in poor health at the time of her incarceration for fraud. She feels that she brought great shame on her family and initially she did not want to survive prison.

Jasmine talks of her AIC artist-facilitator Roberto Chavez with reverence. He recognized her artistic talent and encouraged her to take classes in drawing and painting. Jasmine said that he was "instrumental in helping me and other artist-inmates find their creative inner core while we served time." She described the value of art:

Art is part of my spiritual life. It helped me to be focused, quiet, and centered ... Art in prison helped to shut out the dehumanizing aspects of prison life; to focus on the joy of creating and experiencing my inner spirit, core.

Like Jasmine, "Megan" is well educated. She earned a Bachelor's degree in English, and her father was Chair of English at a local university. She held well-paid and highly responsible positions in business until her daughter died of Hodgkin's disease at age seventeen. That tragic loss launched a sequence of events that spiraled her life out of control. Ultimately, she was sent to prison for possession of heroin and embezzlement.

Although Megan worked in the business world, she always dreamed of becoming a writer. Megan stated that her father's critical and disapproving nature intimidated her, preventing her from putting pen to paper. It was through her incarceration and involvement in the Arts-in-Corrections program that she found her voice as a writer. Megan beautifully expresses her longing for the approval and love of her father in an untitled poem she wrote and published as a student in the AIC program.

When I was pre-preschool, I told my father that I loved him.
He replied, "Likewise, I'm sure."
I told my father that if I was rich, I would give him all my money.
He replied, "It is—if I *were* rich, Megan."
Late one night, I crept into my parents' bedroom and whispered, "Daddy, I snuck in here to kiss you good night."
He replied, "There is no such word as *snuck*,
Remember, Megan, *sneak* and *sneaked*."
I don't tell my father I love him anymore, and likewise I'm sure.
If I were rich, I would undoubtedly give the connection all my money.
And about *snuck* ... I still *sneak* it in every once in a while (Silva, 1987).

As with the other interviewees, Megan attributed her salvation to Arts-in-Corrections and to one particular program representative. For her, it was Ernest Dillihay, the AIC artist-facilitator for her program. She stated:

> *It was Ernest and the program itself that helped me to grow up ... to see that there were better things to do with my life than be a heroin addict, and I haven't been one since my release. I have a lot of years clean and sober. That was the only drug I used, and it ruined my life. It gave me three prison terms and seven violations in a very short period of time ...*
>
> *When I look back on those times, Arts-in-Corrections changed me; it changed my focus and what I thought I could do. And I did it—I became the writer my father never validated.*

"Mickey" was convicted of selling narcotics. While at Soledad Prison, he started a group called The Soledad Clowns and organized classes to teach magic to other inmates. He also became involved in the "We Care Program," through which he told his story to teenagers and young adults in an effort to "scare them straight." Since his release from Soledad nearly seventeen years ago, he has made a good living as a professional magician and life coach, and he has remained clean and sober. The Arts-in-Corrections program, along with other education programs he pursued, gave him hope and confidence for the first time in his life. "You know, I didn't even realize the impact of the program until years later." He now is devoted to helping "wounded children" find their own sense of hope and self-esteem through his magic shows, his presentations to community groups and schools, and related work.

Mickey reflected on how his self-awareness and esteem were enhanced through AIC and the college education he received while incarcerated. He realized that he was "his own worst enemy in laying the blame for his poor decisions on his dysfunctional family and self-loathing." The education programs and the time spent inside Soledad enabled him to discover his identity and capabilities:

> *I no longer defined myself as an angry man who had to turn to drugs and crime to make it in this world. Turns out that I'm smart, talented, and now college educated. I can make a difference in the world through my magic shows and life coaching skills.*

Mickey emphasized that his transformation was underway before he became involved in the art program:

> *I was already working on healing my life by changing my attitude and behaviors when I first enrolled in AIC's poetry and writing classes. However, there is no question that the writing instructors and artist-facilitator, Jack Bowers, were instrumental in helping me to stay focused and to develop disciplined work habits for the first time in my life.*

"David" resorted to using drugs and alcohol to escape his depression and feelings of worthlessness. In his mid-twenties, alone and homeless, he found his way into state prison for possession, after numerous arrests and convictions. Boredom, not a desire to paint, first led him to Arts-in-Corrections, but eventually, he found himself "really getting into it," and he felt absorbed in something for the first time in his life. David spoke about how, with the help of the artist-facilitator, instructors, and other inmate-artists, he transformed:

> *I felt changed from the inside because I had found something of value inside myself. For the first time in my life, I felt like I was capable of doing something worthwhile; that I had some talent and was developing skills. I liked having people acknowledge and praise my paintings.*

As with so many of the men and women interviewed, the longer I spoke with David, the more I appreciated his intelligence, sensitivity, and personal insight. There is little doubt that the AIC program has helped these men and women discover the joy of creating and the satisfaction that comes with purpose and accomplishment. James Rowland, former Director of the California Department of Corrections, expressed his support of the program when he said:

The Arts-in-Corrections program has been shown to have a positive effect upon this problem [the revolving door between prisons and the streets]. I believe this has occurred because the inmates involved have acquired new attitudes about themselves and their capabilities through their work in the arts. The mastery of art skills requires patience, self-discipline and long-term commitment. These attributes are basic to an inmate's ability to function responsibly upon release (e-mail correspondence with Jack Bowers, former artist-facilitator at Soledad state prison, June 30, 2009).

Escaping Into Creativity

Time is precious; it is one of our most coveted possessions. Prison takes a person's time as measured against the crime committed. If freedom is the ability to control time, then it follows that prison time is the most logical form of punishment. As prison blocks off your body, so it suffocates your mind. *Prison:* the very word conjures endless and meaningless days and years spent passing time, doing time. Prison is boring. Inmates are denied their freedom and left alone with their thoughts in a noisy, overcrowded, and dangerous environment. "Alone time" does not have to be wasted time. The men and women who participated in Arts-in-Corrections are proof of this, as their imaginations and ideas were brought to life through the creative process.

In a milieu where only the most restricted liberties exist and where motivation and opportunity for pride in accomplishment is severely limited, uncensored, creative freedom of expression, like that offered through programs such as Arts-in-Corrections, is rare. Creation is a gesture from the void, an affirmation, whether coming from inside prison or a studio loft in the free world. Imagination refuses to submit. We want to live and grow and create. This is no less true for inmate-artists who resist the suffocation of prison life, actively and constructively through the artistic process. They are doing their time meaningfully, renewing themselves, beginning again.

Earlier, I quoted Jake describing how art was meditation for him and how it served to turn off the "monkey mind." Later in our conversation, he told me that he often would awake early in the morning with an idea or vision of what he wanted to create that day and then would proceed to work on the piece until it was done. In his words:

> *I could start early in the morning, seven o'clock, working on a sculpture and stop at seven that night, twelve hours later, and I would still be sitting in my boxer shorts at the table with a mess of soap or some other material, and I look at the time and I say to myself, "Man, I feel like I just woke up' ... because you have no concept of time. My body would be totally relaxed and I would feel good about what I had made that day."*

Others told of similar experiences as they worked on their music, wrote their stories and poems, or painted. They would laugh when commenting on the importance of time in perfecting one's art and how prison life offered nothing but time. "Ray" told me that other inmates would tease him, saying, "Ray, you're not going to have time to do your writing on the outside like you do in here; you'll have to get a real job." Ray told me they were right. Even so, he sees himself as a writer and credits the writing program with helping to preserve his sanity.

"Russ" observed:

> The perception of time is a very important thing. You know, prison time can be a monster, it is oppressive. That changed for me while I was in my art classes, or working at my art in my cell. Time never went as fast as it did during those times when I was focused not on me, or my surroundings, but on my art.

"Chris" spoke at length about how Arts-in-Corrections helped him do his time:

> Oh yeah, I counted on going to classes and working on my art in the evenings and in my cell. It provided a space in which to escape daily prison life. When I was working on my art I didn't have to think about all the other stuff. It was just me and my art.

"Dan" put it this way:

> "It helped to have a creative outlet, a positive activity that kept me off the yard and other places you might be if you didn't have anything else to do with your time—places that may not be safe." All agreed that Arts-in-Corrections helped to keep inmates out of trouble.

Working Together in the Safety of the Art Classroom

The loss of freedom, privacy and the constant tension and threat of danger posed by racially defined prison gangs is emotionally and psychologically draining on even the toughest inmates. Reality prison shows convey some of what it is like to be locked away in overcrowded, cold, and dangerous prisons, but viewers get to turn off their televisions and sleep in comfortable and secure beds. Convicts are forced to sleep in dormitories with hundreds of other inmates or in overcrowded cells. It is nearly impossible for inmates to maintain their emotional equilibrium and self-respect, much less turn their lives around.

The Arts-in-Corrections' classrooms provided a sanctuary for inmate-artists and a place where they—Black, Brown, and White—worked side by side in the classroom, something that would never happen on the prison yard or back home. I observed men of different races in the classrooms. I visited with inmates at San Quentin who told me that they came from neighborhoods where crossing the color lines was deadly. They spoke about how in the art program they simply wanted to hone their skills, share ideas, and learn from one another, regardless of race. They also sought to escape from the gray, regimented, and threatening world that is prison by creating in the classroom or studio or back in their cells writing, drawing, sculpting, playing guitar, creating something, anything using their imaginations and hands.

For example, when I visited the writing class at San Quentin, there were nine men engaged in a lively and thoughtful critique of a book assigned for that night's class. They did not always agree with the others' opinions and expressed their differences in no uncertain terms. They did so, however, with civility, courtesy, and even humor. These men were African-American, Caucasian, and Hispanic. Their love of writing bonded them despite their racial differences. A student in the San Quentin writing program wrote:

> Once a week I sit at a table surrounded by the dregs of society; men banished to a grim Purgatory; men I didn't know three years ago. I sit with them and bare my soul through the words I've written, awaiting their judgment. These men are all convicted criminals, as am I, who have committed robberies, burglaries, and murder. I share my thoughts and creativity with them because they, like me, yearn to make something more of our existence. They dream of becoming more than the sum of their crimes, more than the labels they've become in the eyes of others. Even though these men are criminals I have discovered all of them are intelligent, thoughtful individuals with unique experiences and perspectives on the world we live in. Their voices are the ones you don't hear in polite society; their stories reveal the darkness and demons we all wrestle with, some more successfully than others. These men, who speak from experience of broken homes, abusive relationships, and of life lived on the gritty streets inhabited by gangbangers, drug addicts, hookers and hustlers have helped me to grow as a person, and to expand my horizons. Although they never ask it, I thank these men for their sharing, and it is with equanimity and humility they accept my praise as they struggle to become something more than they are, through writing, as I do. That's what this program means to me; a chance to redeem myself in the eyes of society, and in my own (personal letter, February, 2009).

Others pointed out that the "racial stuff" went away and they "were artists first; part of a community of artists. Arts-in-Corrections was like a subculture." Former inmate Russ described it this way:

... in the AIC classroom, we could sit and kick around ideas. When you're on the yard there's a certain mindset. As much as you think you can ignore it, there's a certain mindset that permeates everything and everyone in prison. You just never know what's going to happen ... but when you're in the art room, everybody's mindset is locked into doing their art, and offering help to the other guys. We can forget being the tough guy. You know, forget doing the rooster thing. It is safe to kick ideas around ... 'Hey, what about this lick [if you're a musician]? What colors did you mix together to get that scene in your painting? What, pastel? Oh man, are you using a thesaurus when you're writing? How're you getting this—how are you finding this stuff, man?' Of course, you are in prison, and you never know what's going to jump off. You never know. Still, locked in a classroom with the teachers and inmate-artists ... it's a beautiful thing.

Preparing for Reintegration

The transition from a life behind bars to becoming productive members of society is never easy, but it has been made even more difficult with reductions in rehabilitation programs due to state budget crises. There comes a time when convicts reach decisions, positively or negatively, about the future course of their lives. When that decision is to change old habits, attitudes, and behaviors in search of a better, more meaningful life, it is imperative that education, vocational training, and inmate support groups are available. The arts are an important alternative in the prison experience and in preparing inmates to return to their communities. It is not uncommon for the ex-cons interviewed to have participated in multiple rehabilitation programs. Many of them enrolled in college and vocational courses or participated in twelve-step and peer counseling programs while studying and practicing their art.

Those who pursued other educational opportunities were grateful for the opportunity to earn a college degree or to become certified in welding or another vocation. However, all of them attributed much of their success on the outside to Arts-in-Corrections. Through their interaction with accomplished artists, they were exposed to models of self-motivated and creative people, examples of universal ideals and aesthetics, and to healing and cognitive development. In the process, they developed empathy and insight into how their actions impact others, and learned to channel their impulses to constructive ends. "Vernon" spoke about art as a love experience, as:

... intimate and innermost feelings projected for public scrutiny. Be it a crudely sketched image on a piece of lined prison stationary, or a line of verse dictated from the heart, or a

haunting lyric speaking of home and family, of love and heartache. Art takes many forms, but all of them is a message from one soul to another: See, we think and feel just alike; our outward differences may not bring us together, but inside we are the same.

"Willie" admits he hurt a lot of people early in his life and deserved to be sent to prison. It wasn't until years into his sentence that he decided to change his thinking and work toward something worthwhile, even behind the razor wire. He explained:

... not until prison did I start to push myself, to do things I should have done in high school and after. I discovered my talent and interest in painting through Arts-in-Corrections. The beauty of prison is that I was able to paint what I wanted because in there I didn't have to chase money. Before entering the program I watched chunks of my life slip away. I was unable to have a family. I was unable to do so any things. It wasn't unjust, but I was fully punished for my wrong-doing. There is so much pain inside prison, but if I hadn't gone there I would never have turned inward. I would still have nothing to say. Now I want to tell a story with my drawings and remain free.

"Holmes," an active member of the San Quentin writing program, has served fourteen years and hopes to leave prison in another three years. He wrote the following in response to me asking why the State should continue funding the Arts-in-Corrections and writing program:

To continue this class [Zoe's writing course] would be a wise investment in a continuing journey for those of us who have little else in our lives. I have written more in this course than I have in my lifetime. It has enabled me to sharpen my writing skills and broaden my scope of awareness. As an inmate trapped in a cage, this program allows me the capacity to feel, to speak, to vent and, yes, even to cry. It is the one thing I look to each week more than anything else. This class is a wise investment ... in its continued embrace I will grow, be challenged and learn. Such experiences are rare indeed. I truly believe that this class and its teacher [Zoe] have changed me for the better and nurtured an artist in me I never knew existed (Holmes, personal letter, February 21, 2009).

Ironically, a few, like "Brad," discussed how they felt "freer" in prison than they did before their incarceration because they now had opportunities to get an education or training and time for honest self-reflection, opportunities not available to them when they were young and poor. They were, of course, anxious to do their time and get out of prison, but they were more relaxed about it and focused on their art and other educational programs. Russ expressed it this way, "I ended up not feeling so attached to getting out ... the programs gave me something to look forward to each week, and I knew I was growing and learning, and I felt hopeful ... all of which were new experiences for me"

A Path of Discovery and Rehabilitation

"Rick," a lifer at New Folsom Prison, wrote a poem about rehabilitation and the artistic process that captures the sentiment of many of the men and women I interviewed. His poem is titled, "Rehabilitation."

> Rehabilitation is said to be a faded memory,
> A lost thought that no longer occurs.
> But I don't care what is said and I don't care what is thought,
> Though it's true day after day and year after year for years and years on end.
> They tried to kill rehabilitation and creation with condemnation and correction, but year after year they still fail to obliterate the passion of an artist's soul.
> And I hear rehabilitation day after day and year after year.
> I hear it in the scratching of pencils across paper.
> I hear it in the newly formed notes of an instrument that still remains, and I hear it boldly announced in the public's words
> 'To hell with rehabilitation, and yet I and many other artists will not be denied the God-given gift to create and to dream, to escape the confines of Corrections on the wings of our passion.
> So when there is a flute, a pen, a paint brush, a guitar or any other artistic paraphernalia in our hands, we are examples of rehabilitation—no longer of condemning or correcting.
> Rehabilitation is found in an artist's passion to create.
> Rehabilitation lives. It lives in me and in every other artist who, in spite of this place, still exercises the God-given gift to be an artist (Rick, personal communication, August 19, 2008).

A Final Word

Severe overcrowding, poor inmate health care, and the Great Recession may be the "perfect storm" that will lead to much needed prison reform and more effective correctional policies. The "tough on crime" approach of the past three decades, leading to lengthy, mandatory incarceration and less emphasis on rehabilitation is under scrutiny. Interest in ideas that have long been out of favor with politicians, law enforcement and correctional officers, and the public are back on the public agenda for consideration. These ideas include: sentencing discretion, discretionary parole release, softening enforcement of technical parole violations, and rehabilitation.

Ironically, California's state correctional authority changed its name to the California Department of Corrections *and Rehabilitation* [emphasis added] (CDCR) in 2005, at a time when funding for education, vocational training, and drug and alcohol treatment decreased and, in the case of Arts-in-Corrections, eliminated altogether after successfully awakening the art spirit in thousands of inmates during its thirty-year run. In the process, it introduced these offenders to hard work, focused discipline, and perseverance through the artistic process and with the help of ACI instructors and staff. The program helped inmates develop self-confidence and self-esteem and to self-identify as artists. Each recalled the journey of self-discovery and determination to live productive and meaningful lives inside and beyond the walls. They took pride in their art and pleasure in the praise they heard from other inmates, fellow artists, family and strangers. Their feelings of self-worth and dignity helped them to imagine a future that was unimaginable before their transformation. These men and women are examples of how art can lead to discovery, redemption, and a healed heart. The words and life of Jake the sculptor sums it up best:

> *I am a 47-year-old African-American male. I'm living with my ex-wife, nine-year-old son, and Katie, our dog. My mother married at sixteen. After my parents divorced, three military stepfathers raised my brothers and me. The military moved us every three years to Texas, Hawaii, Louisiana, Colorado, New Jersey, and California. I'm the oldest, and I had to constantly adjust to new schools, people, places and the 'rules' of how to best fit in. I learned how to make friends, but it has taken me much longer to learn how to keep them. At seventeen, I joined the Army, and received basic training in South Carolina, followed by two years of active duty at Ft. Ord, California. At nineteen, I was arrested for multiple armed robberies. My civil conviction led to a general discharge from the Army.*
>
> *Sixteen years of my life were spent in California State Prisons with a C-xxxx identification number to represent me ... breaking the law to feed my addiction to cocaine caused me and my family a lot of pain. I have learned from my mistakes and I hope to help others make better choices for their tomorrows. I've been out of prison since March 11, 1997 ... creating art has given me the strength to believe in something greater than myself and to move past my addictions and the heartaches of child abuse. Through my ability as a sculptor, mold maker, and wood carver, I have something to give to others and to myself. I am passionate about teaching and creating and making a living doing what I love. Art was my escape when incarcerated and now that I'm free,*

art is the "wind beneath me." Hard work, focused attention, and determination to better myself helped me to develop my talent and provided me with a well-rounded set of skills that can always be made better through experience, education, and the creative process. These are the tools given to me by Arts-in-Corrections, and I've used them to shape various mediums, including my life. We all have strengths and weaknesses and can learn from each other if we are willing to open ourselves. I offer to render my services through the power of creativity, the sharing of truths, and a fair exchange.

Jake's story and so many like his serve as a reminder that we should not, cannot give up on people—perhaps especially those on the "lowest rung of the ladder." Hope may be found in treatment, training, and educational programs; whereas, the "punishment" model that has been dominate for the past three decades merely serves to grow the prison industry at an unsustainable cost to taxpayers.

References

California Department of Corrections Arts-in-Corrections Research Synopsis on Parole Outcomes for Participants Paroled. (1987). *William James Association.* Retrieved May 10, 2009, from http://www.williamjamesassociation.org/

Brewster, Lawrence G. (1983). An evaluation of the Arts-in-Corrections Program of the California Department of Corrections. *William James Association.* Retrieved May 10, 2009, from http://www.williamjamesassociation.org/

Brewster, Lawrence G. (2010). The California Arts-in-Corrections Music Programme: A Qualitative Study. *International Journal of Community Music,* 3(1), 33-46.

Henri, Robert. (2007). The Art Spirit. New York: Basic Books.

Silva, Megan. (1987). Untitled. About Time III: A Third Anthology of California Prison Writing. *William James Association.* Retrieved May 10, 2009, from http://www.williamjamesassociation.org/

Discussion Questions

1. You are the director of prisons for California. What would you tell the governor to continue to fund this program? Include in your answer a discussion of the evidence that the program has rehabilitative benefits.

2. What did Brewster do to maintain anonymity in this report? Why is anonymity important to research?

3. Many program participants described it as giving them self-worth and identity. What is the added value of this in terms of prison administration and public safety?

4. In addition to AIC participation, most inmates participated in other rehabilitation programs. Could this be an issue with regard to assessing program outcome?

5. Consider your response to question #4. How did the inmates compare the impact of those other programs to the AIC program with regard to their success on the outside?

INDEX